# INSTRUCTION
## —— OF ——
# NOVICES

# INSTRUCTION
## —— OF ——
# NOVICES

The Venerable Father John of Jesus and
Mary of Calahorra

# Instruction of Novices

BY
The Venerable Father John of Jesus and Mary of Calahorra
*Third Superior-General of the Discalced Carmelites*

Translated from the Latin revised and adapted
BY
A Master of Novices

**"Blessed is the man whom Thou shalt instruct, O Lord: and shalt teach him out of Thy law."**
Ps. 93:12

Originally Printed in Ireland in 1930 by
M. S. Kelly & Co.
Loughrea, Co. Galway
Benzinger Brothers
New York, Cincinnati, Chicago

First edition with revised typesetting and footnotes
© 2023 Stella Maris Publishing, Inc.
ISBN: 978-1706819295
All rights reserved.

www.stellamarispublishing.com

IMPRIMI POTEST
Fr. Gulielmus A S. Alberto
Praepositus Generalis
Romae, die 24, Oct., 1929

NIHIL OBSTAT
Matthaeus Canonicus MacMahon
Censor Theol. Deput.

IMPRIMI POTEST
Eduardus
Archiep. Dublinen
Hiberniae Primas

Dublin, die 7 Martii, 1930

TO
The Glorious Patriarch
Saint Joseph

Chaste spouse of the Mother of God, Protector of the Universal Church, model and guide of pure, simple and interior souls, this English version of the Instruction of Novices is reverently dedicated.

# CONTENTS

Publisher's Preface ..................................................................11
Preface to the Second Edition................................................13
Author's Introduction ............................................................17

## PART I: THE PASSIONS

I. Passions in General.......................................................21
II. Love, Desire and Joy....................................................26
III. Remedies for Love, Desire and Joy ............................29
IV. Hatred, Aversion, Sadness and their Remedies..........34
V. Hope, Daring and their Remedies ..............................40
VI. Despair, Fear, Anger and their Remedies ..................44
VII. Remarks on the Passions.............................................50
VIII. Temptations ................................................................54

## PART II: THE VIRTUES

I. Theological Virtues .....................................................61
    I. Virtues in General ...............................................61
    II. Faith .....................................................................65
    III. Hope ....................................................................73
    IV. Charity..................................................................80

II. Moral Virtues ...............................................................90
    I. Moral Virtues in General....................................90
    II. Obedience.............................................................93
    III. Chastity..............................................................102
    IV. Poverty...............................................................110
    V. Penance..............................................................116
    VI. Abstinence and Sobriety ...................................123

|      | VII. Humility ..................................................................128 |
|------|---|
|      | VIII. Meekness ................................................................135 |
|      | IX. Patience ...................................................................143 |
|      | X. Modesty ....................................................................151 |
|      | XI. Modesty of the Eyes ................................................156 |
|      | XII. Silence ....................................................................162 |
|      | XIII. Gratitude ..............................................................170 |
|      | XIV. Magnanimity ........................................................175 |
|      | XV. Diligence ................................................................182 |
|      | XVI. Perseverance .........................................................187 |
| III. | Vices .....................................................................................193 |
|      | I. Capital Vices ..............................................................193 |
|      | II. Important Remarks on the Virtues and Vices .................202 |
| IV.  | The Gifts and Fruits of the Holy Ghost...............................210 |
|      | I. The Seven Gifts of the Holy Ghost..............................210 |
|      | II. The Fruits of the Holy Ghost and the Beatitudes ..........214 |

# PART III: THE STUDY OF PRAYER

| I.   | Prayer in General..................................................................219 |
|------|---|
| II.  | Summary of the Practice of Prayer ......................................223 |
|      | I. Advantages and Facility of Prayer................................223 |
|      | II. Parts of Prayer ..........................................................224 |
|      | III. Preparation .............................................................224 |
|      | IV. Body of the Prayer ...................................................226 |
|      | V. Conclusion ................................................................229 |
| III. | Devotion in General.............................................................234 |
| IV.  | Devotion to the Most Blessed Eucharist, The Blessed Virgin and the Saints..................................................................237 |
|      | I. The Blessed Eucharist .................................................237 |
|      | II. The Blessed Virgin ....................................................238 |
|      | III. Saints.......................................................................242 |

# PART IV: THE EXERCISES OF THE RELIGIOUS LIFE

I. Exercises in General ..................................................................245
    I. Observance of the Exercises .............................................245
    II. Daily Exercises ............................................................248
    III. Weekly Exercises .........................................................250
    IV. Monthly Exercises ........................................................250
    V. Yearly Exercises ..........................................................251

II. Direction of the Acts ................................................................253

III. Exercise of the Presence of God in Our Daily Actions .................256

IV. Use of the Sacraments and Examination of Conscience ..............258

V. Manner of Preparing for the Clothing and Profession..................260

Appendix..........................................................................................263

    Instructions for Rendering an Account of the Interior Dispositions to One's Spiritual Director or Superior ........................................263

# PUBLISHER'S PREFACE

As the works could easily be confused with one another, it may help to note that Ven. Fr. John of Jesus and Mary, O.C.D. of Calahorra (1564-1615) wrote: *Instruction of Novices*, *Instructions for the Novice Master*, and *Cloistral Discipline*, as well as other works. A different author by the same name who lived at the same time, Fr. John of Jesus and Mary, O.C.D. of Aravalles (1549-1609), wrote a book by the same title: *Instruction of Novices*. Both were contemporaries of St. John of the Cross O.C.D. (1542-1591).

This present work has been used in the formation of Carmelite Religious for over 400 years.

August 29, 2023

# PREFACE TO THE SECOND EDITION

The Venerable Father John of Jesus and Mary was born at Calagorra in Spain on the 28th of January, 1564. The Christian education which he received from pious parents turned his mind and heart at an early age to God and the practice of virtue, and later led him to embrace a life of Evangelical perfection. From the University of Salamanca, where he distinguished himself by his rare talents, he applied to the Discalced Carmelites for admission into the Order, and received the Religious Habit in the same year in which St. Teresa died (1582).

He received his early religious training in the celebrated Novitiate of Pastrana, where St. John of the Cross was first Novice Master, and studied for the Priesthood at Alcala—the first College of the Discalced Carmelites in Spain. As a student he was a perfect model of religious observance, and was most humble in the midst of the great success which attended his studies. Though not yet a Priest, he was sent by his Superiors to Italy with some other distinguished Fathers of the order to propagate the Teresian Reform there. He completed his studies in the Monastery of St. Anne at Genoa, where he was ordained Priest.

He took part in the General Chapter of the Carmelites at Cremona, and on his return to Genoa was given charge of the Novitiate. Here he imparted by word and example the true spirit of St. Teresa to the Novices, some of whom formerly belonged to the most illustrious families of Genoa, and under his direction they became true models of Discalced Carmelites. He was next sent to the Monastery of *S. Maria della Scala* in Rome, where he was appointed Master of Novices, an office which he held with distinction for several years.

He was elected Definitor-General, Procurator-General, and finally Superior-General of the Order, offices which he fulfilled with great humility, becoming dignity, and rare prudence. In spite of his delicate health and numerous occupations, he labored successfully for the growth and propagation of the Order. He compiled the Carmelite Constitutions, and wrote a series of *Exhortations* on the Rule of the Order, and a treatise on *Cloistral Discipline*.

He wrote many excellent works on various subjects, namely: Mysticism, Asceticism, Monasticism, Exegesis, Canon Law, Rhetoric, Oratory and Literature, which were consulted and praised by Theologians and Saints, among others by St. Francis de Sales and Bossuet, and earned for him the title of "Great Doctor and Great Mystic" (Bossuet). To him is due the defense of the Carmelite Missions, which have survived the vicissitudes of so many centuries, and still endure in spirit and practice as a living testimony of the true spirit of St. Teresa. We owe to him the glorification of St. Teresa, and also the propagation of the Order in Italy, France, Belgium, Russia, Germany, Persia, and in the Indies.

But his special merit lies in his deep knowledge of mysticism, which he lived in practice, and taught in theory to his Brethren and to the illustrious and eminent personages of his time. He was the Spiritual Director of St. Joseph Calasanctius and of Bl. Baptist of the Conception, Reformer of the Trinitarians, and the intimate and deeply venerated friend of Bl. Cardinal Bellarmine. He enjoyed the esteem of the Popes whose counselor he was, of the Cardinals whose teacher he was, and of the King and Princes for whom he wrote a work; yet he always loved to hide himself and to live enclosed in the "House of his own soul," in order to speak to God and to direct towards Him every aspiration of his soul, which was inflamed by love and crushed with suffering.

His chief characteristic was holiness, combined with vast and profound learning. He lived and loved virtue with the keenness of a genius, the ardour of a Saint, the simplicity and humility of a child. His life, though short and filled with labors and suffering, closed in the solitude of St. Sylvester of Montecompatri, Rome, on the Feast of the Ascension, 1615, at the age of 51 years. For three centuries the inhabitants of Montecompatri have called him, "Blessed John" on account of the fame of his virtues and the wonderful preservation of his body from corruption.

The *Instruction of Novices*, of which the following is an English translation, was written by him about the year 1590, when he was Master of

# Preface to the Second Edition

Novices at Rome. It was originally written in Latin, but was soon translated into other languages, in which it was well received. Owing to solidity of doctrine and the methodical treatment of a subject so important as the education of Novices, the book has been extensively used for the last three hundred years, with great spiritual profit, in Religious Communities and Colleges by those charged with the spiritual training of youth.

The object the author had in view in compiling it was to provide Novices with a Manual of sound practical instructions specially adapted to their needs, which would help to initiate them into the spirit of their vocation and teach them those things they will have to observe all their lives. He was convinced, as he states in a letter on the subject to his Superior, Father Peter of the Mother of God, that the whole future life of a Religious will depend on the training he gets during his Novitiate, for, "as the Novice is, so will the professed Religious be." The following are his words: "There is no scourge to which the Divine interests, as well as the interests of the Community, can be exposed in Monastic Institutions more disastrous than negligence in the education of the Novices, for they will bear to their old age the first impressions they received, and thus prepare the way for the certain loss of the perfection attained by the multiplied efforts of their predecessors. And let no one delude himself with the vain hope that the relaxed habits contracted in the beginning—drunk in, as it were, with the milk of the spiritual life, strengthened afterwards in the course of years and degenerated into a crowd of inveterate disorders—can be eradicated either by severe reprimands or by rigorous exercises; for we know that the wisest amongst the Fathers regarded this amendment more difficult to bring about than the conversion of hardened sinners living in the world."

Indeed, all the great masters of the spiritual life who have written on the subject are unanimous on this point. Experience also shows that the Novice who is tepid and negligent during his Novitiate rarely, if ever, changes after his profession; whereas, on the contrary, there is every ground for hoping that the Novice who is fervent and observant in the Novitiate will afterwards continue so, though unfortunately it is not always the case.

A religious vocation is a special call from God to serve him in a more perfect state of life than that of an ordinary Christian. "If thou wilt be perfect," said Our Lord to the young man mentioned in the Gospel, "go, sell what thou hast… and come, follow Me."[1] Two conditions were required

---

[1] Matt. 19:21

of that young man by Our Lord to become perfect: the first, to sell all he possessed; the second, to follow Christ. It is evident that he lived a good life up to the time he met Our Lord, for he was able to say that he had kept all the Commandments from his youth, and asked if he could do anything more. Our Lord's answer was: "If thou wilt be perfect, go, sell what thou hast, and come, follow Me."

Now the whole Religious life, the end of which is the perfection of its members, is based on these two Counsels of Our Lord, namely, the renunciation for Christ's sake of all we possess or might lawfully use, in order thus to become more free to devote ourselves to God and His service; and the imitation of Christ, Who should be the model of every true Religious. By the first we remove the obstacles that are in the way to our perfection; by the second we acquire the virtues or habitual dispositions of mind and heart that fit us for a life of union with God or Divine Charity, in which our perfection consists.

The object of the following instructions is to teach Novices how to do this. The Author points out to them, first, the difficulties they will have to contend with in controlling their passions, or, as he calls them, their domestic enemies, which will declare war against them from the very beginning of their religious career; second, the good habits, or, in other words, the virtues, they will have to acquire before they can attain the perfection of the state to which God has called them; third, the means they are to use in extirpating vice and planting virtue in their souls, which are prayer and the exercises of the religious life. The study and mortification of the passions, he assures them is one of the best remedies against temptations. For since the enemy, when he assails us with his temptations, is accustomed to insinuate himself into the internal senses and increase the natural violence of the passions, if we have the passions well under control we shall find it easier to resist his attacks.

Novices, then, should read attentively these instructions, and put in practice the lessons they inculcate. They shall find methodically arranged therein a complete treatise on monastic discipline, namely, the doctrine of the passions, temptations, virtues, vices, the gifts and fruits of the Holy Ghost, beatitudes, prayer, devotion, and finally the exercises by which the perfection of their state is acquired, so that without the use of any other book they will be able to procure sufficient instructions from this alone to fulfill all their duties.

# AUTHOR'S INTRODUCTION

The religious education of Novices may be divided into four parts, namely, the mortification of the passions, the acquisition of the virtues, the practice of prayer and the acts of community life, general and particular.

In order to become a good Religious it is necessary to subdue those unruly passions, which were nurseries of vice while we lived in the world; to implant in the soul the virtues that we are deficient in; to draw the mind away by the practice of prayer from the perishable things that formerly occupied it and to unite it with God; and, finally, by these means, together with the exercises of the common life, to fulfill the duties proper to our state.

Now, the perfection of the religious state is such that it requires all these conditions on the part of its members, and at the same time furnishes them with the most suitable means for their fulfillment. In the daily exercises of the common life, for example, we have numerous occasions of mortifying the passions, of acquiring the virtues, of advancing in the science of prayer and thus arriving at the love of God which is the end of the whole law.

By means of the three vows we are constantly urged on to union with God. Obedience conforms our will with the Divine Will; chastity excludes all carnal pleasures; and poverty frees us from all solicitude about temporal goods.

Then the prescriptions of the Rule are admirably suited for the perfect observance of the vows. First as regards obedience, the Rule allows nothing, however trifling, to be done, unless "in the word of the Lord," that is, by the command of the Superior. Secondly, it keeps chastity enclosed as it were in a safe asylum by continual prayer, retirement, fasts, abstinence, silence and other similar practices. Thirdly, it provides for the observance of poverty in its full splendour, by permitting the use of necessary things so sparingly that it forbids not only what is superfluous, even the most trivial things, but also the use of any words implying ownership, so that no one can call anything his own.

We have also the admonitions of the Constitutions, which are derived from the Rule, and embrace several counsels of the holy Fathers akin to the Rule itself. They contain all that is necessary for enabling the Religious to attain the perfection of his state; and, lest anything may be wanting, the Instructions or laudable customs are added to complete the work.

Finally, as every Religious Institute has a twofold end in view, namely, charity towards God and charity towards our neighbour for the love of God, it regulates all its laws and exercises in such a manner as to enable its members, not only to attend to their own sanctification but also to labour for the salvation of others, so that nothing may be wanting for the attainment of Christian perfection.

Now if Novices could faithfully practice all these things in the beginning of their religious career, they would not require any further instructions. But since they cannot, it is necessary to make use of a suitable method to initiate them into the spirit of their vocation, and to teach them those things which they will have to observe all their lives. We shall, therefore, treat of the four parts of monastic discipline separately, in the order we have already indicated.

# PART I
# The Passions

# I

# Passions in General

Anyone engaged in warfare cannot expect success unless he knows the strength and stratagems of his enemies; and the more violently they assail him the more necessary this knowledge is for him. Now, according to Sacred Scripture and the teaching of the holy Fathers there is no war so fierce and dangerous as that which our senses constantly wage against us.

St. Paul clearly expressed its bitterness when he exclaimed: "Unhappy man that I am, who shall deliver me from the body of this death?"[2] And again he bewails its extreme danger in those truly Apostolic words: "I chastise my body and bring it into subjection: lest perhaps, when I have preached to others, I myself should become a castaway."[3] As if he would say, my conscience reproaches me with nothing, and I go into the conflict armed with divine strength; yet in order to restrain the concupiscence of the flesh, I take precaution against the revolt of my senses by chastising my body beforehand.

The reason of this is very simple. Our enemies—the passions—are born with us, and as it is impossible to dislodge them, they weary by their importunity those whom they cannot conquer by their violence. This is proved by the unexpected fall of many persons who were once distinguished for sanctity. Hence it is clear that a knowledge of the passions is highly necessary, especially for those who have not yet subdued them.

We will begin, then, by defining passion considered from our point of view. It is a movement of the sensitive appetite, provoked by the imagination

[2] Rom. 7:24
[3] 1 Cor. 9:27

of good or evil, and accompanied by some physical alteration; or to speak more clearly, a passion is that impression which excites the appetite, by the image of good or evil conceived in the interior senses, from which a corporal change results.

Now, passion thus defined has its seat solely in the *sensitive appetite* which is divided into two parts, namely, the *concupiscible* and the *irascible*.[4] The acts of the will which are usually called by the name of passions are not in reality passions but simple acts.

The passions properly so called are eleven in number. Six of them take their rise in the concupiscible part of the sensitive appetite, and have for their object good or evil absolutely considered. The other five, which regard good inasmuch as it is an object difficult to obtain, or evil as a thing hard to avoid, have their origin in the irascible part of the sensitive appetite. But all the passions are fully developed in the heart which is notably affected by their different movements.[5]

The six passions of the concupiscible appetite are love, desire, joy, hatred, aversion, sadness. Love is a movement of the appetite that impels us towards good as soon as that good is perceived or represented to it. When the loved object is not present a movement of desire for it is awakened which necessarily regards an absent good. But if the good object be present,

---

[4] The sensitive appetite is one generic power and is called sensuality; but it is divided into two powers which are species of the sensitive appetite—the irascible and the concupiscible. St. Thomas Aquinas, *Sum. Theol.* I., Q. 81, Art. 2.

[5] Of the various classifications which psychologists of different schools have offered of the emotions or *passions*, that of the Scholastics is perhaps the most reasonable. They distinguish two aspects of sensuous appetency, or perhaps we had better say two appetites in the sensuous soul, one of which they called the *concupiscible* or the tendency towards objects in themselves, and the other the *irascible* or the appetite which seeks objects not directly in themselves but as perceived as subject to some condition of difficulty or danger. The basis for this distinction they found in the fact that the lower emotions have not all the same formal object: some regard a good object precisely as it is cognized as good, an object therefore that is directly sought after as agreeable or avoided as abhorrent—or in other words, that is directly 'loved' or 'hated.' There are others which, though concerned ultimately, it is true with the good, have as their immediate object the removal of some obstacle that prevents a good from being acquired, or it may be, an evil from being averted—in other words, the object is not the good simply, but the *arduous* good; it is something that is formally presented as difficult to be acquired or avoided, and the emotions of love or hatred are now not simple, but complicated by a special affective state which the presence of the obstacle gives rise to in the perceptive subject. The objects in the first case are of the *concupiscible* appetite, and in the second of the *irascible*. Card. Mercier, *Manual of Modern School. Phil. Psyc.* P. II., C. I., Art. I., N. 67.

a movement of joy is experienced which rests in the present good. Hatred is a movement of horror that is excited in the appetite by evil the moment that evil is perceived or represented to it. But if the evil object be absent a movement of aversion for it is excited in the appetite; whereas when the evil is present the appetite on becoming aware of its presence is moved to sadness.

The five passions which have their seat in the irascible appetite are hope, daring, despair, fear, anger. Hope is a movement of the sensitive appetite which inclines us to a good that is difficult of attainment. When the obstacles in the way of attaining that good are great, the movement of the appetite impelling us to surmount them is called daring. But, if they are so great that they seem to be insurmountable, the movement of the appetite by which we are inclined to abandon all hope of obtaining the good is despair. Fear is that movement of the appetite by which we are disturbed at the sight or approach of an evil that threatens us. And anger is a movement of the appetite by which we are irritated or enraged against an evil that befalls us and which we cannot overcome or avoid.

All these passions have for their object exterior and sensible things. They pursue the three sorts of goods which the world seeks so eagerly, namely, the honourable, the useful and the agreeable, and they dread the opposite evils.

Now the concupiscible appetite with its six passions has this peculiarity about it that it estimates these goods, namely, the honourable, the useful and the agreeable and the opposite evils according to their proper nature, and thus remains favourably or badly impressed by them. But as it often happens that numerous obstacles prevent the concupiscible appetite from obtaining possession of the aforesaid goods, human nature is so constituted that the irascible appetite with its five passions comes to its aid, and by overcoming all the difficulties in the way puts the concupiscible in the tranquil enjoyment of them.

It must be remarked, however, that although these goods—the honourable, the useful and the agreeable—are incapable of satisfying the mind of man, yet they excite in him violent emotions by the attraction of the pleasure which they offer. Then the passions, captivated and aroused by the bait, make a furious attack on the superior part, namely, the soul with its faculties. If it is weak enough to yield they overthrow it; if it resists they harass it.

What we have already said will be sufficient to show those who have left the world and its comforts, for the sake of embracing the religious life with its privations, the nature of the interior warfare which awaits them, and the numerous enemies they shall have to encounter.

This may be suitably illustrated by the conflict of Jacob and Esau wrestling in the womb of their mother. Rebecca suffered such violent pain that she almost regretted she had conceived. She consulted God, and He answering said to her: "Two nations are in thy womb, and two people shall be divided out of thy womb. And one people shall overcome the other; and the elder shall serve the younger."[6]

It is exactly the same with everyone who enters into Religion. He carries two peoples as it were within himself. In the world he bore them in perfect concord; but as soon as he crossed the threshold of the house of God he felt them fighting with each other, because he began to oppose the one and take the part of the other. But let him have courage, for peace shall come through war.[7] According to the Divine promise one of the two, as formerly, shall conquer the other; but with this difference, that it is not the younger that shall overcome the elder, but the superior part, that is, the soul with its faculties, shall bring the inferior part, namely, the body with its sense and passions, under subjection.

Now that we have said all that is necessary to be known about the passions in general, we shall proceed to examine each of them in detail. But it is necessary to remark here, that the chapters in the first part of this work require to be read with more attention and reflection than the rest, for every line therein contains so to speak some salutary principle, and he

---

[6] Gen. 25:23

[7] "Dear Mother, you know very well that it was not my wish to turn my companion away from you, I only wanted her to grasp that true love feeds on sacrifice, and that in proportion as our souls renounce natural enjoyments our affections become stronger and more detached. I remember that when I was a postulant I was sometimes so violently tempted to seek my own satisfaction by having a word with you, that I was obliged to hurry past your cell and hold on to the banisters to keep myself from turning back. Numerous permissions I wanted to ask, and a hundred pretexts for yielding to my desires suggested themselves, but now I am truly glad that I did not listen. I already enjoy the reward promised to those who fight bravely. I no longer feel the need of refusing myself these consolations, for my heart is fixed on God. Because it has loved Him only, it has grown, little by little, and now it can give to those who are dear to Him a far deeper and truer love than if it were centered in a barren and selfish affection." St. Thérèse of Lisieux, *Story of a Soul*, Ch 10, Pub.

who does not grasp them fully can never hope to become skilled in the science of the interior life.

# II

# Love, Desire and Joy

It is the unanimous opinion of Philosophers and Theologians that the concupiscible appetite is anterior to the irascible, and, consequently, that the passions of the former are excited before those of the latter, of which they are the principle and the end.

The reason of this is quite natural. For we only hope or despair by the irascible appetite of what we have first loved and desired by the concupiscible. We must likewise hate an evil before we can conceive daring or fear with regard to it. Moreover, we cannot hate anything unless it is opposed to a good we have already loved.

From this it follows that the concupiscible appetite is not only prior to the irascible, but, that all the passions derive their origin from love, which is the first passion of the concupiscible appetite and around which all the others are entwined. Indeed no one desires or rejoices in anything except what he loves. He will only hate, fly from, and grieve over an evil which is opposed to an object he loves. If he hopes or despairs, it is on account of some good that he loves. Every movement of fear, daring and anger will have for its object an evil which is opposed to some good loved by him.

Love, then, is the first movement excited in the appetite by any good object; or in other words, it is the first impression produced in the appetite by the knowledge of some good when that good pleases it.

We have something similar to this in the operations of nature. Every germinating principle first gives a form to its product, and then a movement in harmony with that form. If, for example, fire inflames the air, it first imparts to the air the form of fire, and then a movement which carries it upwards like fire. In the same way, every good object which comes under the observation of the senses, imprints a certain form on the appetite by means of the image which the senses conceive of it; now, that impression is love, which is as it were the form of the thing loved. Moreover, through love it excites a movement of desire by which the appetite reacts and advances towards the good that it loves.

It is now easy to understand the nature of covetousness, which is more properly called desire when it is guided by reason. Desire is a certain extension or progress of love; or, to speak more plainly, it is that step or movement by which the appetite agreeably impressed by a good object begins to advance towards it. When the object pleases the appetite, or, in other words, when it produces in it the movement of love, the appetite expands and stretches forward to seize on it. This is the movement of desire, in which it is evident that it is the good object that draws the appetite.

But the appetite is drawn vehemently because it follows the attraction of pleasure. Now, if it cannot enjoy the pleasure on account of the absence of the loved object, the desire increases until it becomes a sort of ardour which is called fervour; this is an effect of love. Languor, which usually accompanies it, is also an effect of love, and is nothing else than a profound sadness because of the absence of the beloved object; it sometimes brings its victims even to the grave.

But if we possess the desired object then delectation follows, which is called joy when accompanied by reason. Joy is the movement of the soul which is in possession of the good that pleases it; or, again, it is that movement by which the appetite, possessing and embracing the good which it desired, tastes and enjoys it.

This is one of the principal passions, and appears to be the most efficacious of all, since it completes the movement of love, and love seems to exercise all its power in it. In fact, almost all of the numerous effects of love increase in strength by the enjoyment of the present good.

It is evident then that the passion of joy is surrounded by several circumstances which clearly manifest its strength. Experience also proves this, for if you ask anyone what is it that attracts him most, he will answer that "everyone is attracted by the object that pleases him."

In truth, the honourable and the useful would lose their charm for the human heart if they were separated from the agreeable, as the following example proves. If a prince should wish to bring some peasants from the country to his royal city, and there lavish honours and riches upon them, they would probably refuse the offer, because they could not hope to have as much pleasure in the tumult of the city as among the rocks and hedges of the country to which they were accustomed.

Since then the human heart is afflicted as with a burning fever by the love and desire of pleasure, we require some remedy for these three passions. This we shall endeavour to supply in the following chapter, and give some additional advice regarding them as well as other passions of the same kind.

# III

# Remedies for Love, Desire and Joy

As we wish before treating of the remedies for the passions to provide medicine suitable to the disposition of the patient and the nature of his disease, we must first remark that the human heart which is so ardent in its pursuit of the objects that please it—material and sensible things—can only be diverted from the love of them by substituting other objects of a higher order—spiritual things. For, since the appetite cannot divest itself of its natural inclination, it is useless for us to expect that it will not be attracted by what is honourable, useful and agreeable.

Hence, of all others, the most effective means of controlling the passions consists in proposing to the appetite objects of a higher order, such, however, as it is capable of appreciating, and endeavouring to withdraw the human heart from the love of temporal things, and to turn it to the love of those that are eternal.

Now, if we look into the designs of Divine Wisdom in the formation of man, we shall find that the most benign God did not wish to deprive the eleven passions of their proper nourishment, but rather to supply them with food superior to anything they can find here below. And by doing so He has led man to seek after God and aspire to Him with his whole being according to its various capacities, namely, his lower nature—that is, the senses, appetite, and even the flesh itself; and his higher nature—that is, the soul acting through its different faculties.

Hence, all those who renounce the world seek to re-establish in themselves the part which the passions fulfilled in Adam before the fall, and often, aided by the grace of God, have succeeded, as far as is compatible with the weakness of our fallen state. He was one of this happy number who said: "My heart and my flesh have rejoiced in the living God."[8] And again: "For Thee my soul hath thirsted, for Thee my flesh. O how many ways!"[9]

In order to attain the end we proposed in these *Instructions*, we shall illustrate these principles by a few examples, and we shall show how the passions are to be withdrawn from all objects of the lower order—material and sensible things—and directed to goods of a higher order—spiritual things.

## Example

A Religious sees an object which attracts him, a habit, a book, a comfortable cell; it matters not what. As soon as he beholds it a swift movement of pleasure is excited in the appetite; this is the movement of love. Immediately the heart inclines towards the object; this is the movement of covetousness, by which he desires to wear the habit instead of the one he has. If he obtains it he will rejoice, since it is agreeable to the appetite, already allured by love and desire; this is the movement of joy. Hence this habit enslaves the heart that loves it, and flatters it with a sort of enjoyment; this is the end of the passion of joy which completes the movement of love.

He who is tempted in this way should first of all distinguish the fault from the temptation. For as a rule, there is no sin in those sudden movements of love and desire, because they precede the consent of reason. But if through negligence on the part of reason any fault should glide in, it will be only a very slight one. This remark applies to temptations in general and need not be repeated.

As soon as anyone observes that these quick movements of love and desire are excited in his heart, he should strive at once to check the appetite. This can be done in many ways.

Let him, for instance, reason with it thus: Renounce this wicked desire; it is unworthy of a man endowed with intelligence, raised by his soul above material things and destined for the study of wisdom and practice

---

[8] Ps. 83:3
[9] Ps. 62:2

of virtue, to become attached to a vile object which turns him away from the pursuit of such superior goods. This method of restraining the appetite was practiced by the pagan philosophers who sought after virtue; it is the highest mode of restraining of which reason is capable.

There is another method which is worthy of a Christian. It is higher and more efficacious, because it proceeds from faith which worketh by charity. Reason enlightened by faith, thus addresses the appetite: Renounce this evil desire; it is unworthy of a man destined for the enjoyment of eternal goods, and to be adorned hereafter with the precious robe of immortality, to turn away from the pursuit of goods so valuable for the sake of a vile coarse garment.

Finally, there is a more excellent method, and one that is more appropriate for a Religious. It is this: Renounce this evil desire; it is unbecoming for me who profess to imitate the naked Christ to desire this habit.

Of these three methods of restraining the passions, the first is philosophic, the second Christian, and the third religious. But all those who embrace the religious life are not able at once to make use of the third means; for the nakedness of Jesus Christ on the cross will not make much impression in the beginning, on those who are still subject to self-love. Then the second method should be used as it will prove more efficacious, since the hope of a reward generally exercises more influence over those who are lukewarm.

If the appetite does not yield, yet all is not lost, for the appetite is not like the exterior members. It does not obey reason as a servant. It submits only to the voice of authority, and, even then, it is often very rebellious. Now it is certain that this resistance of the appetite increases our merit and furnishes us with an opportunity of practicing mortification by obliging us to fight against it without ceasing until at last it is forced to submit wholly to reason.

But it often happens that the object coveted by a Religious is given to him by his Superior who is ignorant of his secret desire. The three methods indicated above will then be of very little use to him, since, in addition to the movements of love and desire, he already feels joy in the possession of the desired object. The efficacious remedy then, and the one proper for the Novice, is to manifest the hidden disease to his Master, that he may either take the object away from him altogether, or allow him to use it only with moderation.

In case he is permitted to retain it, and in general whenever any object pleasing to the appetite is given to a Religious, the correct thing for him to do is to multiply internal acts of detachment from it and use it with great caution as something dangerous.

The following are a few examples of these interior acts: "Most Merciful God! this object is highly pleasing to my appetite, but I do not wish to take any deliberate pleasure in it. I should prefer, O Lord! that it would cause me displeasure, and then I would use it only for love of Thee. Most Sweet Jesus! grant that this object may soon become wearisome to me, and that nothing may please me but Thee alone."

Finally, all we have said in the aforesaid example of the habit ought to be carefully practiced by the young Soldiers of Jesus Christ regarding every other object, whether it be of the honourable, the useful, or the agreeable, and they ought to take great pains to discover the movements of these three principal passions, namely, love, desire and joy.

We shall conclude this chapter with a brief and very salutary advice. Whoever wishes seriously to inflict a deadly blow on his passions must first conquer the passion of love which is the source of all the others.

By doing so he will, without doubt, gain a complete victory; and what is more, he will obtain it not only in the shortest and quickest but also in the easiest and most meritorious way.

It may be done thus: No matter what he is doing, let him be constantly on his guard not to allow his heart to be captivated by the deceitful appearance of things, lest it may become attached to them. Whenever he sees anything pleasing, let him immediately turn his heart away from it and lift it up to heavenly things. It is impossible for the other passions to increase in strength or to do him any harm if the roots of love are cut off.

To give an example. A Religious sees some useful object, such as a comfortable seat, which excites his love. Let him immediately raise his heart to the eternal thrones and say: How much more comfortable will be the seats of the House of David. He sees an agreeable object, such as food or drink. The moment he perceives a love for it in the appetite, let him instantly raise his heart to heaven and say: How much more delightful to me will be the banquet at which I shall eat of the Bread of Angels and drink of the Fountain of Life. He sees an honourable good, such as the esteem of others for his talents, learning or other natural gifts. As soon as he observes a love for it growing within him, let him lift up his heart to celestial glory, saying: How much more honourable will be the esteem in which I shall be held in the court of the King of Kings before the eyes of all on the last day. But we shall now proceed to the other three passions which are opposed to these.

# IV

# HATRED, AVERSION, SADNESS AND THEIR REMEDIES

As a good object excites love the moment it is perceived, so an evil object, when known, immediately produces hatred.

Hatred is a movement of the concupiscible appetite opposed to evil; or to speak more clearly, it is that feeling of horror which the appetite experiences when anything disagreeable is presented to it. As there is harmony between the appetite and good, so there is discord between the appetite and evil.

Hatred gives rise to aversion, which is that movement of retraction by which the appetite withdraws from evil; or in other words, that receding or recoiling by which the appetite withdraws from an evil that displeases it is called aversion. If the aversion is very intense it sometimes gets the name of abomination. When the evil is presented by the imagination, the appetite first differs or disagrees with it, that is hatred; then it withdraws from it, that is aversion.

Sadness or pain follows aversion when the evil is present. It is called sadness when the evil is interiorly conceived, that is, perceived only by an interior apprehension; but if the evil affects the body, and is apprehended through the senses, it is called pain. Hence sadness can be caused by past and future as well as present evils represented to the mind, whereas pain can only arise from an evil actually affecting the body.

Sadness, then, is that movement by which the appetite is tormented with an evil which is present; in other words, that movement by which the appetite is oppressed by the weight of an actual and pressing evil is called sadness.

These passions are movements of the appetite directly opposite to those we have considered in the preceding chapter. For hatred is a turning away from evil, whereas love is an inclination towards good. Aversion is a withdrawing from evil, desire is an advancement towards good. Sadness is a depression caused by evil, joy is a dilation at the possession of good.

And as love with the two passions of desire and joy inclines towards the good that is honourable, useful and agreeable, so hatred with its two kindred passions of aversion and sadness withdraws from the evil that is contemptible, worthless and unsavoury. By good or evil here we mean either real or apparent good or evil. Whatever pleases the appetite we call good, and what is repugnant to it, evil.

Now, of all the instructions contained in this chapter, particular attention should be paid to the following. Sadness, which is one of the principle passions, since it completes the movement of hatred, as joy does that of love, is the deadly enemy of all true virtue. For besides the injury which it inflicts on the body, which is greater than that caused by any of the other passions, as it produces a movement of contraction opposed to the natural expansion of the heart, sadness, also, seriously injures the soul, as the following reason will show.

The soul loses all energy when it is depressed under the weight of some evil that has befallen it. A cold torpor takes possession of the entire man which almost paralyses all his members. He feels but little inclination for virtue, and often abandons the practice of it altogether; for, since it is arduous, great strength of soul is required to overcome the difficulties. This will be easily understood by the following reason:

It is well known that when the body suffers any pain the whole person is cast down and the imagination cannot occupy itself with other objects, since the pain fetters the spirit. Now, if we take sadness in its strict sense as something distinct from pain, it certainly tortures the soul more than pain does the body, since the sufferings of the soul are more excruciating than those of the body. I shall prove this from the contraries.

Philosophers and Theologians are unanimous in the opinion that the joys of the soul surpass those of the body. For, as joy is a movement that arises from the union with good, it follows that the joy will be the greater, in proportion to the excellence of the good, the intimacy of the union, and the aptitude of the appetite for enjoying the good. Now, it is evident that the goods of the soul are superior to those of the body since they are spiritual. They are also the object of a more intimate union, since this union is effected without the intervention of the corporal senses. Finally, they are more vividly perceived, since the intellect penetrates the essence of good.

For similar reasons the evils of the soul, which are interiorly apprehended, are greater than those of the body, because they relate to the soul, which, by its nature, is superior to the body. The union is also closer, for evil conceived internally touches and opposes the appetite immediately, while that which is apprehended externally first affects the body. Indeed if it only affects the body and does not displease the appetite, it becomes lighter, and sometimes even a source of pleasure. Hence there are many who can bear with joy, even from unworthy motives, hunger, blows and stripes. Finally, the evil is felt more intensely, because the internal senses have greater aptitude.

From all this Novices will clearly understand how diligent they ought to be in plucking out sadness by the very roots, and how important it is for them to apply prudent remedies to the spiritual maladies treated of in this chapter. All persons of experience well know how frequently these passions, especially the third, turn the young Soldiers of Jesus Christ from the way of salvation on which they had already entered. With good reason, then, the Apostle bids us: "Rejoice in the Lord always; again I say rejoice."[10] Indeed, he did well to repeat such a wise counsel. We shall now treat the remedies to be used.

## Example

A Religious sees an uncomfortable cell, the door or window is badly adjusted: it is too warm in summer or too cold in winter. Immediately there springs up a repugnance of the appetite which is hatred. All at once the appetite, as far as it can, turns away from it. This is aversion. If he is ordered by his Superior to occupy that cell he is cast down by the weight of sorrow. This is sadness.

Now if he has his advancement really at heart, as soon as he perceives this movement of hatred he will say to himself: Put away this repugnance, for if you listen to reason you will see that this thing does not deserve hatred.

---

[10] Phil. 4:4

It is only right that one should put up with even greater inconveniences to practice virtue and free the spirit from the bonds of the flesh. Is not man's liberty fettered by these movements since he hates what is not really bad, and fails in the pursuit of good? This mode of repressing hatred was practiced by the pagans, as we have already remarked when treating of love.

Another method which is worthy of a Christian consists in proposing to the appetite real evils, which, from what we know of them by faith, that resides in the superior part of man, fill us with horror. It may be done in this way. Abstain from hatred, for nothing deserves to be hated but sin, and in this there is no sin. Endure the inconvenience and it will be pleasing to God.

There is a third method, also, which is suitable to the Religious. It is taken from the imitation of Christ, and made in the following way. Abstain from hatred. How much more uncomfortable than that cell was the cross on which Jesus Christ voluntarily hung for you? Is it thus you imitate Jesus Christ Crucified, Who, while the "foxes had holes and the birds of the air nests, had not where to lay His head,"[11] so worthy of eternal repose?

By remonstrances of this kind the superior part generally acquires such strength that the appetite is considerably weakened by its commands and influence, and sometimes even, by a sudden change, begins to love what it before hated.

But it will often happen, too, that these methods of repressing the appetite will be of no avail, either because the appetite is but little impressed by such high motives, or it will not submit to reason on account of the heat of passion. Then it will be found useful to represent to the appetite graver evils, which from its experiences of those that are lighter it will be more afraid of, so that if it does not come to love the present inconvenience which it already hates, it may at least patiently endure it in order to avoid worse evils.

Let him admonish the appetite thus: Give up your hatred. Love and embrace this inconvenience. Are you not treated with indulgence who have deserved the torments of hell? Is not this cell preferable to a bed of fire for all eternity?

These and other similar remedies should be used before sadness has taken too deep root. But if it happens that the Novice is grievously troubled, not by such trifles as in the foregoing example, but by something

---

[11] Cf. Matt. 8:20

of real importance, as when persons are afflicted with scruples or troubled on account of the sins of their past lives, then it will be necessary to employ more efficacious remedies.

For a malady of this kind, which affects the whole interior, assumes various forms and paralyses, as it were, all the powers both of soul and body, it is not so much written and, so to speak, lifeless counsels that should be made use of as the living voice of the Master of Novices, who will prescribe a remedy according to the nature of the evil. Hence those Novices who are severely tried in this way, should have more frequent recourse to their Master than others. They are much to be blamed if they allow themselves to pine away in unprofitable sadness instead of availing themselves of such an easy remedy.

How many powerful motives have they not for driving away sadness! The royal Prophet exulted with joy when he said: "The Lord has brought me out of the pit of misery and the mire of dregs; and He set my feet upon a rock, and directed my steps."[12] As if he would say, I have good reason to rejoice, for I was wallowing in the mire, and the good God not alone drew me out of it gratuitously, but to prevent me from falling in again He has set me on a rock which is Christ. And that I may happily advance by this sublime way, He has directed my steps by His Divine teaching, so that nothing may be wanting to me that is necessary for the attainment of the happiness to which I aspire.

Indeed, Novices have already received all these advantages if they are only faithful to them. For they could never find in the world among its riches, honours and pleasures, causes for rejoicing equal to those they have in religion, unless they deliberately close their eyes to them. Moreover, they shall not find elsewhere such a copious supply of the remedies which spiritual writers prescribe for overcoming sadness. For it is evident that God nowhere provides friends so faithful, hearts so devoted, corporal wants and assistance so readily, in a word, everything that contributes to man's well-being and happiness, as where Christian charity intimately unites the bodies as well as the souls together.

But to conclude this chapter, it must be remarked of the three passions we have just considered, that they can not only be restrained by the remedies assigned, through which the superior part brings them into subjection; but the true followers of Christ can and ought to provoke them frequently

---

[12] Ps. 39:3

according to the instructions laid down in the preceding chapter. For as love, desire and joy are excited in the pursuit of spiritual goods, so hatred, aversion and sadness ought to be aroused in order to detest spiritual evils. This can be done in the following way by which the superior part instructs the inferior, that is, our higher faculties lead on the lower.

When the superior part remarks in the lower appetite a repugnance for labour, contempt, or austerity of life, let it address the appetite thus: If you wish to indulge in hatred, hate the deformity of sin, not those things in which there is no disgrace. If you wish for aversion, fly from sin as from the face of a serpent. If you are sad, let it be on account of the offense you have offered to God by your sins, not for the punishment due to them, that thus your sadness may be changed into salutary penance.

But if the appetite cannot sufficiently realize the deformity of sin to feel a horror for it, let the terror of the last judgment and the pains of hell which the imagination can picture more vividly be represented to it, in order to excite therein hatred, aversion and sadness. We shall now pass on to the passions of the irascible part of the appetite.

# V

## Hope, Daring and their Remedies

The irascible appetite, as we have already said, is the support of the concupiscible. Since divers obstacles are to be met with in the pursuit of the object desired by the concupiscible appetite, the irascible appetite, armed as it were for the combat, attacks these obstacles, overcomes them, and establishes the concupiscible in the free enjoyment of the object that it desired.

Hope holds the first place among the five passions of the irascible appetite. It is nothing else than a movement of the appetite towards a good which is difficult though possible to be obtained; or in other words, hope is that movement by which the irascible appetite is excited to pursue a good object which the concupiscible appetite loves, and though surrounded by difficulties it believes it can obtain.

After hope comes daring. Daring is a movement of the irascible appetite which contends with an imminent evil hard to be overcome; or perhaps better daring is that movement by which the irascible appetite advances against a proximate evil. It is then a sort of progression of hope, as desire is an advancement of love.

When we say daring is a movement against an evil, we understand by the word evil the difficulty that it endeavours to overcome and surrounds the good object which is, properly speaking, the object of hope. But daring also extends to the difficulty of a serious evil which there is hope of conquering.

We must remark, however, with regard to these two passions, that those who are most prone to love are likewise better disposed for hope and daring. For as each of these passions is a movement of progression and the ardour which is proper to love helps by its power of expansion a progressive movement, it follows that those who love are more susceptible of hope and daring. This is specially true of those who take a delight in spiritual things, for the purity of their conscience, supported by the Divine aid, begets a certain security which wonderfully conduces to hope and daring.

From this Novices will clearly understand that it is by a special privilege of God they have been called to a state, where the love of God and heavenly things united with the testimony of a good conscience begets hope and daring, passions which they can henceforth exercise with great profit.

But we must be careful to distinguish the true from the false in such matters, as these passions when badly employed may easily deceive the imprudent. Indeed, we should not hope for anything unworthy of an imitator of Jesus Christ. And it is not meet to use daring towards that which is not an evil. This may be explained by the following example.

## Example

A Religious sees that his Master or Superior reprimands him oftener than the others, and hence he concludes that he is not loved as much as they are. Meanwhile, he wishes to be loved but finds that it is no easy matter to gain the good graces of his Superior. For in order to do this he must study the best means of pleasing him, and try in this way to anticipate his corrections. But all this requires time, thought and trouble. However, the end seems possible to be attained. So without making any account of the loss that his prayers, the various observances of the religious life and the exercise of the presence of God may suffer, he decides seriously to undertake the difficult task. Hope stimulates and daring urges him on. But he can repress these passions in the following manner.

Let him say to his disordered appetite: To what do you aspire? That which is not a real good is unworthy of exciting the hopes of man. Now, the desire to be loved in order to escape correction is an unreasonable thing, and hence cannot be a true good. God forbid, therefore, that I should spend my time and energy in trying to secure the good graces of a man. Far be it from me to strive courageously to put away what mortifies the flesh and to seek for what indulges its inclinations at the expense of virtue. This first way of resisting belongs to the natural order.

It is clear from this example that a Religious who allows himself to be governed by the passions of hope and daring would be sadly deceived. For by hope he longs for his Superior's indulgent love, which, though apparently good, is in reality an evil, and by daring he strives to surmount the difficulty in his way as if it were an evil. Hence he should correct the lower appetite in the following manner by the aid of his higher faculties.

If you wish to exercise hope, why not hope for amendment of life by correction, which is a real good? If there be question of daring, why not strive bravely to overcome the obstacles which oppose this amendment? Arm yourself against the movements of sadness. Attack them courageously and put on a countenance that your Superior, seeing in you the fruit of his correction, may continue to correct you, for it is written: "The just man shall correct me in mercy, and shall reprove me; but let not the oil of the sinner fatten my head."[13] That is, let not the horrid and deceitful word of the flatterer have any charm for my heart.

We shall now give a second method of resistance which is proper to a Christian, and which we can employ by exercising our reason thus: Abandon this hope of acquiring the favour of man, rather "trust in the Lord and do good, and dwell in the land; and thou shalt be fed with its riches."[14] God's friendship will be more honourable, useful and agreeable to you than that of man. You will certainly enjoy it if, despising the good graces of men, you endeavour to establish your hope and portion in heaven. Courage, then, and withstand boldly all that can hinder you from enjoying the sweet embraces of Jesus Christ and you will be happy.

Finally, there is a third manner of resistance which is worthy of the followers of Jesus Christ. Did Christ place His hope in men, or ambition their favour? Did He seek after the friendship of the great? Did He avoid rebukes? How often, on the contrary, when He had power to change embittered hearts and save Himself from chastisements, did He not prefer to keep silent, and thus accomplish the work of my salvation? God forbid that I should differ from such a Divine Model.

---

[13] Ps. 140:5
[14] Ps. 36:3

We ought then, to place all our hope in God and elevate ourselves to so great a good by the efforts of a holy daring. Here we intended to give some advice concerning these two passions of hope and daring, but as the same applies to despair and fear, we shall reserve all we have to say on the subject for the next chapter.

# VI

## Despair, Fear, Anger and their Remedies

Three passions still remain to be considered before bringing this treatise to a close, namely, despair and fear, which are opposed to hope and daring, and anger, which has no contrary passion. For if the difficult evil no longer exists since it has been overcome and possession of the good obtained, no difficulty is then present for the passions of the irascible appetite to attack, hence delectation follows which is a passion of the concupiscible appetite.

Despair is a movement of the appetite withdrawing from a good which we believe we cannot acquire; in other words, that movement by which the appetite is afflicted or cast down when we think we cannot obtain a good which we love is called despair.

It gives rise to fear which is a movement of the appetite receding from an approaching evil; or if you will, fear is that movement by which the appetite is contracted and depressed when a difficult evil is imminent, though not yet present. It is not a simple withdrawing from the evil as aversion, but a depression of the appetite on account of the difficulty of the evil with which it is threatened.

But when the difficult evil is present and has the quality of an injury, it gives rise to anger. Anger is a movement of the appetite seeking revenge; or in other words, it is that movement by which the wounded appetite burns to revenge an injury. It has a twofold object, namely, vengeance as a good, and the person who inflicted the injury as an evil.

These three passions are often the cause of much annoyance to those who have enrolled themselves among the Soldiers of Christ. It is but reasonable then, that they should study these carefully and try to find out their proper remedies since they are so important.

Despair is caused not alone by the evil of the difficulty that opposes us which is present, but also by the superiority of the desired good which is so far above our reach. Although both of these causes may be said to amount to the same thing, yet they show the different movements of despair that arise in the hearts of cowardly soldiers, which are excited at one time by the difficulty of the enterprise, and at another by the thought of the preeminence of the good which they desire. Hence, those who are influenced by this passion will never propose anything great to themselves, without which they shall make but very slight progress.[15]

Fear is wont to so oppress and weaken all the natural operations and fetter, as it were, the entire man, either by a dread of the exalted virtues to be acquired, or an apprehension of the immense labours to be endured before attaining them, that a sort of stupor results; that is to say, an extraordinary imagination of evil which blunts the senses and organs and afflicts them with a sort of paralysis. Hence arise suspicions and consultations on account of those imaginary evils which in all probability will never happen. Finally, fear is the most deadly enemy of true virtue which, as a rule, is acquired only by generous souls.

Anger is a most furious passion and is excited by contempt, or that which is calculated to bring one into contempt. Its ravages are all the greater on account of its affinity to the pernicious vice of pride. Indeed, it rages as often as its victim believes that he is despised. But when the injured person sees that the offense proceeded from ignorance or passion and not from contempt, he is not so much exasperated. The more just his indignation appears to him the more violent the irritation it causes in the appetite, since evil is sought after as a good. This evil is vengeance, which assumes in his eyes the appearance of justice, on account of the imperfection of his reason influenced by passion, by which he tries to balance the revenge with the

---

[15] "Now, O my Lord, the fault is not Thine that those who love Thee do not do great things, but in our cowardice and littleness of mind!" St. Teresa of Avila, *Foundations*, Ch 2. "We must have a holy boldness, for God helps the strong, being no respecter of persons; [Acts 10:34] and He will give courage to you and to me." St. Teresa of Avila, *Way of Perfection*, Ch 16. "Always make courageous resolutions, for then God will give you grace to act accordingly." St. Teresa of Avila, *Conceptions of the Love of God*, #23, Pub.

contempt. Reason, indeed, compares the vengeance with the injury, but it stops too soon before it has accomplished its work. For if it continued it would understand that revenge is not lawful. But the light of reason is so extinguished by anger that this passion is of all others by its extreme vehemence the one which causes most darkness in the mind and judgment.

In conclusion, let us strive with the aid of God's grace to conquer these three passions, which may be compared to three wild beasts, and to apply them as far as possible to Divine things. We shall show how this can be done by the following examples.

## Example of Despair

A Religious is frequently admonished by his Superior to acquire modesty of the eyes. The instruction and exhortation please him. He has already made many efforts, offered up prayers and mortifications for that end, but, so far, has not succeeded. He then falls into a state of dejection and becomes a prey to the evil suggestions of the appetite. Why, it asks, do you torment yourself in vain? You have frequently made use of the remedies prescribed by the holy Fathers yet you have always relapsed again. Having already exhausted all the resources at your disposal, what prospect is there that you will succeed better in the future? Cease, then, to labour any longer for that which is impossible to attain. And from this you may conclude that as you cannot succeed in a small matter like the present, you need never expect to imitate the saints in the practice of the sublimer virtues.

When the appetite is badly disposed in this way, reason should come to its assistance and make use of the second method for controlling the passions by saying: Why are you sad, O my soul, and why do you come to trouble me with your despair? Hope in the Lord, for, after all the faults which, through frailty, I have committed, I shall still confess to Him; I shall praise Him by my hope, Who is the salvation of my countenance; that is to say, the remedy to which I shall look for help.[16] Finally, to express all in one word, He is my God to Whom it belongs to lift up those that are cast down; and since He can easily enrich the poor man in an instant, I could not despair without sin.[17]

There are many consoling examples in which despair has been conquered. Several remedies have also been provided for discouragement.

---

[16] Cf. Ps. 42:5-6
[17] Cf. Ecclus. 11:23

We have most efficacious reasons to excite us to hope which can be found in the treatise on the Theological virtues in the chapter on hope. We shall now pass on to fear.

## Example of Fear

A Religious sees that in the ordinary course of events his Superior will soon impose on him some very disagreeable duty, such as the care of the sick, rising at midnight to call for Matins, or some other similar charge. Immediately the appetite is seized with fear and horror as if it were threatened by some violent tempest, or the sudden fall of an edifice; for it loves ease and fears labour. Reason should then make use of the second method for overcoming the passions as follows.

Let it say: "The Lord is my light and my salvation. Whom shall I fear? The Lord is the protector of my life," that life for which I have renounced the world, "of whom shall I be afraid?" Indeed, I shall not fear to undergo those labours undertaken for the love of God; even "if armies in camp should stand together against me, my heart shall not fear."[18]

But if the sensitive appetite still resists, then the third method which consists in the imitation of Christ, should be used. For when Christ felt in the inferior part such a fear of the sufferings of His Passion that it caused Him to sweat blood, He excited in Himself by a deliberate act of reason the passion of daring in order to combat and surmount the fear. He rose up and said to His disciples: "Rise; let us go. Behold, he is at hand that will betray Me."[19] It is thus that the Soldier of Jesus Christ should act, saying: Let us then arise, and as, in a panic of fear, we almost fled from the evil that presented itself to us, so, animated by fresh courage, let us bravely go to meet this approaching trouble. Is he worthy of Christ who will not accompany Him into the battlefield?

## Example of Anger

A Religious sees that one of his Brethren, perhaps an inferior, has but little respect for him, which he shows by his gestures and words. Immediately, his anger is excited, and in order to avenge the injury, he desires to pay him back in the same way. The appetite complains thus: This Brother ought not

---

[18] Ps. 26:1, 3
[19] Matt. 26:46

to make little of me; he ought to stand up; he ought to uncover his head; he should not condemn what I say; he ought not to contradict me; he ought not to correct me; he ought to answer my questions with greater civility; and many other similar things which pride is accustomed to suggest.

But the superior part should reprehend it thus: Calm thyself down, O fierce appetite! It does not become a man endowed with reason to act like a wild beast and lose his judgement in an intoxication of fury. The hideousness of this passion reveals itself in the countenance, for the eyes flash, the lips tremble, the speech is broken with excitement, and the entire man is estranged from meekness, which, since he is a social animal, is natural to him. But this mode of subduing, however efficacious it may appear, does not exceed the limits of natural reason.

The second method is worthy of a Christian. "Blessed are the meek for they shall possess the land."[20] Shall I deprive myself of a right to a celestial inheritance which faith points out to me to gratify this unruly passion?

But the third means is particularly appropriate to the imitators of Jesus Christ. He was dumb as a lamb before the shearer; He was led as a sheep to the slaughter.[21] "Who, when He was reviled, did not revile; when He suffered He threatened not, but delivered Himself to him that judged Him unjustly."[22] Should not I try to bear all contradictions for love of Him?

Other motives may be sought in the treatise on the virtues where we shall speak of meekness. Here, however, it must be observed, as we have already remarked about the other passions, that these passions can be usefully exercised by turning them to Divine things. And even despair may be made use of, though less easily than the others, according to the counsel of the Royal Prophet, since there is no spiritual good to be despaired of because it is difficult to attain. "Put not," says he, "your trust in princes, in the children of men, in whom there is no salvation."[23] As if he would say: hope not, yea, even despair of obtaining salvation from men who have it not to give. With good reason ought we to despair of that salvation which a deceitful world insolently promises us.

There is a very wide field for the exercise of fear; for, if we dread monastic discipline, we should fear much more a sudden death, the torments of hell and the severity of God's judgement. Indeed, no evil of the present life,

---

[20] Matt. 5:4
[21] Cf. Isa. 53:7
[22] 1 Pet. 2:23
[23] Ps. 145:2-3

however great, should afflict us with fear; for Our Lord bids us "Fear ye not them that kill the body and are not able to kill the soul, but rather fear Him that can destroy both body and soul in hell."[24]

Anger, in like manner, can be exercised in many ways: against sin, against the enemies of the soul, and especially against the passions themselves, which are our most formidable adversaries and wage incessant war with reason. Jesus Christ Himself has taught us how anger can be very profitably employed against enemies of this kind, when, though the meekest of men, He was filled with indignation against the profaners of the Temple. Here we shall bring to a close all we have to say about the passions in particular.

---

[24] Matt. 10:28

# VII

## Remarks on the Passions

From what we have said in the preceding chapters the Novice will clearly understand the difference between those who strive to know and overcome their passions and those who neglect to do so. The former, like the guards who surround the bed of King Solomon, are of the number of the sixty valiant ones of the most valiant of Israel.[25] Military prudence makes them keep their swords by their sides because of the fears of the night. The side signifies here the inferior part or the senses which must be guarded by the sword of mortification, lest the night of sin, indicated by the nocturnal fears, take them by surprise. The latter, on the contrary, so despise the nuptial bed of Solomon, that is to say, their own souls, that their state soon becomes like that of the profaned Temple which provoked the tears of the Machabees, uncultivated soil which produces only brambles and briars.[26]

Let each one, therefore, study carefully the origin, progress and decline of his own passions, for, in addition to what we have said, he will find therein many other things useful for his spiritual progress. He will observe how one passion now, and another again, issuing, as it were, from different sources, produce strange effects, as the following example will show.

Nothing, indeed, seems to be more at variance with anger than delectation, and yet it often springs up conjointly with it, as when one intoxicated by fury satisfies his desire of revenge. Sadness is even more directly opposed to delectation than anger is, yet in the very movement

---

[25] Cf. Cant. 3:7
[26] Cf. 1 Mach. 4:38-39

of affliction caused by the absence of the good object, sadness begets delectation by awaking the remembrance of the thing loved.

Other instances are even clearer, as when the love of some good object begets a hatred of the opposite evil, and the desire of a good deferred increases sadness on account of the delay. We know also how two passions make war on each other regarding the same object; for example, when silence or fasting is concerned, the appetite shows at the same time courage since it hopes for the victory, and fear because it is frightened by the difficulties. All this will help us to understand the various alliances of the passions and to apply the different remedies.

But each one should be careful to find out his predominant passion, that is, the passion which assaults him most violently. For some are more grievously tormented by love, others by hatred, some again by fear, whilst others are more subject to anger. And as the soul, when it applies all its strength to one act, has less energy for performing others, in like manner, when the inferior part is violently agitated by one particular passion, it is usually less troubled by the rest.

As soon as he discovers his capital enemy, let him immediately declare war on it; for, by defeating it, he will disable all the others and bring them to subjection. Let him select for this purpose the remedy which he considers the most efficacious from those we have prescribed in the preceding chapters, or from others which he will easily find by the aid of His Master.[27]

Here it will be necessary to make a general remark about external acts, as the methods of which we have hitherto treated have reference principally to interior acts which are the source of the exterior. An external act of one passion can be made use of as a remedy against the opposite passion, if that passion and the circumstances permit it. Now, we do not think that external acts of this kind are necessary for all the passions; for instance, despair and hope correct each other by internal acts. But what we mean is, when the circumstances are favourable it will be expedient to employ those external acts which will beget a contrary affection, or even extinguish the passion altogether. We do not use the word contrary here in its rigorous sense. Indeed, anger has no contrary passion, yet it can be extinguished.

There are several examples of this, and as a rule of frequent occurrence. When, for instance, any one is affected with a childish fear of the dead, if

---

[27] In Part II., Sec., III., Ch. II., where we shall treat of the selection of a particular virtue, we will also point out the method to be made use of in overcoming the predominant passion.

he boldly touches dead bodies several times as is customary in hospitals, he will soon get rid of it. If a person who is prone to anger be frequently exposed to insults, he will grow less irritable daily, according to the proverb "habitual things do not excite passion," and finally become an example of meekness. If one who is slothful, which is a species of sadness, be violently sprinkled with water or aroused from sleep in any other peremptory way, he will soon shake off the drowsiness. If one is carried away by the desire of a new and becoming habit let him wear an old and patched habit, and in a few days he will overcome all affection for the new one. These are a few of the external remedies for the passions, but we shall add many others in the treatise on the virtues. He who desires to conquer his passions should not only endure with a good will those remedies that have been prescribed for him, but he ought even to ask them sometimes of his Master.

But if we unite the spirit of prayer to these external remedies and the interior means we have prescribed, we shall infallibly succeed. It is, indeed, evident that the practice of prayer is a most efficacious remedy against the passions. For the effort that is made to raise the heart to God, by a natural consequence, weakens the inferior part of man and turns it away from the objects that charm it.[28] Now, the passions are not excited unless the knowledge of their objects has first entered by the senses. But if we apply the interior senses to the images of Divine things, we cut off, as with a sword, the roots of that knowledge of the passions. This remedy is provided by our Rule which ordains that we ought to be assiduous in prayer. Indeed we may add that of all the remedies it is the most efficacious.

Finally, we must remark that the eleven passions, if allowed full scope, will become the sources of as many vices, whereas on the contrary, if governed rigorously according to the dictates of reason, aided by the grace of God, they become, as it were, nurseries of as many virtues. For the movements of the passions produce habits of vice when they rule reason, but habits of virtue when reason rules them. The vice of anger, for instance, arises from the passion of anger unsubdued, whereas the virtue of meekness is acquired by repressing the same passion. Hence it is that several virtues and vices are called by the names of passions; for they take their names from those passions, whose acts or defeats have given them birth.

From this it naturally follows that we should next treat of the vices and virtues, which, with the help of God, we shall do after we have made

---

[28] "The more we pray, the more we wish to pray." St. John Vianney, *Catechism*, Intro., Pub.

a few remarks on temptations. We could, of course, treat separately of the vices in the following treatise on account of their affinity to the passions, but it appears to us more useful to devote it to the virtues, and afterwards insert what pertains to the vices, especially the capital vices. That method of treatment is indeed shorter and more convenient in practice, which teaches us at the same time how to acquire virtue and extirpate vice.

# VIII

## Temptations

One of the chief advantages to be derived from the study and mortification of the passions is beyond doubt a knowledge of temptations and the victory we get over them. For it is evident from the various remedies which we have given for subduing the passions in their infancy, that the most powerful and efficacious means among all others of repelling temptations, according to the holy Fathers, are the same as those which we have indicated in several places in the preceding chapter for overcoming the passions.

Now, if Novices, as soon as any of their passions is excited, no matter from what cause it may arise, make use of the means which we have already prescribed for restraining it, the temptation which they experience at the time can do them no harm, but, on the contrary, it will considerably increase their merit. For when temptations are repelled at the first attack, they only serve to afford valiant Soldiers of Christ an occasion of subduing the passion, acquiring virtue and extirpating the contrary vice.

But in order to know where temptations have their seat and how they insinuate themselves, we shall here give a division of the powers of the soul, according to the common teaching of Theologians.

There are two powers in man which contribute to the attainment of knowledge, and he has also a twofold appetite which corresponds with them in regular proportion.

The first, which is called the sensitive power, embraces all the senses both external and internal. The internal senses are the common sense, imagination, estimative sense, and the sensitive memory. The sensitive appetite, which is made up of the *concupiscible* and *irascible* parts, follows the knowledge imbibed by the senses. We have already treated fully of it with its movements or eleven passions.

This power is called the inferior part of man. The Apostle calls men animals, who, despising the light of their higher reason, are guided by it.

The second power, which is called the rational, comprises the intelligence and reason. It is known as intelligence, when it apprehends first principles which are understood by merely grasping the terms, and it is called reason, when it deduces fresh knowledge from knowledge already possessed. The rational appetite or will corresponds to this power. It is called the superior part of man.

When the second power of man, with the concurrence of the superior appetite, is applied to truths of the moral order, it is called *Synderesis* or Conscience. Synderesis is the habit of the intelligence by which it readily grasps the most fundamental moral truths. Conscience is the judgment of the reason concerning the morality of an action we are about to perform. The will has a natural tendency towards the good represented to it by the simple concept of the intellect.

The reason then or intelligence with the corresponding appetite or will applies itself to check and control the superior part, to regulate the interior and exterior senses, and to govern the inferior appetite. This, however is accomplished in different ways, for the mind commands the exterior senses and members with a sort of despotic power, that is, as a master commands his slaves; but over the inferior appetite it has only a sort of political authority, and commands it in the way that citizens are wont to be governed. Indeed the members and exterior senses are powerless to resist, but the inferior appetite can offer an obstinate resistance.

The best means of repressing it is that which we have indicated in the third chapter, when treating of the remedies for love. It consists in doing violence to love as the chief of all the passions, by proposing to the appetite a better good which will attract it. If, for instance, the sight of carnal beauty excites the love of the concupiscible appetite, then, let the imagination, at the command of reason, represent to the appetite a beautiful image of our Lord, and thus by changing the object it will delight it considerably without depriving it of its food.

It must be remembered that the enemy of our salvation assails with greater fury the true Servants of Jesus Christ than other Christians, who give him but little trouble. Hence, it behooves them to understand fully his attacks and stratagems. He is accustomed to insinuate himself into the interior senses, and increase the natural violence of the passions by fiercely agitating the inferior appetite. But if we do not wish to let the evil grow, we must repel vigorously all temptations as soon as we perceive them.

Thus, for instance, a Novice may be tempted by an unchaste thought, as ordinarily happens, in any of the three following ways. The object is either perceived by the exterior senses and conveyed to the imagination, or the image is formed by the imagination alone without the aid of the external senses, or finally the devil is its author. In every case, he ought with the greatest caution, to refer it immediately to the office of his superior reason, and from it as the seat of authority to govern all the other powers.

If then, while the temptation disturbs the inferior part by its attacks, his reason in any way neglects to prevent the passions excited in the sensitive appetite from being carried towards the unchaste object, he commits a fault, but it will be only venial if he does not do it with full deliberation.

If on the contrary, the reason consents even tacitly but with sufficient deliberation, he commits a mortal sin, unless the matter be light; for in a light matter the consent of reason is only a venial sin.

In like manner the fault will be only venial even in a grave matter, when the superior reason does not act with perfect deliberation, as ordinarily happens in sudden movements or temptations of infidelity which pertain in a special way to the superior reason.

From all this it clearly follows that it is universally true to say that all sins, especially those that are mortal, arise only from the consent of the intellect and will, either formal or tacit. Hence it will not be a mortal sin, if from inadvertence, distraction or any similar cause, the sensitive appetite and even the intellect itself be occupied without the consent of the will with vain, illicit or unchaste thoughts, for a whole hour or even longer, as often happens during the recitation of the Divine Office and other functions.

Let us suppose the case in which a person is distracted by an unchaste or an idle thought, which is very violent and lasts for a long time; and at the same time, he has a strong will firmly determined to drive it away as soon as he adverts to it and to become recollected interiorly, in such a case there never will be a mortal sin.

Hence, when Novices by the grace of God are in such good dispositions that they would not even think on evil objects, much less commit bad deeds they should not allow themselves to be troubled with scruples, which are only a sort of vain but most injurious temptation.

They should be very careful to distinguish between the temptation and the consent, and accustom themselves to resist bravely the first attacks.[29] As long as they preserve a true knowledge of temptations and a firm will to resist them, they may confidently trust that God in His goodness will not allow them to fall without their knowledge into grave sins.

If they are assaulted by violent temptations, they should have unshaken confidence that God, in his liberality, will give them not only sufficient strength but even more than they require, and enable them to turn the temptation to their spiritual profit. Let them hold themselves in readiness, and love to be tried, so that when they have been proved they may receive the crown of life.

Such indeed is the happy issue of temptations as the Son of God testified, when, after He was "tempted in all things like as we are, without sin,"[30] He addressed His followers in those consoling words: "You are they who have continued with Me in My temptations, and I dispose to you, as My Father hath disposed to Me, a Kingdom; that you may eat and drink at My table."[31] Called to the delights of such a splendid banquet, what more should be necessary to encourage us to fight bravely? Let the young Soldiers of Christ then pass through fire and water, that they may be brought forth into refreshment so sweet.[32]

---

[29] "Just so when God intends to perform some act of love in us, by us, and with us; He first suggests it by His inspiration; secondly, we receive that inspiration; and thirdly, we consent to it: for, like as we fall into sin by three steps, temptation, delectation, and consent, so there are three steps whereby we ascend to virtue; inspiration, as opposed to temptation; delectation in God's inspiration, as opposed to that of temptation; and consent to the one instead of to the other." St. Francis de Sales, *Intro. to the Devout Life*, Part II., Ch. XVIII. "But again, as to the pleasure which may be taken in temptation (i.e. delectation), inasmuch as our souls have two parts, one inferior, the other superior, and the inferior does not always choose to be led by the superior, but takes its own line, it not infrequently happens that the inferior part takes pleasure in a temptation not only without consent from, but absolutely in contradiction to the superior will. It is this contest which St. Paul describes when he speaks of the 'law in my members, warring against the law of my mind,' and of the 'flesh lusting against the spirit.'" Ibid., Part IV., Ch III., Pub.

[30] Heb. 4:15

[31] Luke 22:28-30

[32] Cf. Ps. 65:12

# PART II

# The Virtues

# I

# Theological Virtues

## I. Virtues in General

In beginning this treatise on the virtues we cannot make use of a principle better calculated to express its excellence than the definition which is commonly given: "Virtue is a habit of the mind by which we live righteously, of which no one makes bad use."[33]

Surely that must be something very beautiful, and supremely worthy of praise and love, which procures for man the sovereign good of human life, namely, *rectitude*, and preserves it so inviolably that there is no fear of him abusing it.

He anticipated this truth who said that virtue is in itself so excellent that if men only understood it fully they would be enamoured of it. Yet the man who said this did not know Christ, without Whom there can be no true virtue. But in speaking thus, he clearly shows what he would have said of true virtue if he knew it.

Indeed, Christian virtue is so beautiful and shines with such celestial splendour, that if we contrast it with the virtue of the pagans, so admirably eulogized by their philosophers who were destitute of the light of faith, we shall see it rise almost to an incredible height, far above the limits of nature where the ancient sages could never reach.

---

[33] St. Thomas Aquinas, *Sum. Theol.* I-II., Q. 55, Art. IV.

In reality, by a singular favour of Jesus Christ, it contains in itself as regards the honourable, the useful and agreeable, even more than the world, so eager for these three kinds of goods, could ever have imagined.

What nobility is comparable to that which virtue begets? It renders those who practice it worthy of eternal honour. It tramples under foot, as vile and worthless, the glory and pomp of the world. It so elevates the heart of man that nothing but God can satisfy it.

Where, then, are such precious advantages to be found as in true virtue, since it leads to the possession of eternal goods and riches which will neither decrease nor end?

And what pleasure can be compared to the pure joys of that virtue which springs from Jesus Christ, the Fountain of Life, and contains the hope of eternal bliss?

Now, Christian virtue produces all these goods more plentifully than can be expressed by tongue or pen. They are its natural fruit, most delicious, not only to him who practices it, but even to God Himself.

The beauty of virtue is so perfect that it has power to charm even the Holy Spirit. The holy Scriptures, in clear terms, show us how He delights in it. Almost the entire Canticle of Solomon, to say nothing of the other books, is a description of divers virtues forming a perfect beauty by means of a crowd of images, which men accustomed to sensible representations can well understand.

How lovingly does not the most clement God express the delight He takes in those images of the various virtues. Surely nothing can be found better calculated to exalt its beauty.

It is, then, but just that the Novice—the intended Spouse of Christ—should be enamoured with the beauty of what captivates God Himself, and earnestly seek after the plentitude of all those goods of which virtue is the source.

The following passage from Baruch is most appropriate to our subject: "Learn, O Israel! where is wisdom, where is strength, where is understanding: that thou mayest know also where is length of days and life, where is the light of the eyes and peace." And again: "O Israel! how great is the house of God, and how vast is the place of His possession."[34]

Yes, the house is great, and very rich is the inheritance which Novices are called to share. In the sight of such an abundance of spiritual wealth,

---

[34] Baruch 3:14, 24

it would be the height of folly on their part not to engage valiantly in the combat for virtue. What lasting honour can he have in this land of exile who does not direct all his aspirations to eternal goods?

But it is well to give some general principles regarding the virtues to those who are preparing for this glorious enterprise.

To begin, no one can ignore the fact that the virtues, considered in their nature, are the same in beginners, in those who are progressing, and in the perfect. But if we consider them separately, we shall find there are many degrees of difference in the virtues of these three great divisions of souls aspiring after perfection.

Indeed, beginners, and it is to them chiefly these *Instructions* are addressed, should obey the great precept of the Divine law: "Thou shalt love the Lord thy God with thy whole heart,"[35] under pain of being excluded from the first division. If they fulfill this commandment they are evidently in the exercise of the virtue of charity, in which the advancement of the second division and the perfection of the third consist. The same may be said of the other virtues which accompany the love of God.

But it is clear that within the limits of charity, which is very extensive, and also within the limits of the other virtues, those who are progressing are far in advance of beginners, and the perfect are farther still.

Hence it follows that they ought to make use of different methods in practicing virtue. Beginners should apply themselves principally to overcome their passions and eradicate vices, those who are advanced should labour to become more enlightened by the splendour of the virtues, and the perfect should strive to live in uninterrupted union with God.

From this the young aspirants will learn how to direct their energies. They have implacable enemies to contend with, and must arm themselves with the virtues to resist the violence of their assaults.

But though God in His goodness is wont to deal indulgently with those new soldiers, by lightening the difficulties of virtue and restraining the attacks of their adversaries, lest, intimidated by obstacles so formidable, they withdraw from the conflict; still, it is true that the enemies are there, although held in check, as the following example will prove.

Let us take a person who a few days ago was assaulted by temptations and harassed by the rebellion of his passions. At present he finds a facility and pleasure in the practice of good works; yet he has performed no heroic

---

[35] Matt. 22:37

deed, nor has he made use of any violence in overcoming his senses. What then has happened? Suddenly he experienced the unction of devotion and immediately all difficulties disappeared.

But let him who has not yet much experience in the spiritual warfare bear well in mind, that although the enemies without are repressed the enemies within are not dead, but only asleep; and if devotion is withdrawn which holds them in suspense, they will again attack him furiously. Hence he should apply to the practice of virtue with the same diligence in seasons of peace as in time of war.

Now as the virtues are so numerous, and it is not necessary for our purpose to explain them all, we shall treat only of those that are most appropriate to our state, and, taking into consideration the circumstances of time and place, conduce to the end of our religious vocation.

It is true each virtue is excellent in its kind, honourable, useful and agreeable for all, and serves every occasion; but as the capacity of man is limited it would prove rather a hindrance than a help in acquiring them if we were to treat them all.

Indeed, there is no virtue, when properly considered by one who is capable of appreciating its excellence, that does not excite in him a desire to possess it, for virtue belongs to a Divine race, and nothing is more amiable. However, as regards the number and degree of the virtues to which each one, according to his capacity, ought principally to apply himself, it is necessary to follow a safe method. We will speak however of this at the end of the treatise.

But in order to give a full exposition in these instructions of the doctrine of the virtues which is the principal part of wisdom, first, we shall treat of the Theological virtues, secondly, of the moral virtues but with special reference to the religious life.

In our treatment of each virtue we will aim specially at three things; we will give the definition of the virtue, with the motives which should urge us to practice it; we will combat the opposite vice or passion; and we will indicate the acts by which the virtue may be acquired or increased. Thus, under the auspices of the Author of all virtue Jesus Christ and of the Blessed Virgin Mary, we will begin our exposition of the virtues we have chosen.

# II. Faith

## 1. Nature and Excellence of Faith

Faith ought to hold the first place among the virtues, as is evident from the definition which the Apostle gives of it: "Faith is the substance of things to be hoped for, the evidence of things that appear not."[36] As if he would say that faith is the foundation of the edifice constructed in heaven and which we on earth hope to possess; for that is the meaning of the words, "the substance of things to be hoped for." And since the things that are not seen usually make but a slight impression on the mind, St. Paul adds that faith is the evidence or conviction of things that are not seen; whereby he means the authority of God which makes us believe what we see not more firmly than what we see by natural light.

Now the holy Fathers in saying that obedience is a work of faith, teach us that faith is necessary for those who are living under obedience in a far wider and more sublime degree than for ordinary Christians.

Indeed the obscurity of faith harmonizes wonderfully with the voluntary blindness which gives perfection to the "State of Obedience,"[37] wherein we allow ourselves to be conducted not by reason but by the authority of God. It is not meet then to separate two virtues which God has so united in the same spirit. Hence the Apostle, in the chapter which contains the definition of faith, attributes to the virtue of faith the heroic act of Abraham in preparing to immolate his son, although it was a sublime act of obedience. Indeed to the mind of St. Paul this was the same as if he attributed that act to obedience itself.

Since then Novices aspire to the State of Obedience, they are obliged by virtue of the engagements they desire to contract to love faith, and become experts in the practice of it. To dispose themselves to do so they have but to consider the excellence of this virtue.

It is certain that faith belongs to the number of those noble virtues called Theological; that is to say, it is elevated above the other virtues not belonging to this order, and has with hope and charity, in the language of the schools, God Himself for its object. And as it pertains to hope and charity to turn the affections of the will towards the Divine essence, so it

---
[36] Heb. 11:1
[37] By the state of obedience here is meant the Religious state.

belongs to faith to enlighten the understanding with the knowledge of Divine truths.

Now to form an idea of the sublimity of the teaching of faith it is sufficient to know that, not only all the Schools of Philosophy so vainly renowned for their pretended wisdom, but even the angelic spirits themselves if left to their natural perspicacity, could not attain to the knowledge of one revealed truth.

And yet illustrious men through so many ages, desiring to satisfy their innate thirst for science, have esteemed so highly the knowledge of those things that are shrouded in the clouds of darkness, but which man in his fallen state is yet capable of acquiring, that some have renounced riches, others have undertaken long voyages to famous Universities, others again have half blinded themselves by hard study, regarding it as a praiseworthy thing to procure even at the cost of so much labor a little knowledge of philosophy.

What then should not the Religious do to acquire or increase the knowledge of the sublime truths of faith, especially in these days, when it would seem that God has chosen us to spread its light? What chastisement would he not merit who neglects to learn the mysteries of faith, and does not strive to augment daily these treasures of Divine wisdom? Indeed, it is faith that leads to God and thus it is an immense help to salvation. What can be more precious than a sure guide in the way which conducts us to the riches of eternity? Now faith is this guide, and those whom it directs will arrive infallibly at the region of life and spiritual wealth.

What shall we say of the pleasure it brings us? Indeed, when we consider that faith satisfies fully our thirst for knowledge far more than human science can do, we are filled with inexpressible joy and can with greater reason than the Hebrews glory in those words: "He hath not done in like manner to every nation, and His judgments He hath not made manifest to them."[38] It is indeed a wonderful thing, and well calculated to move our hearts, that even uneducated persons who hardly know how to express their thoughts, should be initiated by faith into the "secrets and mysteries of Divine wisdom."[39]

That great admirer of faith, the illustrious St. Augustine, after he was divinely enlightened by its teaching which dispelled the darkness of his former errors, was never tired considering the depth of God's counsels in

---

[38] Ps. 147:20
[39] Ps. 50:8

the salvation of the human race, on account of the marvelous sweetness he experienced therein.

And indeed there is a source of ineffable joy in the certitude of this virtue, which reveals to us, without any danger of error, the Author of our felicity, and how elevated and powerful, how sweet and propitious He is. Let others learn worldly prudence and acquire a useless knowledge of various things, in order to be ranked among sages and celebrated for their science; but we, enrolled among the humble disciples of Jesus Christ, shall submit ourselves to the teaching of this great Master, and guided by the torch of faith which enlightens our darkness, shall pursue the path to eternal life.

This is the wisdom that has conquered the world, ravished the most subtle genius of man, and brought the most eminent of all ages and nations to Jesus Christ Crucified. By the sole confession of this wisdom, a simple man, ignorant of all else but strong in faith, confounded the clever and perfidious eloquence of a philosopher at the Council of Nice, to the astonishment of that grave assembly, and thus accomplished by the power of faith alone what many learned arguments had failed to do.

Let Novices then have a great esteem for the virtue of faith, and diligently apply themselves to acquire a profound knowledge of the mysteries contained in the Christian doctrine. Thus armed, even without any other weapons in their hands, they will be able to carry on the spiritual combat and will be sure to obtain the victory. We will now give some examples of acts of faith.

## II. Practice of Faith

*Acts of faith which we cannot neglect without danger in sudden attacks ought to be exercised in the following manner:*

O my Jesus, Author of Faith, I firmly believe that all Thou hast revealed through our holy Mother the Church is true, and I would freely give my life to confess this truth.

O God of infinite truth, it is impossible that anything false could be revealed by Thee to Thy Church; I am ready to seal this truth with my blood.

It is quite true that there are Three Divine Persons in the Blessed Trinity, and that They are but one God. Would that I could shed the last drop of my blood in testimony of this truth!

O most loving Lord Jesus, it is certain that Thou art truly God and truly Man in one Person. I would willingly offer my body to be burned rather than deny this truth.

It is equally true, my most loving Saviour, that Thou art really present in the Blessed Sacrament of the Altar, true God and true Man; neither fire nor sword could shake my faith in this mystery.

Novices should bear well in mind that every thought, word or action, no matter to what virtue it belongs, if conceived, said or done, with the intention of strengthening or increasing faith, and still more of professing it, is an act of this virtue. The same must be said of the other virtues, as the acts by which they are produced contract the splendour and merit of the virtue to which they are directed. We shall explain this more fully in another chapter.[40]

Hence acts of faith like these should be frequently exercised. And in order to acquire a more vigorous faith it will be useful for them to represent to themselves occasions of martyrdom, as if they were actually in the presence of the tyrants, to excite the heart to produce these acts with greater courage. Moreover, they should be careful to profess the truths of faith with great courage and determination.

We shall give in the third part of this chapter an abridgment of the principal considerations furnished by the holy Fathers for perfecting this virtue, and overcoming the contrary vices and temptations.

Indeed for a soul that is well grounded in faith it will be profitable for the increase of that virtue, to consider attentively the foundations of Divine truth, not in order to believe them but to get a higher conception of them. Hence, Novices should try to acquire a full knowledge of the following motives on which faith rests, so that they may be well prepared for every emergency.

---

[40] We refer the reader for an explanation of this principle to P. II., S. III., C. II.

## III. Motives of Faith

Of all the truths that have ever appeared worthy of faith, there are none that have come down to us surrounded by so many circumstances calculated to attract the belief of man as the truths of Christianity. This we shall briefly prove by a few general considerations.

*First Motive:* The belief in any truth can be established either by the authority of him who proposes it, or by the testimony of others, friends or enemies. If the author is a wise man, of noble extraction and incontestable probity, it would in the common estimation be imprudent to reject his teaching. Now to consider our Lord Jesus Christ merely from a human point of view, it is certain, if we consult the writers of His time, that He was filled with wisdom. He gave proof of it in the Temple when He was but twelve years old; and afterwards during His public life it was said of Him: "How doth this man know letters, having never learned?"[41] and again: "Never did man speak like this man."[42] He was noble. His extraction could not remain unknown, since the marriage of the Blessed Virgin and Saint Joseph was public. Moreover, we read in St. Paul: "It is evident that our Lord sprung out of Juda."[43] Now this was the royal line. He was without reproach. His greatest detractors even could not convict Him of sin. He did not commit those wicked sins then of which He would have been guilty if what He taught was not the truth, for He treated of those things that related to Religion without which the worship of God or the salvation of man cannot exist.

Since Jesus Christ then, being wise, illustrious by birth, irreproachable in His conduct, has formally preached the mystery of the Blessed Trinity, that He was Himself the Son of God, the Sacrament of the Blessed Eucharist and other points of faith, and has suffered death in testimony thereof; it follows either that He was a blasphemer, worthy of condemnation, which is incredible for the reasons we have given; or that He is the true Son of God and that His doctrine is true which is the only legitimate conclusion.

*Second Motive:* The works which anyone accomplishes to confirm his doctrine must also redound to the authority of him who teaches it. For if to wisdom, nobility and probity, the Divine testimony of miracles is joined, no one can object to it unless he is idiotic. Now Jesus Christ as

---

[41] John 7:15
[42] John 7:46
[43] Heb. 7:14

His enemies had to acknowledge wrought several miracles: "What do we for this man doeth many miracles? If we let Him alone so, all will believe in him?"[44] Therefore He preached the truth. And not to speak of all the other prodigies He wrought, the famous resurrection of Lazarus moved the minds of all in Jerusalem and its neighbourhood.

*Third Motive:* If we take the testimony of friends, nowhere shall we find friends more upright than the four Evangelists, whose writings contain a record of public events which are known to everyone. No sane person can deny that these four historians are worthy of belief, since their lives were blameless, they converted a great part of the world, during so many centuries no enemy of the faith has been ever able to convict them of falsehood, and their relics even to the present day bear all the marks of sanctity. Moreover, it is as eyewitnesses that these writers have recorded the mysteries of the life of Christ. What they have said then is true.

*Fourth Motive:* That is not all. We can rightly count among His friends as witnesses properly so called the innumerable Martyrs, who, renouncing nobility, fortune and pleasures, have given their lives for Jesus Christ. How many delicate maidens have courageously spurned the offers of Princes and the goods of this world so agreeable to flesh and blood, and joyfully faced a cruel death! What except the truth of the doctrine taught by Jesus Christ their heavenly Spouse could enable them to do so?

Among His friends are also reckoned those illustrious Confessors and Solitaries, who, trampling under foot the delights of courts, have clothed themselves is coarse garments and given themselves to lives of penance in inaccessible grottoes. We are told in the history of their lives that it was the truth of the doctrine of Jesus Christ alone that moved them to embrace such austerities.

*Fifth Motive:* What shall we say of the miraculous preservation of holy bodies and the sweet perfume they exhale? What of the miracles we have witnessed in our own times, not to speak of the prodigies wrought in the past by the Apostles and other Saints?

It would take too long to go through all the ranks of our Saviour's friends. It is then quite evident that either there is no reason among men, or considering the matter merely from a human point of view, the Christian faith is alone true.

---

[44] John 11:47-48

*Sixth Motive:* Now, we must add to all this the testimony of His enemies. We can count among them Pilate who condemned Him to death and his wife. But Pilate avowed in the presence of the citizens of Jerusalem that he found no fault to reprehend in Him. And his wife sent him a message: "Have thou nothing to do with that just man."[45]

The princes and priests of the Pharisees, furious enemies of Jesus, desired not only to put Him to death but also to kill Lazarus whose miraculous resurrection so glorified the Divine Master. And though they often tried their stratagems against those divine prodigies which confounded them, as the healing of the man born blind; and at another time Jesus Christ Himself even challenged them saying: "Which of you shall convince Me of Sin?"[46] yet they never had the satisfaction of convicting Him of the least fault. Finally, those who put Him to death, seeing how the very earth itself expressed its horror at the death of its Creator, cried out that He was a just man and the Son of God. All this is clearly related by the Evangelists.

*Seventh Motive:* How speak of the adoration of the oriental Kings at His birth, or the bread miraculously furnished to so many thousands in the wilderness? How speak of His glorious Resurrection, the earthquake, the terrified guards, the bribe given by the priests to the soldiers, the Ascension, followed by the Coming of the Holy Ghost, and many other prodigies, so public that it would be the height of folly to deny them?

What shall we say of the public apparitions of our Saviour to His Apostles, that is to say, to men so truthful, so upright, so celebrated all over the world, the testimony of whom could never be questioned even by the most incredulous?

*Eighth Motive:* What of the uninterrupted series of the Vicars of Jesus Christ, the Successors of St. Peter, who have outlived the fierce opposition of the world and the wiles of satan? What of so many empires and notably that of Rome, which after it had conquered all others was itself in turn conquered, not by the power, resources or eloquence of poor men but by the faith of Christ?

What of the distinguished men of so many different nations, illustrious alike for sanctity and wisdom, who by their writings and by their worship have wonderfully concurred in professing the same faith as Jesus Christ, and who, although they have never seen one another face to face, yet have always displayed both by word and writing the same phase of the faith?

[45] Matt. 27:19
[46] John 8:46

And even if we had not the foregoing reasons in favour of the truth of the Christian faith, there is yet another reason which ought not be kept back, which Christians cannot ignore, and which is of a nature to convince those who are outside the Church no matter to what sect they belong. It is as follows.

*Ninth Motive*: Either there is no worship of the true God on earth or there is. No one except an atheist can deny the first part of this. For how can anyone assert that the Author of all things has not inspired men with Religion, since the natural law imposes a duty on them to render homage to their Creator? Then if this worship exists, it is evident that the true God could only reveal a Religion in harmony with the idea of infinite wisdom and goodness, which all sects attribute to the Divinity. Consequently, it is necessary that this Religion should exact of its followers true sanctity, and the practice of all virtues proper to the nature of man. The Divine purity cannot take delight in aught that is sullied. Now in order that the Servants of God may be unspotted, virtues must take the place of vices in their hearts. The absence of one virtue suffices to tarnish their souls.

Then, as it is only faith or the Christian Law which exacts of us real and mature sanctity by the perfection of all virtues, and reproves every thought even the slightest contrary to right reason, it follows logically that the Christian truth alone is Divine, and that all the other doctrines opposed to it come from the demon. We can easily be convinced of this by comparing these doctrines with the doctrine of Christ; by considering the vain ceremonies which they authorize in their worship, the infamous things which they admit as lawful, and many other points which we must pass over in silence in this brief instruction. For the rest it suffices to know that these doctrines or laws are different from the Christian Law, which was upheld from the beginning by the perpetual confession of the faith. If then the law of Jesus Christ is as we have proved the true one, all others apart from it are false.

*Conclusion:* Undoubtedly it is necessary that Religious, who are called not only to embrace most firmly the faith of Jesus Christ and to root it deeply in their own hearts, but also to propagate it among others, should furnish themselves with all these considerations as with so many tried weapons. And in order to provide first for their own spiritual interests they should attach themselves so strongly to the practice of this virtue, that from their entrance into the "State of Obedience," that is, the Religious life, they will manifest to their Superiors a docile, supple mind, disposed to believe what they see not, and to lean on the authority of God not on human reason. By this means they will not fail to make from day to day such marked progress in the practice of faith, that if an occasion should present itself they would gladly give their lives to defend it.

# III. Hope

## 1. Its Nature and Excellence

Hope is a *Theological virtue* by which the will wherein it is seated, aided by grace, raises itself towards God to acquire the possession of Him.

What we have said of the passion of hope will help considerably to make this definition clear. Indeed Theological hope fortified by the Divine aid, tends towards the good which is infinite and for this reason difficult to attain, and its act is a sort of flight of the will aspiring after great things. The *Theological virtues* have this peculiarity, that what the human heart undertakes through their efforts surpasses in grandeur the object of the other virtues.

This will enlighten us as to the nature of the noble virtue of hope. The intellect illuminated by the light of faith has no sooner proposed to the will the excellence of the eternal good, than by means of Divine hope the will raises itself up, and trusts that it will come to the enjoyment of this good. The Apostle might then well say in formal terms of hope that it "goes before," that is, by its acts as by so many degrees, it constantly draws nearer to the good which faith has shown to it.

Grave dangers show how advantageous to us it is to acquire the habit of this virtue. For instance, if a man has not frequently exercised himself in acts of hope, it is astonishing into what an excess of fear and almost despair he will fall when suddenly exposed to the danger of death.

The reason of this is very simple. Since these grave dangers come but rarely, he who thinks of making acts of hope only when his life is at stake, neglecting to do so in the ordinary circumstances of every day, will find himself powerless and inert, like a blunt and rusty sword which has remained long idle in its scabbard and cannot be drawn out without difficulty.

INSTRUCTION OF NOVICES

On the contrary, he who habitually makes these acts, acquires a disposition of mind that is prepared for every emergency and is according to the Royal Prophet peculiar to the just man: "His heart is ready to hope in the Lord." Then, to show the happy fruits of this preparation he says: "His heart is strengthened, he shall not be moved until he look over his enemies."[47]

The necessity of hope is certainly very great, for it gives firmness to the heart of man and enriches him with solid goods. It is in these advantages which are reserved to the Saints that the Apostle rejoices when he says: "We have hope as a sure and firm anchor of the soul."[48]

The Saint indicates the sweetness of the consolations imparted by this firm hope of immortality when he says: "Rejoicing in hope."[49] Nothing so cheers the soul buffeted by the storms of the world as the assured expectation of heaven.

This hope gives strength to undertake great things, and by the excess of joy which it causes inspires a contempt for all meaner pleasures.

Moreover, this Divine virtue is so noble that it renders hearts large and magnanimous making them forget their natural vileness. The soul, freed in some sort from the burden of the body, raises itself towards God with a vigorous movement as it is written: "They that hope in the Lord shall renew their strength, they shall take wings as eagles; they shall run and not be weary."[50]

Novices then should apply themselves with much care to the practice of this virtue. Let them strive to anticipate those difficult occasions which rarely occur, by exercising frequent acts of hope. They should not be content with that faint languishing hope which seems to satisfy many Christians, but will endeavour to have a strong hope which will be proof against all difficulties; like that holy man who, besieged by immense evils, rebuked by God, tormented by his friends, driven to despair by his wife, a burden to himself, expecting death as it were each moment, said: "Although He should kill me, I will trust in Him."[51]

If men only knew how worthy of the most clement God it is, on account of His infinite goodness and mercy, to have pity on those who

---

[47] Ps. 111:7-8
[48] Cf. Heb. 6:19
[49] Rom. 12:12
[50] Isa. 40:31
[51] Job 13:15

humble themselves before Him, and how easy it is for Him in an instant to lift up the poor from abjection and misery, there is no doubt but they would rest on Him with perfect confidence amid the gravest dangers of sin.

Indeed it is the characteristic of a generous heart like that of God to be bountiful; and nothing so contributes to His glory, which is the end of all His works as to show Himself propitious to those who hope in Him. Whenever He sees a soul overpowered by the guilt of many grievous sins with which his conscience upbraids him, yet confiding in the Divine goodness which, beyond all doubt, promises him pardon, He seems, as far as it is lawful to conjecture, to act with it thus.

This sinner, although burdened with debt which he was not able to pay, hitherto thought only of provoking Me to anger, and yet now when I am ready to take vengeance on him at any moment he firmly hopes in Me. Since he knows for certain by the testimony of his own conscience that he does not merit pardon, he would never trust so firmly in Me unless he was convinced of My excessive generosity and disposition to forgive. I will pardon him then, "because he hopes in Me; I will deliver him; I will protect him because he hath known My name."[52] It is thus that God has in reality pardoned a great number of sinners.

From all this Novices should conclude that, since by the grace of God they have been preserved from such grievous sins, it would be disgraceful and altogether unworthy of the Servants of Jesus Christ not to have a firm hope in Him for things of less importance, such as a victory over some passion or the acquisition of a virtue. But it is time to give the acts to be used in the practice of this virtue.

## II. Practice of Hope

O most clement God, relying on Thy grace and the good works accomplished by Thy aid I firmly hope one day to enjoy eternal glory.

However grievous my sins may have been, O God of infinite goodness, I am confident Thou wilt pardon me.

No matter how often in the day I may fall into sin, it is certain that with Thy grace I can still acquire Christian perfection.

---

[52] Ps. 90:14

Even if I had the misfortune to commit the most grievous sins, O gentle Jesus, Thou wouldst still be able to draw me out of the abyss of misery.

If I were laden with all the sins committed since the beginning of the world, O my God, in Thy great goodness, Thou wouldst willingly pardon me.

Yes! O my most merciful God, I hope with the help of Thy grace, to overcome all the difficulties of this life, and to possess Thee for ever in the land of the living.

If armies were encamped about me and ready to destroy me; were I even at the gates of hell, I should still rely on Thy great mercy.

Acts of this kind ought to be made with a holy energy. It is wonderful how they raise the courage of a heart which leans on the Divine aid. But we will indicate in the third part of this chapter the means to be employed in order to extinguish the vice, passion and temptations against the virtue of hope.

## III. MOTIVES OF HOPE

Here we are encountered by a multitude of considerations so efficacious and well calculated to encourage us in our warfare against all kinds of vice, passion and temptation, that they would move even the most stony hearts. We shall select from among them three of the most powerful.

*First Motive:* Putting aside altogether the Incarnation, Passion and Death of the Son of God, the remedies which man possesses in the Sacraments, the protection of the Blessed Virgin and the Saints, and considering only in God His goodness and His natural inclination to do good, we find that He is infinite in mercy, and that He can manifest His goodness and mercy in no other way so highly as in granting pardon. Indeed the supreme degree of bounty and mercy consists in doing good to those who have offended us. Then, since God has made all things for Himself, that is, to manifest His goodness and promote His glory, and nothing contributes so much to this end as to have pity on man, especially those who have grievously offended Him, we may confidently hope that He will hear the sinner's prayer and grant him pardon, grace and glory.

*Second Motive:* Let us add yet more to the force of this reason. God is more inclined to do good than fire is to burn. Consequently as fire, if allowed to act without hindrance, never fails to consume every combustible material that is submitted to it, so God exercises His mercy whenever it meets with no obstacle. Now man puts no obstacle in the way so long as he seriously wishes that God would have pity and bestow His graces on him. Hence there is reason to hope, that even the greatest sinners if they seriously wish it will obtain pardon of all their sins.

*Third Motive:* But we shall endeavour to render this truth still more clear. Since the beginning of the world, there never was a man, however addicted to wine or any other form of self-gratification he may have been, who found as much pleasure in satisfying himself as God does in showing mercy. If then the drunkard or intemperate man not only seeks gladly his criminal pleasure but even runs impetuously after it, God also without any unseemliness to His Divine Majesty, nay even with sovereign dignity, hastens as it were to enjoy the delight of showing mercy. Have we not sufficient proof of this? Indeed, it is because He found pleasure in showing mercy promptly that He sent His Word, that is His Son on earth. Why His Son? Because as it is written: "His Word runneth swiftly."[53]

*Fourth Motive:* God in showing mercy performs an honourable act, that is, one that conduces to His own glory; an agreeable act, since it is conformable to His nature and inclination; an advantageous act, since He gains thereby as many servants as He has forgiven sinners. Who then will be so unreasonable or foolish as not to conceive a firm hope, that he will receive from the infinite munificence of the Divine Majesty whatever he asks?

*Fifth Motive:* From all eternity, before there was any creature to pray, God foreseeing the fall of Adam and moved by His goodness alone decreed the Incarnation of Jesus Christ, our Redeemer. And when the time was accomplished the Son of God made man was born of the Virgin Mary, suffered for thirty-three years all sorts of privations, and finally by shedding His Blood, paid to His Father the price of my salvation; offering Himself wholly for me the same as if there was no one else to be redeemed. In other words, Jesus Christ so offered the price of all His Blood for me, that it was shed for my salvation no less than if He did not offer it for any other. And, moreover, I was not deprived of one drop of His Blood any more than if He shed it all for me alone. This the Apostle must have felt when he said: "I live in the faith of the Son of God, Who loved me, and delivered Himself

---

[53] Ps. 147:15

for me."⁵⁴ Here he seems to express something more special than when he said: "Christ hath loved us, and hath delivered Himself for us."⁵⁵

Now in order to weigh well the force of this consideration let us for a moment imagine that Jesus Christ, in presenting to His Eternal Father the whole price of His Blood, His sufferings and His death, intercedes with Him for me alone, and asks with loud cries and tears by His sweat of Blood in Gethsemane, not for the salvation of other men, but only for my salvation; for the offerings and prayers He makes for others detract nothing from those He makes for me.

Is there anyone then so senseless, who, when he meditates on those things, will not courageously rise from the abyss if dejected and establish in his heart an invincible hope? Surely this thought is capable, not only of restoring health to the sick but even of raising the dead to life. Indeed that heart must be obdurate which will not be moved by it.

*Sixth Motive:* Besides the infinite love which God has shown us in giving us His Son Who is the foundation of our hope, Jesus Christ Himself has said many things eminently calculated to excite this virtue in us: "Ask and it shall be given you; seek and you shall find; knock and it shall be opened unto you. For everyone that asketh receiveth; and he that seeketh findeth; and to him that knocketh it shall be opened."⁵⁶ This is certainly a great promise. What follows is still more magnificent. "If you ask the Father anything in My name He will give it you."⁵⁷ It is thus that He, through Whom we ask, counsels us to affix the seal of His name to our petitions.

*Seventh Motive:* There is another very wonderful promise recorded by Saint Mark. Jesus Christ at first said: "Have the faith of God, Amen I say to you that whosoever shall say to this mountain, be thou removed and be cast into the sea, and shall not stagger in his heart, but believe that whatsoever he saith shall be done; it shall be done unto him." Then He added: "Therefore I say unto you, all things whatsoever you ask when ye pray, believe that you shall receive; and they shall come unto you."⁵⁸

Indeed these words are so well calculated to excite courage and beget a vigorous hope even in the most languishing hearts, that it is impossible to imagine anything more efficacious for the purpose. For this mode of

---

[54] Gal. 2:20
[55] Eph. 5:2
[56] Matt. 7:7-8
[57] John 16:23
[58] Mark 11:22-24

expression "Therefore I say to you," is on the part of Jesus Christ, Who is ever faithful to His promises, like the written engagement by which He has in some sort bound Himself to us, on condition that, unheeding our own weakness, we conceive exalted sentiments of His Father's goodness, and believe firmly that He is disposed to grant us our requests. Now this as we shall undertake to prove is quite conformable to reason.

*Eighth Motive:* There is not a prince in the whole world so wanting in liberality and probity, if he promises that he will give an alms or any other gift on his birthday or another festival, to those who ask it of him with confidence, firmly believing that he will keep his word, who will not give what he promised. No one can reasonably doubt this, even if that prince acted only from political motives, and although he may suffer pecuniary loss thereby.

Then if Jesus Christ, the Sovereign Master of all things, Whose riches can never diminish—nay, even humanly speaking, the more He bestows the richer He becomes—has promised what after all will cost Him but an act of His will, who is there so foolish as not to hope firmly, or not to ask with confidence what he desires?

*Conclusion:* To conclude, if, as we have seen in the first consideration, God is by His very nature inclined to do good; if, as has been said in the fifth, He has, of His own free will, delivered His only Son to a most cruel death, in order that I may obtain the graces that I ask; if, in fine, this Son Who is Himself our God and Redeemer has with a generosity worthy of Him, engaged Himself to grant what I ask; I must either have a firm hope of obtaining the eternal goods that I ask, or else I am a complete stranger to the dictates of right reason and teaching of Christianity.

Reflecting then on these reasons which are so numerous and so solid, let Novices endeavour each day to make frequent acts of hope, and thus strengthen this virtue more and more in their souls by its constant practice.

# IV. Charity

## I. Nature and Excellence of Charity

Charity, the mark of the children of God, which distinguishes Jerusalem the City of Peace from Babylon the City of Confusion, is a virtue whereby the will attaches itself to God because of His infinite goodness.

It is the queen of all the virtues. Theologians say that it is the form of virtue, since all other virtues, not excepting faith and hope, are crude and unformed if they are not clothed and embellished with the splendour of Divine charity.

Since this excellent virtue is the true friendship of God, all the rest without it have some deformity, as they lack the pure disposition of heart which inclines us to seek, not our own interests, but those of God alone.

It follows that charity, like in its flight to the eagle which bears aloft her young, lifts up the acts of the other virtues to the rays of the true Sun. For when borne on the wings of this sublime virtue they arrive at the term which they could not attain by their own strength.

Hence the Apostle justly extols charity as being the life of the other virtues and even of the soul itself. He declares that the tongues of men and Angels, the gift of prophecy, the power of miracles, the distribution of alms, and even the torment of death itself are, in the absence of charity, of no price or merit for eternity.[59]

Since then charity is life, vivifying by its contact the virtues which form its cortege, it should be sought and preserved with the same ardour and care as life itself.

Our Lord Jesus Christ, Who declared that He came on earth in order that men might have a greater abundance of life, teaches this truth clearly when, forgetting in some sort the other virtues, He says: "This is My commandment, that you love one another as I have loved you."[60] As if He would say, seek this one good, charity, which gives life and I shall have attained the end for which I came down from heaven.

This admirable commandment of Jesus Christ was so deeply engraved on the hearts of the Apostles and of all the Fathers of the Church that they have exalted charity by almost an infinite number of eulogies.

---

[59] Cf. 1 Cor. 13:1
[60] John 15:12

Even if all these testimonies were wanting, charity has in itself a splendour and marvelous charm which constrain us to love it. One should have a heart of iron to resist its beauty.

Now what is charity? It is a brilliant ray escaped from the Divine Light and communicated unsullied to the heart of man. Its beauty is so extraordinary as to render it a fitting ornament for the resting-place of the heavenly Spouse.

Nothing created touches it; no earthly interest guides it; no fear agitates it save that of sin. It is, in fine, of such finished perfection that, unlike faith or hope, it will never end[61], since it has nothing imperfect in it that can exclude it from the celestial Kingdom.

The character of charity is certainly very noble; but this is perhaps to our eyes its least merit, as the advantages it procures will doubtless have a more efficacious influence on our hearts. Indeed, there is no middle course; we must either fully observe the law of God or perish eternally. Is it not more prudent, then, to apply ourselves to the practice of love which is the observance of Divine ordinances[62] and the fulfilling of the law[63], and thereby to increase by charity the merit of those acts which otherwise would have been produced, but with less profit? For it is certain that the merit of our acts depends on the degree of love with which they are performed.

This is not all. The heavenly virtue of charity produces another marvelous effect in those who cultivate it; for not only does it increase the merit of each action, but it also fills the soul with superabundant consolation. We know that acts of love are the most agreeable, and thus the easiest and most lasting; since the very inclination of our nature attaches us more quickly and irrevocably to the things which give us pleasure.

Seeing, then, that this way of charity, which the Apostle St. Paul praises so highly, is the most excellent by so many titles, Novices should strive as far as possible to fulfill most perfectly everything that belongs to the province of this virtue. From the beginning of their career they should have the most filial affection for God, and let themselves be conducted by His love in all that they think, say or do.

According to the unanimous teaching of Philosophers and Theologians, we should first form an idea in our mind of the end we have in view; for in human affairs the end is the principle which determines the act.

---

[61] Cf. 1 Cor. 13:8
[62] Cf. Wis. 6:19
[63] Cf. Rom. 13:8-10

It is only fitting, then, that Novices should first engrave in their hearts the sovereign good towards which they tend, and for Whom alone they have embraced the religious life; and that afterwards, without ever relaxing, they direct all their efforts towards the attainment of this end by performing all their actions for the pure love of God.

Now, in order that they may begin in real earnest to love this immense good which is the source of all love, they should weigh well these powerful motives for charity which will be found in the third part of this chapter, for these considerations will help them to fight generously against the temptations they will be exposed to from the world, the flesh and the devil. We shall give some examples of acts of charity.

## II. Practice of Charity

*Charity produces two kinds of acts; acts of love towards God, and acts of love towards our neighbor. We shall begin with the former.*

### Acts of Charity Towards God

Most gracious God, I entreat Thee, take full and entire possession of my heart.

O most loving Lord, I immolate to Thee my whole being.

O my most desirable God, far be it from me ever to love anything save Thee.

O most sweet God of my soul, I seek Thee alone as my most precious inheritance.

Most amiable Author of my life, I sacrifice my whole heart to Thee.

O Beauty surpassing all earthly splendour, inflame me with the fire of Thy charms.

Most gracious Prince of my heart, draw me irresistibly to Thee.

O King all radiant with beauty, I desire no other heritage than Thee.

O most pure Spouse of my soul, may all other affections depart that I may seek Thee alone with all my heart.

Live, O supreme Emperor of my heart, and reign over it as it becomes Thee to do.

Most high King of Glory, reign for ever on the eternal throne of Thy Majesty.

O God of my heart, God Whose riches are infinite, it is altogether just that Thou shouldst be most happy in Thyself.

I desire sincerely that Thou, O Eternal King shouldst reign for ever and ever.

O supreme Lord of my heart, would that I could subject to Thy yoke all the children of Adam, and prevail on them to seek only Thee.

Would that I had all the millions of hearts that ever pleased Thee, or could please Thee, in order that I might be able to give them wholly to Thee.

My most sweet Saviour, grant me the grace that nothing may give me pleasure save Thee alone.

The Saints advise us to produce these acts not only in time of consolation, but also when the soul is arid and everything seems to be in vain. For, whatever may be the repugnance of the inferior part, the superior part profits by them, provided we have an intense desire to please God. The same may be said with regard to the acts of the other virtues.

## Acts of Charity Towards Our Neighbour

To love our neighbor is simply to desire with a sincere heart that he may attain eternal beatitude and the things which lead thereto. We can make acts of this love in the following manner.

## Interior Acts

O most clement God, may all sinners be converted and give themselves to Thee.

O most merciful Lord, grant that all the enemies of the Church may submit to Thy Vicar.

I implore Thee, O Lord, through Thy infinite mercy, to turn the ambition of those who seek after earthly dignities to Thee.

I beseech Thee, O Lord, to convert all those who are slaves to carnal pleasure.

O most loving Lord, grant that the avaricious may become detached from perishable goods and seek only the riches of Thy love.

These acts may be thus made in a thousand different forms. Ordinarily they are produced with more fervour when they relate to something that happens to a particular person; for instance one who falls into sin, an illness, dishonour, persecution, or anything similar.

## Exterior Acts

With regard to our neighbour, we must also practice exterior acts of charity when he needs our services. This, however, ought to be done with discretion; for in a Convent the practice of charity should be ruled by obedience. But beyond this, we should always show ourselves ready to render him the services permitted to, or imposed on us. These services include the care of the sick, relieving those who are fatigued, consoling the afflicted and other acts of the same kind.

As to spiritual acts of charity, Novices should rejoice in doing good to others, grieve for the evils which befall them and pray for their welfare; but their age does not permit that they correct, instruct, or exercise other similar acts towards them. If anything in the conduct of others should scandalize them they will try to believe themselves mistaken; and if they cannot overcome this temptation let them manifest it to the Superior. Their chief study in the exercise of charity towards their neighbor should be to accommodate themselves to the manners of others, as far as it can be done without prejudice to virtue; to correct in themselves what is displeasing to others; and, finally, to bear patiently the faults and defects of others without showing any repugnance. Such are the elements of which the true love of our neighbour is composed. But we shall proceed to the third part of this chapter.

## III. Motives of Charity

The love of our neighbour, or more properly speaking, the entire economy of the human heart, depends on the love of God. It is this love which sweetens all that is bitter in our neighbour; it is this love which opposes a victorious resistance to the attacks of the enemy. The first born of charity, then, the love of God, is the subject on which we propose to instruct Novices, by the following considerations.

## Love of God

*First Motive:* Of all the amiable qualities which we can imagine there is not one which God does not possess in an eminent degree. But to make a fitting choice from such a vast number, we must first remark that all love has reference to either of two heads, namely, the person or the acts. One can be loved for what he is in himself, or because of his deeds.

See, for example, what sometimes happens. As soon as we see a Prince eminent for nobility, beauty and wisdom, we feel drawn towards him, though we expect no favour from him. On the other hand, we spontaneously love a man of the people without beauty or wit, from whom we hope for some service. Now, if we add to the charms of the prince the motive of usefulness to us, we shall then, it seems to me, have condensed all the force of love.

*Second Motive:* The sovereign Lord of the world is nobility itself, wisdom itself, beauty itself. With what ardour, then, should not those especially who aspire to eternal blessings seek after the love of such an immense good? Is it not true that nobility alone suffices to turn the heads of a great number of men? They try to represent to themselves something (I know not what) divine which they think they will find in it. We find a proof of this in the fables of ancient writers. When they wished to exalt their heroes they represented them as belonging to the family of the gods. We see it even daily in the courts of the great; everyone seems desirous of insinuating himself into the good graces of the most illustrious Princes as if contact with these would ennoble them. How far wiser is the desire of the Royal Prophet: "My soul hath stuck close to Thee."[64] This, indeed, is the source of true nobility, as it is written: "Come to Him and be enlightened," that is, you will become noble and illustrious. "And your faces shall not be confounded,"[65] that is, you will not have to blush for shame, since all dishonour is annihilated by that ancient nobility which never had a beginning, by that beauty of infinite purity, by that greatness which is so sublime that beside it the loftiest heights of the blessed spirits appear but as a low valley.

*Third Motive:* What shall we say of wisdom? The esteem of even a little of it drives men from their country, and leads them across wide seas and into vast solitudes. Thus the whole East sighed after Solomon; a

---

[64] Ps. 62:9
[65] Ps. 33:6

crowd of illustrious men flocked around Plato and Aristotle; and the most brilliant among the Fathers of the Church travelled over several kingdoms animated with the same sentiment. Why, then, should we not strive to enter into communication with this Infinite Wisdom that is alone capable of quenching the burning thirst which consumes us? Why should we not endeavour to gain the good graces of a Master so eminent, Who in one moment can impart to our souls the plenitude of wisdom; not the wisdom which enfeebles the mind of man by eager speculation, but the most delicious wisdom whose torrents rejoice the city of God. Indeed, nothing on this earth can be more desirable than its sweetness.

*Fourth Motive:* What shall we say of beauty? There is no one so senseless as not to feel and admire its power. In fact, its very name inspires joy, and many for the sake of it despise not only riches and other goods of an inferior order, but even nobility and wisdom. Experience has proved this to be but too true.

Beauty has a powerful magnetic force; for it draws hearts, delights and exercises a sweet empire over them. Now, even earthly beauty does all this, although subject to corruption and mingled with a thousand deformities.

Why, then, does not the Divine Beauty, Whose name alone has the power to melt the very rocks, captivate the hearts of those who have trodden underfoot all the beauty of the world to give themselves up to the pursuit of the one thing necessary? In truth, the splendour of the Saviour's Body alone incomparably surpasses all the beauty of the entire universe. What, then, must be the beauty of His Soul? What must be the beauty of His Divinity, a beauty without shadow of imperfection and capable of softening all hearts.

Here, words are too weak, and serve rather to diminish than exalt the greatness of these things. But, faith fills up the void, and believes even greater things than can be expressed by words which charity pursues in her lofty flight.

It is the same with regard to the second head or viewpoint of love, that is, the benefits which God has granted to, and still reserves for, each one of us; as it is in this the Divine Bounty shines specially. Indeed, Jesus Christ, Who makes eloquent the tongues of little ones, must guide my pen, or I shall not be able to speak adequately on the subject.

*Fifth Motive:* There is no nature so savage that it cannot be softened by kindness. We see every day even lions and bears tamed by good treatment and fawning on their master. Why, then, should not the heart of man be touched by so many and such glorious benefits as faith tells us God has bestowed on him? Man had deserved eternal chastisements. Is it, then, a little thing, not only to have drawn him from the abyss, but to draw him by means full of sweetness, and as if the Divine interests were concerned, to protect him, console him, make him advance in the way of salvation, and confer on him the rights of a child to eternal beatitude?

Man had multiplied his offenses; he had insolently fought against the goodness of God; his ingratitude deserved a sudden and unhappy end. Is it a small thing, then, that God in His mercy should have called him into the sublime state of the Religious life?

Is it a small thing that God became man and, after immense labours and suffering all sorts of ignominies, died for an ungrateful sinner, and satisfied His Eternal Father for all his sins?

Is it a small thing that God should give His Body and Blood as food to one who was wont hitherto to feed on the husks of swine?

What shall we say of all the helps that He has gratuitously bestowed—the protection of the Blessed Virgin, the guardianship of the Angels, the prayers of the Saints and the grace of preservation from serious or fatal accidents?

What shall we say of His Most Sacred Heart, which is so placed at the disposal of man, that if he is not wanting to It, It will never fail him, but will faithfully give him the heavenly inheritance?

*Sixth Motive:* Every Christian worthy of the name recognizes that at each moment he is indebted to God's liberality for a multitude of benefits. Every evil that he escapes; every virtuous act that he performs by thought, word, or deed; everything, even to his natural respiration, is but a chain of signal favours from the very Heart of his great Benefactor.

If, then, on whatever side he turns, man sees himself weighed down by the benefits of God; if, moreover, it is to him quite natural to love a benefactor; what, I ask, would not be the barbarity of one who should neglect a return of love and withdraw from God as if he owed Him nothing? What would not the folly of that Religious be who does not strenuously endeavour to feel and testify to his Benefactor the gratitude He merits?

*Conclusion:* Let Novices then exercise themselves actively in the practice of Divine love. They should devote themselves in heart and soul to this infinitely amiable God, and receive from Him as from a loving Father, pains and consolations alike. In all their actions they should strive to avoid even the least fault and seek no other recompense than that of pleasing so generous a benefactor. Thus, having kindled in their hearts the Divine flame, they will fulfill also with great exactness all the duties of charity towards their neighbours.

## Love of Our Neighbour

*First Motive:* Indeed, if the love of God, whence the love of our neighbour derives its origin, once takes possession of our hearts, we shall find in it motives more than sufficient to love our neighbour, even though he may be uncouth, insolent, passionate, importunate, rude, and subject to many other vices which usually beget dislike. The Divine perfections, such as the goodness, beauty, sweetness and wisdom of God, shine with a wondrous splendour and incite us to love our neighbour though he has none of these qualities. For, when we love, the charm which attracts us makes us endure all sorts of labours, fatigues and contradictions.

*Second Motive:* Do not say that our neighbour, not being amiable, can only displease us. He displeases our natural inclinations, it is true, but if we will he can please our reason. Without repeating here the motive given above, which is drawn from the Divine beauty and perfections, let us ask ourselves is not this man the child of God, called to eternal beatitude, redeemed by the Blood of Jesus Christ? Moreover, he is useful to me for the exercise of patience and the merits he procures for me. Is it not, perhaps, in the designs of God that my salvation should depend upon him? Assuredly, such considerations are capable of moving the hardest hearts.

*Third Motive:* Let us develop one of them; it will help to show us the force of the others. Would it not be a senseless thing to hate, offend, or even not to love a man whom we regard as predestined to an eternal kingdom? Now, we ought to believe that it is really so with each of our Brethren. Can this body which will one day enter heaven and be clothed for all eternity with beauty and light ineffable, be displeasing to me, since I hope for the same happiness? Should I not, then, always receive him graciously, and hasten to contract with this future king an alliance of unalterable peace?

*Fourth Motive:* Finally, even if all other motives failed, the authority of Jesus Christ should suffice to triumph over our repugnance: "This is My commandment," says He, "that you love one another as I have loved you"[66] Let us ponder these words, "as I have loved you"; that is, as I Who

---

[66] John 15:12

am God, wise, mighty and beautiful, have loved you who are only foolish, plain, uncouth men, and have suffered for love of you sorrows, ignominy, and death; thus ought you to love one another. Such is the testament of the Son of God; those who do not fulfill it will have no part in His inheritance.

# II

# Moral Virtues

## I. Moral Virtues in General

There are two sorts of moral virtues, namely, infused and acquired. They are called moral because they have for their object the regulation of manners.

They rule or perfect man in all his parts. Thus prudence and its attendant virtues perfect the intelligence; justice with the virtues which depend on it, the will; temperance with its train, the concupiscible appetite; fortitude and the virtues which belong to it, the irascible appetite.

These four Cardinal virtues rule the whole man in such a way that prudence, which is right reason applied to moral action, prescribes for all the other moral virtues the proper means by which they may directly attain their end; while these virtues previously dispose the soul in a suitable manner with regard to the end towards which prudence directs them.

The infused virtues and the acquired virtues bear the same names and are the same in number; however, there is a great difference between them. The acquired virtues relate to the practical and speculative principles of natural reason; whereas the infused refer to the Theological virtues as to their principles.

From this arises another difference well worthy of notice, namely, in their manner of operating. The acquired virtues receive their impulse from natural reason; the infused virtues from faith and the Divine Law. Let us make this clear by the example of temperance.

In the use of food or drink according to the acquired virtue of temperance, reason prescribes the manner, and makes one avoid all that can be hurtful to health or hinder the functions of the mind. If one acts according to the infused virtue of temperance it is the Divine Law, known by faith, which prescribes the manner, in order to mortify the flesh and, as the Apostle says, bring it to subjection.

From this illustration Novices can easily discover the kind of virtues with which God has adorned their souls; and they will learn at the same time how to use the natural virtues in a way far superior to what nature requires.

Indeed they should not exercise acts of the acquired virtues solely because these are conformable to natural reason, but also, and more especially, because they are in harmony with faith and contribute to the end of the Theological virtues.[67]

One thing, however, must not be lost sight of by those who wish to judge of their progress, namely, that the acquired virtues, though less noble than the infused, have this property peculiar to them, that they extirpate the contrary vices by the very efforts which are made to acquire them, and establish the soul in an admirable calm.

The infused virtues, on the contrary, allow the old habits of the opposite vices to remain. However, they give greater strength for the numerous combats that have to be undertaken so that peace may be established by war.

This is a certain but strange fact. A man hitherto given up to the most grievous sins is suddenly converted, leaves the world and embraces the religious life. At the very moment of his justification he receives in his soul all the infused moral virtues, prudence, justice, fortitude, temperance and a host of other virtues of which these four are the parents; yet he still

---

[67] "Since charity is the Queen and the soul of all virtues, every act inspired by it will have by far more merit than acts inspired by fear or by hope. It is important, then, that all our actions be done out of love of God and neighbor. In this way even the most ordinary actions, like meals and recreations, become acts of charity and share in the merits of that virtue. To eat in order to restore our strength is lawful and, in a Christian, it is meritorious; but to do this in order to work for God and for souls is to act from a motive of love which ennobles our action and bestows on it greater meritorious value… It is, therefore, useful in performing our actions to propose to ourselves several supernatural motives. We must, however, avoid all excess and preoccupation in seeking to multiply intentions, for this would disturb the soul." Fr. Adolphe Tanquerey, *The Spiritual Life*, P. I., Ch 2., Art II., §II., #240-241, Pub.

retains the vicious habits which he contracted in the world and has the same passions.

What happens? Being but ill instructed in the interior movements of the soul, he is astonished to feel in the Cloister the same vicious tendencies and the same irregular movements which he experienced in the world. Nay, even although he has become better, in reality it seems to him that he is worse than formerly. The reason of this is very simple. It is because the desire of advancement and the warfare to which he has given himself up, have discovered to him the disorders which hitherto had not troubled him.

All this should enable Novices to distinguish truth from falsehood in this matter, and ought to show them how to make use of the infused virtues to obtain the acquired.

This is the work of the just, who, clothed with the armor of the infused virtues and fortified by the Divine aid, are conducted by the Spirit into the desert in order to win a thousand crowns shining with the whiteness of purity or the purple of suffering.

It is the work of intrepid soldiers whose combats are the glory of Monastic Institutes and who with much labour and sweat strive to merit the joys of heaven.

This is the touchstone which discerns the true Religious from him who is one but in name. Both, it is true, at the appointed time assist at the community acts, both pronounce the solemn vows. But it is much to be feared those of the latter are only vows and not virtues.

Indeed the vows which we make to God are sacred promises by which we engage ourselves to practice the virtues that are, in philosophical language, the objects of the vows. But, alas! it may happen (and it is this we wish to guard against) that a Religious remains for twenty whole years bound by the vow of obedience without having acquired a single degree of the virtue of obedience.

Hence Novices should, from the beginning of their religious career, so act that they may acquire the virtues before they pronounce the vows. Then with God's help they will afterwards perfect the work which they so happily began.

The moral virtues are very numerous. We shall select from the four Cardinal virtues only the following which are more in keeping with the religious life:

| **Cardinal Virtues** | **Sub-Virtues** |
| --- | --- |
| Prudence | Diligence or Vigilance |
| Temperance | Humility, Chastity, Meekness, Abstinence, Modesty, Modesty of the eyes, Silence |
| Justice | Penance, Religion, Prayer, Devotion, Obedience, Gratitude |
| Fortitude | Patience, Magnanimity, Perseverance |

The explanation of these virtues will be quite a treatise on Monastic Discipline, for we shall sum up in it all that pertains to the other virtues whose acts are more in use than their names. As to poverty which ranks among the beatitudes we shall speak of it in detail.

Finally, we shall employ nearly the same reasons we made use of for subduing the passions and rooting out the contrary vices in constructing the virtues. As to the order in which we shall treat of the latter, we will follow that which seems to us the most conformable to our vocation, our renunciation of the world and monastic discipline. I am well aware that the origin of the virtues and their mutual connection are differently considered by Theologians and may seem to demand a different method, but order is subordinate to utility and ought to contribute to it.

# II. Obedience

## I. Nature and Excellence of Obedience

After having spoken of the Theological virtues by which the soul is united to God, and which, though common to all Christians, ought to be more religiously cultivated by those who make profession of despising the world, our vocation requires that we treat of the particular virtues that distinguish Religious, as regards their state of life, from the rest of the faithful. We will take them in due order. And as it is to arrive at the perfection of faith, hope and especially of charity that Novices have embraced the state of obedience,[68] we will treat of obedience immediately after the Theological virtues.

Now obedience, as it concerns us, is a virtue by which we submit to Superiors as holding the place of God in our regard. This virtue then participates in the nature of justice; for it renders to those who govern what is their due.

Obedience is almost as sublime as the Theological virtues; for though it has not God for its immediate object, nevertheless through it, we act with regard to those who command us in the name of God as if we treated directly with God Himself.

Indeed it is from this that the virtue of obedience derives that heavenly splendour which sheds on those who practice it an admirable luster, and raises them above human things. They mingle with men and perform the ordinary actions of everyday life, but in a Divine manner with heavenly views.

What can be conceived more sublime than the most pure regard of the obedient man, who judges of nothing by human reason which is too short a measure for him, but who, in order to see more clearly, borrows his light from the Theological virtue of faith?

What more noble than to treat always with God, to converse with Him, to communicate to Him all the sentiments of one's heart? It is this which takes place when the Superior is considered with the eyes of faith. Indeed we see in him then, not the person of such or such a man in particular, but the Divine Majesty Himself.

What more precious than this virtue which, although one, introduces all the other virtues inseparably with it into the soul and conserves them in an indissoluble alliance? For each time that we perform an act of any of the other virtues in order to obey God, in addition to the virtue of obedience we practice also the proper acts of those virtues which are commanded by the Superior.

---

[68] The Religious state is called the State of Obedience. P. II., Sect. I., C. I., 1-3.

What more agreeable than to be conducted through the waves of this stormy sea of life by God's own rule, Who does all things according to the counsel of His will?

What greater security of conscience can there be than to be free from illusion and deceit in the important affair of salvation? For it is impossible to be deceived when one acts through obedience.

The obedient man is immortal and cannot suffer injury. Behold that perfect model of obedience, Acatius, who, from the depths of the sepulcher in which his body but not his soul was buried made his voice heard, to the great astonishment of the ancients.

The abundance of spiritual goods which this virtue begets is so great, that the Fathers who laid the foundations of Monastic Institutes never ceased to recommend it.

Even if obedient men, of whom there are many in our own days, did not proceed from victory to victory, or attain the summit of Christian perfection more promptly by this way than any other, reason alone should convince us that we ought to give great care to the practice of this virtue.

God in his infinite goodness seems to have renewed with obedient men the compact which He entered into with Adam in the state of original justice, namely, that the inferior part would be subject to the superior part as long as the superior part would be subject to God. For the senses of the obedient man are submissive to his spirit whilst the latter adheres to God and he enjoys in anticipation the peace of heaven.

All that we can express in words, however, in praise of obedience falls far short of what it deserves. But we will substitute for a multitude of encomiums what has come down to us on the authority of Jesus Christ Himself.

"And whereas indeed He was the Son of God, He learned obedience by the things which He suffered: and being consummated He became to all that obey Him the cause of eternal salvation."[69]

Hence all who desire eternal salvation should strive to understand how to acquire this virtue by the exercise of suitable acts such as will be found in the following examples.

---

[69] Heb. 5:8-9

## II. Practice of Obedience

The holy Fathers have treated of the acts of this virtue in various ways. To proceed methodically, we must distinguish between what relates to the understanding and that which concerns the will. It is on these two points that all obedience turns. We must submit our will, the less perfect do so; we must also submit our understanding, as the more perfect are wont to do. Let us explain this more clearly.

Several have learned to obey, either with or without the repugnance of nature; however they reserve their own judgement in such a way that they do not approve with the understanding what they embrace with the will. Their virtue is imperfect; for, though they judge that he who commands is a Superior and that they cannot refuse to obey him, nevertheless, they think themselves more enlightened than he.

The perfect, on the contrary, so obey that they judge that what is commanded them is best, not only when they see clearly that such is the case, but also when the thing commanded is evidently unreasonable. Now Novices will have no difficulty in practicing this renunciation, if they consider attentively that Superiors are acquainted with many things of which inferiors are ignorant, and that it would be extremely rash for them to blame a thing without knowing the hidden circumstances which may render it good and praiseworthy. Moreover, it is certain that Superiors receive from God abundant lights and secret impulses to try those under them and make them advance in virtue. Would it not then be folly on the part of the subject who has not received these lights to pass judgment on a matter of which he is ignorant?

As to the various ways of practicing obedience, we must never lose sight of this common distinction, namely, it is one thing to act *with obedience*, another to act *by obedience*. In the first case the inferior has expressed his desire beforehand to the Superior; in the second the Superior commands of his own accord.

The first manner does not exempt the inferior from fault; the second is perfectly blameless, unless perverted by some imperfection. Thus for example, one asks a book, a habit, a lamp, or something similar. The Superior grants it and then the inferior acts with obedience. But this obedience does not render the act good in itself, if it was not good already. It leaves it still in the same nature. Now this act may be good in a case of necessity, or bad in the contrary case.

In order to be convinced that an act does not become blameless by the connivance of the Superior, we have only to consider that very often the Superior, knowing the imperfection of his subject, grants what he asks in order to avoid a greater evil. Herein he acts prudently whilst the inferior acts foolishly.

On the contrary, when a thing is done by obedience, that act by its nature cannot be bad. It may, however, be vitiated by the intention of him who obeys. It is therefore we have made the reservation, "unless it is perverted by some imperfection." This happens by an abuse of the will, as when the inferior willingly embraces what is commanded by the Superior because it is agreeable to his own inclination, but would perform it only with difficulty if it did not please him.

There are other circumstances of obedience such as the cheerfulness, promptitude, or diligence with which one obeys. Sometimes the inferior submits at once his will and understanding; for he desires to accomplish what has been commanded him and, moreover, he judges it right. But the sensitive appetite which is opposed to the law of the mind, allows itself to be pressed down by sadness or disturbed in other unseemly ways, and thus becomes a burden to the soul. A certain languor is the result, and this causes delay in the execution of the command. The truly obedient should banish far from them this pernicious languor.

Finally, everything that turns the mind from the pure and simple view of God speaking by the mouth of the Superior, so as to make one seek any other thing than to obey God for the love of God Himself, is a corruption of obedience. If, on the contrary, one has only in view the good pleasure of God, whether He commands by the Superior or sends a direct inspiration, whether He sends prosperity or afflicts by adversity, one will practice that most pure degree of obedience which the Saints call resignation. After having weighed well the preceding and purified the heart, let us practice acts of obedience in the following manner.

## Interior Acts

O most clement God, since Thou hast made known to me Thy will through my Superior, I firmly resolve to obey him as I would obey Thee.

O God of infinite wisdom, no matter who my Superior may be, I shall regard whatever he says to me as a message from heaven.

O my God, I shall always recognize Thee in my Superior, and on Thy account I shall submit myself wholly to him and with a good heart.

It is most certain, O Lord, that my Superior holds Thy place in my regard; consequently, I shall seek no other wisdom or knowledge.

Though my Superior may sometimes appear according to my worldly views to speak and act foolishly, I shall still regard him, O Lord, as Thy representative.

Yes! O Lord, I shall obey my Superior as I would obey Thee if I saw Thee with the eyes of the body.

Far be it from me, O Lord, to disapprove of what my Superior approves.

Acts of this kind are very salutary; but we will now say something about external acts.

## Exterior Acts

Though, as we have already said, acts imposed are preferable to those that are asked for, there are, however, certain acts which it is more perfect to ask; for example, bodily mortifications and painful labours, which Superiors through prudence and charity do not wish to impose on their subjects. The truly obedient, however, are not content with accomplishing the expressed will of their Superior; they even anticipate his desires and freely offer their services saying: "Lo! Here am I, send me."[70]

When, therefore, the Superior has commanded or the inferior has asked and obtained leave to do some painful work, he should undertake it cheerfully and accomplish it as perfectly as possible.

It must be remarked here that the laxity of the sensitive appetite gives birth to sloth and a false exaggeration of the difficulties to be encountered in the performance of our work. We should avoid fear, and rest on faith which teaches us that God never tries any of His creatures above their strength.

Now one of the most excellent of all the obligations imposed on Novices by the virtue of obedience is to render an account to their Master of the state of their conscience, in such a way that they conceal nothing from him.[71] If, indeed, they ought to be sincere and simple with everyone without a shadow of dissimulation, duplicity being incompatible with the true religious spirit, it is especially with regard to their Master that this

---

[70] Isa. 6:8
[71] This can be one's confessor or spiritual director. Also, see footnote on Appendix, #1. Pub.

candour should be exercised. And let them be thoroughly convinced that by observing this counsel alone they will be able to avoid all the snares of the evil one and obtain every good.

Away then with all false shame, away with fear and human reasonings, even when there is question of serious things and of temptations against Superiors themselves. Indeed the affection of the latter will not be diminished by such a manifestation, nor will any other harm result, quite the contrary. But the devil, who knows and fears the good results of this confidence, employs all his cunning to try and turn away the Religious from it, either by fear or under pretense of virtue.

But the truly obedient should be so constant and faithful to his Superior that he is even ready, not alone to reveal to him but even to the whole city if he wishes, all his faults and imperfections. Indeed, he will easily attain to this degree and overcome all the difficulties in the way, if he regards God Himself in the person of his Superior. This is the most excellent of all the counsels of obedience. From this principle spring love and reverence; reverence that excludes resistance, and the love that begets promptitude in the execution. These are the two columns that sustain the entire edifice of the Religious state. We earnestly recommend them to Novices.

We now come to the third part of this chapter, in which we shall give suitable reasons to excite our ardour in the practice of obedience and the extirpation of the vices and passions that are opposed to it.

## III. Motives of Obedience

*First Motive:* The principal part of man, namely, his understanding and will, is sacrificed by obedience; hence it is a most noble and agreeable holocaust to God. It is indeed a painful sacrifice; for the more excellent an object is in itself, and the more a man is by nature attached to it, the more difficult it is for him to renounce it.

But what is this pain to that which weighs down worldlings? For some slight recompense, sometimes a mere nothing, they serve the Princes of the earth for many years, whose least caprices they carefully obey, often at the expense of sleep, honour and peace. And then, when they have grown old in a prolonged servitude, they die, perhaps in hospitals, and who knows if they are not buried in hell?

Is it not much more prudent to govern oneself by rendering filial obedience with the hope of an immense reward to the meekest of Princes, the most loving of Fathers?

*Second Motive:* Among all those things that are highly esteemed by men we must include the decrees of Senates and the decisions of the wise. We see kings of the earth full of anxiety in important business affairs because they know not what is most expedient to do, and if they make a mistake they fear the loss of their kingdom. How happy then should not Religious esteem themselves, in the midst of the anxieties incidental to the important affair of their salvation, for receiving from heaven by the medium of their Superior for each of their actions, oracles so certain that in conforming to them they can never go astray, even when, through frailty, the Superior may be deceived! This consideration is, without doubt, more than sufficient to compensate for the pains attached to obedience.

*Third Motive:* Besides, although a Religious may be endowed with extreme prudence and capable of guiding himself, it is much more honourable for him to be directed by God in a particular manner which is wanting to the rest of the faithful; and to be conducted by Him in a more sublime way than he of himself, no matter how holy he may be, could select. We know that there is a great difference between the acts performed even by holy men according to their own will, and those that are done through obedience; indeed the first can never attain the perfection of the second. How important is it not, then, for those who have formed great designs, to apply themselves with their whole heart to obedience?

*Fourth Motive:* Moreover, in the midst of the temptations which sometimes oppress and almost deprive us of the use of reason, if a suitable remedy is to be found anywhere on this earth it is certainly in obedience. For God does not content Himself with giving to the Superior, however unworthy he may be, the celestial lights that are necessary to direct faithful subjects; He also inspires him with sentiments of the most tender affection in their regard, so that when he sees any of his subjects in trouble he procures for him with special attention spiritual and corporal consolation. If then the Superior has received from God with regard to his subjects a mother's heart, why should they not obey him with great exactitude? And what temptations can hold out against this antidote?

*Fifth Motive:* He who does not studiously cultivate the virtue of obedience, not only abandons the practice of the Saints, all of whom ardently loved their Superiors, but he even acts in opposition to the very nature of the human heart. For all the goods to which it is sensible, honour, consolation, advantages of all kinds, it finds united together in one man who holds for him the place of God. But were there no other reason to persuade us to love this virtue, the sole authority of Jesus Christ, our Model, should gain all hearts. He willingly obeyed His Mother and Foster Father; for, as the Evangelist says: "He was subject to them."[72] From the first instant of His conception until His death on the Cross He never withdrew from the practice of this virtue, as it is written: "He was obedient unto death, even to the death of the Cross."[73]

*Sixth Motive:* Indeed He compensated so fully for the disobedience of Adam, that we see clearly the evils caused by the first sin have been repaired by the exercise of obedience. He who will not embrace this doctrine shows clearly that he does not belong to Christ. Then as others in the world submit to masters in order to become learned, to officers in order to succeed in becoming good soldiers, to pilots in order to become good seamen; let us have no other Master, no other Captain, no other Pilot, than the God of all goodness, to Whom we shall offer each day on the altar of our heart the sacrifice of obedience, after the example that has been shown us on Mount Calvary.

Such is the road that leads to life though it seems to lead to death. It is a military way on which we cannot go astray and which terminates in a happy issue. In truth, God conducts His people, not as heretofore by the hands of Moses and Aaron, but by His only Son.

Yes, this wise Master has set up obedience to direct them as He formerly did the Israelites in the wilderness "with a cloud by day, and all the night with a light of fire."[74] He leads and brings back His people as a shepherd his sheep; He gives them instructions; He guards them as the pupil of His eye.

All these privileges of obedience are the property of monasteries. They are denied to those strange children who have wavered from their youth, on account of their infidelity; and rightly so, "because it is like the sin of witchcraft to rebel, and like the crime of idolatry to refuse to obey."[75]

*Conclusion:* Hence, Novices who desire to advance in the knowledge of Jesus Christ, should endeavour to have for their Superiors as for God Himself a profound love and respect. Let them make it a point to regulate

---

[72] Luke 2:51
[73] Phil 2:8
[74] Ps. 77:14
[75] 1 Kings 15:23

not alone their actions but even their words, and, as far as possible, their thoughts according to the instructions they receive; that, after having completed their career in Religion by a life of faith which makes them like the most obedient Son of God, they may obtain as a recompense the incomparable joys of eternal beatitude.

# III. Chastity

## 1. Its Nature and Excellence

Chastity, as we understand it here, is the virtue which represses concupiscence of the flesh and rejects unlawful pleasures.

The dignity of this angelic virtue is indeed celestial. A special beauty distinguishes it from all others.

In raising man above the condition of the flesh it gives him sublimity of mind and the nobility of the Angels; precious advantages which are, undoubtedly, proper only to the blessed in heaven.

From this we can clearly see what splendour this virtue sheds on man, since, elevated by it above his nature it invests him with a celestial luster like that of the angelic spirits.

This splendour gives birth to a fascinating beauty which attracts with marvelous power all eyes and hearts; for as the hideousness of the contrary vice inspires horror, so the loveliness of chastity charms and ravishes us.

This is true, not only of creatures but also of the Creator Himself. Jesus Christ was not alone a Virgin, but He willed to be born of a Virgin and showed a special predilection for virgins. Witness St. John who was singularly loved by Him on account of his prerogative of chastity.

For the rest, it is fitting that He Who is the "brightness of eternal light and the unspotted mirror,"[76] should pursue with special marks of affection those hearts which resemble His in purity, and lavish His favours on them. It is thus He has acted with a legion of virgins, on whom He has been pleased to shed the riches of His bounty.

---

[76] Wis. 7:26

Hence we can estimate the priceless value of this beautiful virtue, since it has at its disposal the Heart of Jesus Christ the greatest and richest of all treasures.

But so great a good is not the portion of all kinds of chastity; indeed perfect chastity alone enjoys it. It is this then that Novices should strive to acquire, relying on the aid of heaven without which no one can be continent.[77]

Chastity is of ravishing beauty and exacts the most ardent desires of those who cultivate it, such as a vast number of illustrious Christians have laudably conceived. Were there not in the highest ranks of society thousands of young girls and young men, whom the world invited to brilliant entertainments, but who preferred to lose earthly beauty by bodily austerities or by the torments of death, rather than be deprived of the sweet charms of chastity?

It seemed to them much more honourable to be the object of the contempt of men, to incur the hatred of their nearest and dearest friends, or to suffer persecutions, famine, stripes and other cruel torments, than renounce their first resolution and let themselves be torn away from the embraces of this sweet virtue.

Certainly, these young souls, matured by heavenly inspirations, would not have displayed such heroism if the practice of chastity were not the source of extraordinary goods.

Inflamed by these considerations, Novices will strive to reproduce in themselves the splendour of this angelic virtue; and let them be convinced that it alone can secure for them the incomparable title of true Spouses of Christ. We will now treat of the acts.

## II. Practice of Chastity

Chastity admits of many degrees; but for greater clearness, we shall reduce them to two categories. The first comprises those who limit themselves to abstaining from forbidden pleasures and is proper to seculars; the second is made up of those who renounce even lawful pleasures and is proper to Religious, though there are many in the world who attain this degree.

---

[77] Cf. Wis. 8:21

INSTRUCTION OF NOVICES

With regard to this second degree, it may be remarked that some abstain only from lawful pleasures that relate to the body, without renouncing the spiritual joys which they experience in the exercises of the spiritual life; whilst others carry their renunciation even to these interior joys.

Novices should not only embrace wholly the resolution of the former, but they should be generous enough to aspire to the perfection of the latter. Just as a man who is seriously determined to restrain his tongue abstains sometimes from saying good words through fear of being insensibly led to utter those that are evil, so he who desires to be truly chaste should refuse himself lawful pleasures in order that those that are unlawful may not insinuate themselves by degrees into his heart.

Authentic histories teach us that the ancient Fathers abstained with great exactitude from speaking to their relations, lest they might be thereby exposed to the danger of conversing also with other persons; such was the reverence with which they guarded their virtue.[78]

---

[78] "And often there is more to be feared—as experience has often shown, and shows every day—where intercourse seems perfectly legitimate, as with relations, or in the discharge of duties, or with persons who from their virtues ought to be beloved. For with this too frequent and unguarded intercourse, the poisonous pleasure of sense insinuates itself; gradually instilling itself, until it penetrates into the very depths of the soul, and darkens the reason more and more, until things which are most dangerous are regarded as of no account; such as loving looks, words of mutual endearment, and charms of conversation; and thus, step by step, a ruinous fall approached, or at the least some painful temptation which is with great difficulty overcome... At the time of the temptation to carnal indulgences I do not recommend you to meditate upon certain points—as many books suggest—as a remedy against this temptation; such, for instance, as the vileness of this vice, its insatiableness, the loathing and remorse which follow upon it, the peril and loss of goods, life, honor, and all such things. For this is so far from being a sovereign remedy against such temptations, that it may prove hurtful rather than otherwise; for if, on the one hand, the mind dispels these thoughts, on the other, it affords the opportunity and exposes us to the danger of taking pleasure in them, and consenting to the delight. Therefore the sure remedy is flight in all these cases, both from the thoughts themselves, and from every thing—however contrary to them—which may bring them to the mind again. Take, therefore, for your subject of meditation the Life and Passion of our Crucified Redeemer for this purpose. And if, during your meditation, the images of the same thoughts come before the mind's eye against your will, and molest you more than ever—as is frequently the case—do not therefore despond, nor leave off your meditation, neither turn your attention to these thoughts with a view to resisting them, but pursue it with all possible intenseness, taking no notice of these thoughts, which in no sense belong to you. There is no better plan of resisting them than this, however frequently these assaults may come... Never, at any time, stay to dispute with such temptations, whether you have consented or not; for this is a device of the Devil, who seeks, under the guise of a good motive, to harass you and

And it was not without reason. For the most skillful amongst them in spiritual warfare, who were not in the least afraid of the assaults of other enemies, when treating of chastity always counseled flight. Indeed the corruption of the senses is so great that in this warfare they considered flight of the dangers conformable to reason which is the part of valour, and proved it by many examples.

Our Novices shall reach the highest degree of chastity by observing this sole advice. Let them be very vigilant not to allow their hearts to become attached to any creature, no matter how beautiful, and to regard it as a serious breach of fidelity not to give themselves wholly and everywhere to God alone. Every other love always injures, if *not* the chastity of the body, at least that of the heart. But we will give some acts.

## Interior Acts

O God of infinite purity, and most worthy of all love, I resolve to abstain from all carnal pleasure for love of Thee.

O most chaste Son of the Virgin, even if I could enjoy without sin all the pleasures of the flesh which are so much sought after by men, I would abstain from them for Thy sake.

O most pure God of my heart, I not only renounce all the pleasures of the flesh, but also all occasions of them.

O most amiable Jesus Christ, I make a compact with my eyes not to let them rest on dangerous objects.

O most chaste Beauty of my soul, for Thy sake I will abstain as far as possible from all pleasure, even in corporeal things.

O most sweet Saviour, I renounce not only the pleasures of the flesh but also, as far as it depends on me, the delights of the spirit.

These acts ought to be made with great fervour. We shall now proceed to external acts.

## Exterior Acts

The practice of exterior chastity may be reduced to two chief heads, namely the mortification of the senses and the maceration of the body.

---

render you distrustful and despondent; or hopes, by keeping your attention on such questions, to plunge you into some wrong pleasure." Fr. Lorenzo Scupoli, *The Spiritual Combat*, Ch 19, Pub.

INSTRUCTION OF NOVICES

It is necessary in the first place to mortify or repress the senses as often as any delectation arises, so that each Religious should make a firm resolution to renounce the pleasure as soon as he adverts to it. This will be better understood by the two following examples.

A Religious sees a secular or another Religious remarkable for his beauty. Immediately by a natural movement without any fault on his part he feels a sort of delectation. Then out of love for chastity turning away his eyes he shall exclaim: "God forbid that I should wish to take any delight in the sight of this beautiful body. Turn away my eyes that they may not behold vanity, quicken me in Thy way."[79]

Let us take another example from the sense of touch. It can happen at recreation or elsewhere that one of the Religious without thinking of it touches the hand of another from which he derives some pleasure. As soon as he perceives it he shall immediately withdraw his hand and raise his heart to God in the following manner. "Far be it from me, O Lord! to seek any satisfaction outside of Thee."

From all this Novices should learn with what care they ought to avoid in their intercourse with others all familiarity that could give rise to unseemly movements. And what is more, if they have a true love for chastity and for themselves, they should avoid doing anything unbecoming or hurtful to the sight or touch when in the cells they take off their habit, retire to rest, or perform other similar acts.

And what we have said with regard to the senses of sight and touch in the preceding examples ought to extend equally to the other senses. For one should use the senses of hearing, smell or taste only from necessity or utility and not for pleasure. But with regard to the sense of taste there is much greater difficulty in conquering it.

The same is to be said of the internal senses or powers. Everything that causes pleasure must be rejected if it is not necessary or useful. But when it cannot be rejected or there is no obligation to do so, the intention should be purified and entirely directed to God.[80] We shall proceed to the second head, namely, the maceration of the body.

---

[79] Ps. 118:37
[80] "Now sweetness and delight enter into the senses in two ways; either from the mind through some interior divine communication, or from outward objects represented to them. But according to the text just quoted, our lower nature cannot know God either in the way of the spirit or in the way of sense; for having no capacity for so great a matter, it receives that which is of the mind and spirit in the senses only. Therefore, to occupy the will with the joy that

"Vain is the horse for safety; neither shall he be saved by the abundance of his strength."[81] The friends of chastity should be careful to practice works of penance, such as vigils, fasts, rough beds, hair shirts, hard chairs, and others of this kind, of which we shall treat in the chapter on Penance. Here we wish only to remark that all the acts of austerity and mortification of the senses practiced with a view to chastity, are also acts of chastity, and that without their aid it will be difficult to maintain this virtue in its vigour.

Hence the ancient Fathers, though consummate in virtue and strangers to every irregular movement of the flesh, delivered themselves up to cruel macerations in their grottoes and deserts, not so much to repel present attacks as to prevent future ones; and they never relaxed in these practices during their whole lives.

What is specially remarkable in the lessons they have left us is, that without heeding the pretexts of necessity or sickness alleged by the flesh, they persisted in the struggle at its expense to save the spirit.

Since the contests of chastity are full of difficulties, for man has to arm himself against his own flesh which no one ever hated, and one is exposed to all sorts of combats, fears, fatigues and weakness; it will be profitable to furnish in the third part of this chapter a collection of solid arguments for the defense of a virtue so excellent.

---

has its sources in any of these apprehensions, will be at the least but vanity, and a hindrance in the way of employing the strength of the will upon God, by rejoicing in Him alone. This is what the soul can never wholly do unless it purifies itself from and makes itself blind to joy in the things of sense, for if it should rejoice herein at all, that, as I have said, will be but vanity. When the soul does not rest here, but instantly, as soon as the will becomes conscious of any joy in any object of sense, raises itself upwards unto God—that joy supplying motives thereto and power—it is well with it, and then it need not suppress such movements, but may profit by them, and even ought to do so, so as to accomplish so holy an act; for there are souls whom sensible objects greatly influence in the way of God. Such souls, however, must be very cautious, and watch the issues of this conduct, for very often many spiritual persons indulge themselves in these sensible recreations, under the pretense of giving themselves to prayer and to God. Now what they do should be called recreation, not prayer, and their pleasure in this is their own rather than God's. Though their intention be directed to God, yet the effect is sensible recreation, and the fruit of it is weakness and imperfection, rather than the quickening of the will and the surrender of it into the hands of God." St. John of the Cross, *Ascent of Mount Carmel,* Book 3, Ch 23, #2, Pub.

[81] Ps. 32:17

## III. Motives for Chastity

*First Motive:* Self-love alleges the difficulty of the enterprise as if the labour would be immense to wage continual war with such an implacable enemy. But what are these pains compared with all those that voluptuous men have to suffer to taste by stealth a momentary pleasure. They squander their patrimony; they obscure their honour and the nobility of their birth; and by their undue indulgence they deliver their bodies to corruption and their souls to eternal torments, which they begin to experience even in this life.

Is it not more prudent, then, to acquire by a little labour and by war, the beauty of chastity and eternal felicity than to purchase, by very short and deceitful pleasures, exhaustion of body and dishonour in this world and everlasting death in the next?

*Second Motive:* Worldlings spare no pains to please Princes and to gain their good graces, by wit, nobility, or courage. Why then should not Religious use all their efforts to excel in chastity, since it is certain that the ineffable and sweet beauty of this virtue, for this is its privilege, renders exceedingly dear to God not alone their hearts but even their bodies?

*Third Motive:* Besides, all the children of holy Church implore the help of the Blessed Virgin as a sure means of salvation; and if they have found grace with her they believe they have won their cause. Now it is certain that this sole virtue of chastity infallibly obtains for us the favour of this great Queen. What labours then should not those who are enrolled among the number of her chaste children be ready to undergo for the preservation of this glorious virtue?

*Fourth Motive:* The noblest part of the human race consists of those who give themselves up to the study of wisdom, and who, disengaged from every other occupation, esteem it just to apply themselves with their whole hearts to the understanding of Divine things. For the knowledge of heavenly things however limited it may be, far surpasses that of all inferior sciences. For this end they choose a single and austere life, in order to keep their minds detached from even the lawful pleasures of the state of wedlock. The example of the holy Fathers furnish many well known proofs of this. It is then but reasonable that Religious so happily called to the study of wisdom should neglect the care of the flesh, in order that chastity, which of all the virtues best disposes the mind for that study, may shine in their bodies; for a single drop of heavenly wisdom contains more sweetness than the practice of chastity brings labour and pain.

*Fifth Motive:* Moreover, the love of life is greater than the love of science or wisdom, and everyone knows how carefully man avoids what is detrimental to his life. Now, it is certain that chastity is as much opposed to death and corruption as impurity is to life and the integrity of the body. Hence, if anyone wishes for life, and is anxious to preserve it at any cost, even through fire and sword, he ought also to love chastity, which is acquired by many labours.

*Sixth Motive:* But what shall we say of the issue of the combat? Indeed, chastity is not only rewarded by magnificent gifts in the future life; for, even here, in *this* life, when our Lord sees that they have been sufficiently tried, He is pleased to favour chaste hearts with His sweetest delights. Novices should often meditate seriously on this point.

*Seventh Motive:* Indeed, it is the opinion of all Theologians, considering the thing merely from a philosophical point of view, that the joys of the mind and heart are much greater than those of the body. Novices, then, will lose nothing if they receive Divine joys in exchange for the pleasures they have renounced.

*Eighth Motive:* For the rest, even if they were to derive no other advantage from the practice of this beautiful virtue than the incomparable glory of making themselves conformable to Jesus Christ, Novices should be willing to undergo continual labour and fatigues to attain it.

*Conclusion:* But since it is necessary that they must nourish daily this domestic enemy, the flesh, and at the same time suffer from its attacks; let them bear well in mind that they must pray earnestly that the Lord may grant them without ceasing help proportioned to the greatness of His bounty and of their own frailty.

By assiduity in prayer and pious exercises they will arm themselves for the combat; and neither terrified by difficulties, nor dejected by sadness, they shall carry on the warfare, keeping ever before their eyes the splendour of this virtue, the magnificence of the reward, and the likeness to Jesus Christ which it begets.

# IV. Poverty

## I. Its Nature and Excellence

Jesus Christ, the Master of true wisdom, desiring to teach us the way to eternal beatitude, began by the lesson of poverty. Poverty consists in the voluntary renunciation of temporal goods for the sake of the eternal kingdom. It is the sacrifice of exterior goods, as obedience and chastity are the immolation of interior.

Now, it is not an easy matter to speak fittingly of poverty, the true seal of the Religious state. It is incomparably greater than a simple virtue, since it generously tramples under foot the goods which men adore.

With good reason has Our Lord, in order to recommend it, placed it among the beatitudes rather than among the virtues. By this He teaches us that the truly poor in spirit have not only acquired a virtue, but they have attained, even in this exile, to a certain degree of felicity.

This, indeed, ought to inflame our hearts. All desire happiness, and we know that in every nation the most illustrious of men of antiquity have sought, with much labour, the path that leads to it. For this reason Religious, having learned from the mouth of God Himself that Christian poverty is for those who practice it the direct road to happiness, should apply themselves to it with the greatest ardour.

But besides this oracle, the poverty of Christ carries with it many other advantages which are capable of softening our hearts. The poor in spirit have a special right to God's adoption; for those whom the world seems to despise receive from Him a paternal care and support, since they are the children of the Most High. Is there any glory comparable to that which the renunciation of this world's goods procures by making us the children of the noblest of Fathers? This truth was well known to him who said: "My father and my mother have left me; but the Lord hath taken me up."[82]

This most honourable protection of the heavenly Father is not the only fruit of detachment from riches; many other consolations likewise flow from it. The Holy Spirit Who comforts the hearts of men is especially the consoler of the poor. And as He is the Gift of God, He gives Himself chiefly to those who give Him empty hearts, after having first cast out of

---

[82] Ps. 26:10

them all earthly things, that He may fill them with Himself alone. Hence, after the words: "Come, Father of the poor," is immediately added: "Come, Giver of gifts."[83]

This will show how prudent those dealers are who exchange the miserable goods of this earth for the magnificent treasures of heaven.

We must not be surprised that such powerful reasons in favour of Christian poverty make no impression on worldlings. Indeed, they are above the understanding of the world, and lean on the rock of faith. One must despise the world in order to grasp their meaning.

It is to this happy state that Religious have been gratuitously called. It only remains for them to have a profound contempt for temporal goods, and to learn the acts suitable for acquiring Christian poverty.

## II. Practice of Poverty

Christian poverty consists of two parts, namely, exterior renunciation and interior detachment. Exterior renunciation is the abandonment of earthly things, which is common to all those who enter the cloister. Interior detachment consists in the extirpation of covetousness or cupidity, and is not possessed in the same degree by all.

Our Lord indicated this double renunciation by saying: "Poor in spirit." The word "Poor" of itself would only have expressed the exterior privation of riches; by adding "in spirit," He signified the movement of the will which produces interior detachment.

Now, when a man has renounced temporal goods in will and in deed, he is not by this means made perfect all at once in the practice of poverty. Indeed, many things still remain which he must do in Religion in order to arrive at this perfection, as we shall see further on.

The substance of this world is adhesive, and the human heart easily attaches itself to all that surrounds it. Thus it is that covetousness, seeing itself deprived of the goods it enjoyed in the world, turns vehemently to the little comforts to be had in the cloister, and directs towards the most trivial things all the activity it formerly bestowed on the riches of the world. A habit, a book, or an image becomes an object of avaricious affection, and once allowed their use we are unwilling to give them to anyone else.

---

[83] See Hymn, *Veni Sancte Spiritus*.

What a deplorable stumbling-block! A man has perhaps given up a rich patrimony, yet he lets himself be overcome by the love of a mere trifle. We should be careful never to allow ourselves to be misled by such insignificant objects. Let us purify our affections by the following interior acts.

## Interior Acts

O most clement God, I desire to possess nothing but Thee alone.

O most amiable Father, would that I had the riches of a thousand worlds, not to enjoy them, but to abandon them for love of Thee.

O most sweet Lord, as far as it depends on me, I renounce with all my heart, for love of Thee, everything that is less than Thee.

O most merciful Lord, deprive me even of the very garment that covers me, if my want of it should be more pleasing to Thee.

O most bountiful Father, I am unworthy to inhabit this cell. Would that I were allowed to pass the night under the stairs, or in the most inconvenient corner of the house.

O Lord, permit me, I beseech Thee, if it be pleasing to Thee, to dine on the crumbs that are left on the table of Thy Servants.

O Thou Who art my sole inheritance, do not allow me to be prevented by an inordinate love of a book, a cell, a habit, or anything else from desiring only Thee.

These acts, as is evident, can be made in various ways, but we will proceed to the external acts.

## Exterior Acts

Many of those who make profession of poverty deceive themselves grossly by thinking there is nothing more to be done after they have renounced their fortune, and practiced some interior acts, without suffering themselves to be deprived of any exterior comfort. This is a grave error. For how can we be poor if nothing is wanting to us? The Saints teach us that the inseparable companions of poverty are the privation of necessary things, heat, cold, thirst, hunger, nakedness and other inconveniences. It is then to be feared, that those who are never in want to necessaries are not truly poor according to the teaching of Jesus Christ.

If, then, it should happen that Novices have to endure some privation in health or in sickness, they should return thanks to the mercy of God for giving them an occasion of tasting the sweetness of the poverty they profess.

But this God of goodness has pity on our weakness, and does not usually permit us to be in need. This is no reason, however, why we should be less diligent in the practice of poverty; on the contrary, we ought to apply ourselves to it with greater fervour, so that, if the occasion for exercising poverty is taken from us, we may not on that account lose its merit.

Consequently, Novices should ask of their Superior as often as they can, or accept willingly, old and worn habits, inconvenient cells, hard beds, old books, or insipid food; in a word, everything that can liken them to the poor.

If they receive things that please them they should be careful not to become attached to them; but they should use them, as well as everything else, with reserve, as things that do not belong to them; and with great respect and care, as things consecrated to Jesus Christ.

Such are the principles of the poverty of Jesus Christ; once they have taken possession of a heart they bring with them a wonderful increase of monastic perfection; for besides their own excellence they bear with them the splendour of several other exalted virtues. But since they contradict the flesh, which is often unduly loved, we shall furnish some solid reasons calculated to fortify our hearts in the love and practice of poverty.

## III. Motives for the Virtue of Poverty

*First Motive:* People will say the practice of such strict poverty is painful, and a kind of slavery. But how much more painful is the life of many men in the world, who, being poor, not of their own choice but of necessity, have hardly enough bread to eat, and waste away without hope of recompense. And withal they are men, redeemed by the Blood of Jesus Christ.

It may be objected that many of those who are called to the Religious life have left great riches to embrace poverty, and that, consequently, they must suffer more than those who are poor by necessity. This worldly way of reasoning is utterly false; and even were it true, how many men, either through their own fault or by accident, fall unexpectedly from opulence to extreme destitution, without any consolation to soften their misfortune.

It may be said it was their own fault. Granted; but among those called to the cloister, who is there so just that his conscience does not reproach him of sin on account of which he merited, if not imprisonment in this life, the fires of hell in the next? It is not enough to consider temporal things; we must also think of eternal.

*Second Motive:* And then, those who have gloried in their riches, what pleasure will they experience when they sleep their last sleep? In death they can no longer enjoy their goods; and they will only find in their hands the thorns of their sins. And since they have bent their back under the burden of earthly things, "they sunk as lead in the mighty waters,"[84] as a punishment for their covetousness. Is not this the fate that is reserved for them? "Do men gather grapes of thorns?"[85] Is it not said that "the rich man also died and he was buried in hell?"[86]

It is, then, far more profitable to abandon these false goods than to be abandoned by them[87], and to procure eternal repose with Lazarus who was once poor.

It is more delightful and glorious to apply to ourselves the words of him who said to Jesus Christ in the name of all the others: "Behold, we have left all things and have followed Thee,"[88] and to be seated with the poor Apostles on brilliant thrones of glory. Certainly this honourable prerogative sufficiently shows that it is not a useless exchange to abandon all for that which is above all.[89]

*Third Motive:* Besides, lest it may be said that the mere promise of future goods makes but little impression, let us add that the riches of this world are only useful to procure bodily sustenance; for what is expended on luxuries is not exempt from fault. Now, setting aside luxuries, what is wanting to the Religious, since God provides for his subsistence with special care? Solicitude, sins and covetousness are doubtless wanting to him; but it is a happiness for him not to have these things.

*Fourth Motive:* Earthly goods may perish by some accident, and leave in their place extreme misery; but no calamity can deprive the Servants of Jesus Christ of their bread; for it is written: "I have not seen the just forsaken, nor his seed seeking bread."[90] And not alone bread, but any other

---

[84] Exod. 15:10
[85] Matt. 7:16
[86] Luke 16:22
[87] St. Bernard
[88] Matt. 19:27
[89] St. Bernard
[90] Ps. 36:25

good shall not be wanting to them, whereas even bread is often wanting to the rich of this world; as it is also written: "The rich have wanted, and have suffered hunger; but they that seek the Lord shall not be deprived of any good."[91]

The rich take care of themselves; but God provides for the poor, and, as He is attentive to every detail, He numbers, weighs and measures what He places on the table of His children. How much more profitable to the body will not the food be which is provided by Him with so much love and wisdom than that which is prepared by intemperate men, who are, perhaps, aided by the demon!

*Fifth Motive:* Moreover, it is certain that the delicious nourishment of interior consolation which, by intervals at least, is given to the poor of Jesus Christ in this land of exile, is not shared by the rich of this world. The latter have, it is true, comforts here below, but our Lord has said: "Woe to you, rich, for you have your consolation."[92] How much better, then, to enjoy on this earth Divine consolations and, at the same time, turn our hopes towards those which are eternal.

*Conclusion:* For the rest, even if the foregoing motives were not sufficiently convincing, the love with which the son of God, Who, being rich, made Himself poor for love of us, ought to urge us vehemently to apply ourselves heart and soul to acquire poverty of spirit. If God, in the effusion of His tenderness, has said to us, "I am poor and in labours from my youth,"[93] is it fitting that a Religious should say: I do not care to practice strict poverty?

What shall we say of the Immaculate Virgin Mary, whose poverty were better described with tears than with ink? Oh, how rich has poverty become on account of her predilection for it! These two examples ought to soften the hardest hearts.

Religious, then, who are the special children of the most chaste and most poor Virgin, should ever seek the company of so excellent a Mother, and without letting themselves be impeded by passion or temptation, aspire incessantly to the heritage of the poor, that is, the kingdom of heaven.

---

[91] Ps. 33:11
[92] Luke 6:24
[93] Ps. 87:16

# V. Penance

## I. Nature and Excellence of Penance

After Novices have been called from the slough of the world to the sublime height of the religious life, and understand that they can attain the end of the Theological virtues by the exercise of obedience, chastity and poverty, God exacts of them before all things, that as they have now a favourable opportunity in their new state, they should strive to expiate the sins they have committed in the world by the practice of penance.

Penance is a virtue by which we detest our sins for love of God, with a firm purpose not to commit them again, and to make satisfaction to Him for them according to our strength. It has the nature of justice. The sinner, having irritated God by his offenses, makes a resolution to appease Him by good works, and to exercise vengeance on himself for his faults[94].

3. Herein we see clearly the nobility of this virtue. For what could be more generous than to chastise ourselves willingly, and constantly to uphold the cause of God against ourselves through pure love of Him?

The excellence of this virtue raises it almost to the rank of a Theological virtue; for in this detestation of sin, and in this vengeance exercised on ourselves, the intention is directed not towards our own utility, but towards God Himself sovereignly loved; and this constitutes a sort of sublime affinity with Divine charity.

Thus it is that those who were before slaves to the demon are raised by it in an instant to the select number of the children of God. Such is the power of this virtue.

Can anyone, then, be so insensible as not to be attracted by its charms, or refuse to blot out his sins by it, and recover that spotless innocence by which he is raised to the dignity of the children of God which is the greatest of all honours?

---

[94] "It should be noted here that it is not the difficulty itself of penance which merits, but rather the virtue we exercise by bearing the cross well out of love for God" (Fr. Adolphe Tanquerey, *The Spiritual Life*, Part I., Ch 2., Art II., §II.). Insofar as we resist crosses, they take on the character of vengeance, insofar as we embrace them, of satisfaction (*Catechism of the Council of Trent*, Q. LXI). "Penance also helps to uproot the causes of sin" (St. Thomas Aquinas, *Sum. Theol.*, Supp., Q. 15., Art. 2-3), Pub.

It is undoubtedly a great gain to purchase a right to the heavenly Jerusalem, and to repair the loss of primitive liberty destroyed by sin[95].

Such was the gain of Magdalen, of Peter, of Paul, and of the good thief who conceived in one moment such a lively sentiment of true penitence that he gained paradise by it. There is no crime, however enormous, that cannot be effaced by a single act of this virtue.

It has no sadness about it though it appears clothed in sackcloth, for there is joy in heaven when a sinner does penance; and the sinner himself, animated with a new spirit, like an invalid who has recovered perfect health, rejoices at his happy state.

Man cannot desire any good which this fruitful virtue does not produce; and there is no evil which it cannot remove. It is but just, then, that Novices should purify themselves of the old leaven, since God in His mercy has called them to be a new paste; for it befits the just who are wholly cleansed from their sins to feast on "the unleavened bread of sincerity and truth."[96] Let us now indicate some acts of this virtue.

## II. Practice of Penance

Novices should strive to penetrate well the excellence of this counsel: "Be not without fear about sin forgiven."[97] They know indeed that they have sinned; but while confident that pardon has been granted them, they cannot, however, feel an entire certainty in the matter. For this reason they should never cease to implore the most clement God for forgiveness of their sins, just as if they believed these sins were not pardoned; imitating in this those prudent men who, in affairs of great importance, fail not to employ, if there is the least suspicion of danger, the means they would use were they to know that danger menaced them for certain.

Moreover, even if they were certain of having obtained pardon, they would be wrong in thinking themselves exempted from the sufferings of Purgatory, and they would act foolishly if they did not strive to extinguish its terrible flames by works of penance.

Besides, even though God had remitted the offense and the punishment, they could not without reproach dispense themselves from chastising their

---

[95] "Unless you shall do penance, you shall all likewise perish." Luke 13:3, Pub.
[96] 1 Cor. 5:8
[97] Ecclus. 5:5

bodies[98]; the immense goodness of this merciful God acts as a sharp spur to generous hearts urging them on to endure sufferings. Thus the most illustrious Saints macerated their flesh with greater severity after having obtained pardon than before.

But let us go further and suppose that our young athletes have never been guilty of any sin. It is even then prudent for them to restrain the restless horse of concupiscence, lest it may precipitate them into sin.

In fine, even if they had never sinned and were sure of never committing sin, the spiritual profits that accrue to the soul from the mortification of the body should induce them to give themselves generously to the practice of penance.

The principal act of true penance is contrition. But in order not to torment themselves with scruples, Novices should know that true contrition consists not in a sorrow of the appetite and senses, but in the serious detestation for God's sake of the faults committed, with a firm purpose of never committing them again.

## Interior Acts

O most merciful God, I detest my sins because they displease Thee, and I am resolved to die rather than offend Thee again.

O most clement Lord, I hate and abominate my iniquity, for it is against Thee alone that I have sinned; and I resolve to love Thy law and not to transgress it any more.

O God, infinitely amiable, I abhor my sins because they displease Thee, and I resolve to punish myself for them for Thy sake.

O most bountiful Lord, would that I had died rather than have offended Thee. I now wish to die sooner than offend Thee again, even venially.

O my God, my sins displease me above every other evil; I hope I shall never be so unfortunate as to commit them again.

O God of all gentleness and sweetness, would that I could efface with my blood the sins I have committed! For all the riches of this world I would not again commit even a venial sin.

O most loving Lord, I deserved hell by my sins; would that I had never committed them! Grant me grace never to offend Thee again.

---

[98] "But I chastise my body, and bring it into subjection: lest perhaps, when I have preached to others, I myself should become a castaway." 1 Cor 9:27, Pub.

We may produce these acts in various ways. But we must make a remark here which applies equally to the other virtues. When pronouncing the words, or conceiving them interiorly, it is necessary to excite a movement or affection of the will; for it is vain to say with the lips: Lord, I detest my sins, if interiorly we turn not the heart from sin as we would turn the eyes of the body from the sight of a serpent, otherwise we shall not have made a true act of penance.

## Exterior Acts

The Holy Scriptures furnish us with many examples of these acts. David was accustomed to haircloth and ashes; the king of Nineveh covered himself with sackcloth, as did all the inhabitants of the city. Saint Mary Magdalen retired to the grotto; Mary of Egypt lived in the desert; indeed, all those who wish to live godly in Christ suffer for Him.[99]

It is certain that if sinners will not do penance they shall, without exception, perish; now, the more holy a person is, the more sinful he esteems himself to be; consequently no one can dispense himself from the law of penance.

For this reason, the more perfect a Religious Order is the more rigorously it treats the body, and imposes on the flesh many ordinances which it maintains with great exactitude; indeed, it is the custom among its members never to seek any indulgence as regards health, sleep, or clothing, unless there is a grave necessity of which the Superior is ignorant.

Hence the use of hair-cloth, fasts on bread and water, extreme moderation in the use of wine and food, prolonged vigils, long prayers on bare knees, severe disciplines, iron chains worn on certain days of the week, the courageous endurance of heat and cold, and various other practices familiar to Religious.

All these exercises of penance, undertaken for the love of God, wonderfully advance the work of religious perfection; and whilst they increase and fortify interior penance they fill the soul with joy, and excite in those who behold such exercises performed a holy emulation. But let us consider the reasons which ought to induce us to desire and practice penance.[100]

---

[99] Cf. 2 Tim. 3:12
[100] "If I should deliver my body to be burned, and have not charity, it profiteth me nothing. Charity is patient, is kind: charity envieth not, dealeth not perversely; is not puffed up; Is not

# III. Motives For Penance

*First Motive:* The first motive is drawn from the majesty of God, Who has been offended by sin. Worldly people have a high idea of the greatness of princes, and would consider it a disgrace to be wanting in the respect due to them. Natural reason teaches us that it is not meet to offend those who have a right to our reverence, and it inspires us with a kind of repentance which urges us to humble ourselves, and use all our efforts to appease the Prince whom we have offended. What, then, should not the vehemence of our sorrow be for having provoked the supreme Majesty of Him who has a right to our sovereign love and respect?

Let us remark that this first motive is drawn from the gravity of the offense, measured by the greatness, wisdom, beauty, and other perfections of God. The excellence of this Infinite Being is, indeed, so sublime that even if He never did good to us we should still owe Him sovereign honour. Men render homage to the dignity of strange kings when they meet them, though they may never have received any benefit from them; and if they refuse to do so they commit a fault and incur censure.

*Second Motive:* Now, as the Divine Majesty is not only infinitely great in Himself but has laden us with immense and innumerable benefits, how cruel it would be not to conceive any sorrow for the offenses offered to so loving and so generous a Benefactor. There is no nation in the world, however uncivilized or barbarous, that is not extremely grateful to those from whom it has received benefits and fearful of offending them.

*Third Motive:* The favours expected from kings and princes exercise a singular influence on men. The hope of enjoying them produces such deep impressions on illustrious personages who have grown old in courts, that if they receive from these princes an uncourteous reply, or even an indifferent look, the great chagrin they feel often causes illness, and sometimes even death. Consequently, since God the great King of kings, to Whom all impiety is an object of hatred, no longer regards with a favourable eye the sinner who has offended Him, but on the contrary detests him and holds

---

ambitious, seeketh not her own, is not provoked to anger, thinketh no evil; Rejoiceth not in iniquity, but rejoiceth with the truth." 1 Cor 13:3-6. "The Christian, therefore, if he will direct his rejoicing to God in moral goods, must keep in mind, that the value of his good works, fasting, almsgiving, penances, and prayers, does not depend on their number and nature, but on the love which moves him to perform them for God." St. John of the Cross, *Ascent of Mount Carmel*, Book 3, Ch 26, Pub.

him in abomination, should not that sinner, when he sees all that has been lost to him, be seized with a profound sorrow, and reduced to the last extremity? The force of this motive is still more increased by what we see in the case of wicked men. It is, indeed, wonderful, when they have incurred the anger of an earthly monarch, how they fly far away from his presence, and while traveling in foreign lands or distant seas suspect every noise they hear to be the approach of his officers. How, then, can those who have offended an immortal King, from Whose presence there is no escape either by sea or by land, continue to rest and laugh and play in their own homes? How is it they do not hasten to implore His clemency? Why is it they are not afraid of a sudden death?

*Fourth Motive:* But even if death were not to be feared, and if we consider only the injury that man does to himself when he commits sin; should it not be deplored on account of its enormity? For besides the friendship of God, the blessed Virgin Mary, the Angels and Saints which he loses, if we consider the interior deformity of soul that sin causes, the loss of Divine grace, of the infused virtues, of the gifts of the Holy Ghost, of the right to the heavenly inheritance, and of the merits of his good works; what can be more lamentable? Truly, his fate is so deplorable that it could not be sufficiently mourned by all the tears of the entire world.

*Fifth Motive:* What shall be said of the other evils entailed by sin? As a child of God, man was clothed in a robe of brilliant whiteness; when he sinned he became at once the slave of the demon; all the interior beauty which delighted the eye of God was changed into foul deformity. And just as when in the state of justice he was drawn towards heaven by a natural movement of grace, so in the state of sin he is drawn to the infernal abyss as to his center, by the natural weight of his fault, which agitates him that he may fall into it, like another Judas who made haste to hang himself, "that he might go to his own place."[101]

Since then so many and such terrible evils menace the sinner, his gravest interests are at stake, while time is left him to do penance. He should see in this a kind of warning from God Who, after having drawn the sword of His justice, is not, however, in His anger, forgetful of His mercy.[102] But if he will not be converted, the Lord has already "bent His bow, and made it

---

[101] Acts 1:25
[102] Cf. Habac. 3:2

ready. And in it He hath prepared the instruments of death, He hath made ready His arrows for them that burn."[103]

*Sixth Motive:* God in His clemency offers to sinners the choice, either to endure a light penance in this life, or if they remain obstinate in sin, to burn in eternal flames. Can we imagine anyone to be so foolish as not to prefer to suffer a little pain in this life rather than everlasting torments in the next?

*Seventh Motive:* Let us consider how great is the clemency of Him now towards sinners Who will one day punish them very severely. Very often men are condemned to death by their fellow men for robbery, murder, or other crimes, which is equivalent to reducing them to nothing, as regards the present life. O prodigy of Divine mercy! The sinner has deserved eternal chastisements, yet God invites him to submit to a light punishment, in which he will find the amendment of his life.

*Eighth Motive*: Let us think of the consolations of penance. Were there no other motives to engage sinners to embrace it voluntarily, the sweetness it brings with it should make them practice it. Indeed, nothing is more true than the following: "According to the multitude of my sorrows in my heart, Thy comforts have given joy to my soul."[104] When true penance exists, and the sinner embraces an austere life to repair the injury done to God, joy, the daughter of hope, which then increases in vigour, springs up in the inmost heart and gives sweetness to all the pains to which he voluntarily submits.

*Ninth Motive:* What happens then? The vicious habits which corroded the soul, as rust corrodes iron, disappear with the contact of penance; and the soul freed from their evil influence enters with ardour on the career of Christian perfection, and hastens to repair its former losses.

*Tenth Motive:* Finally, if the preceding motives are insufficient to make us practice penance, where is the Christian heart that will not be touched at seeing Jesus Christ expiate our sins by such cruel suffering? Ah! without doubt, when He was struck, spit upon, mocked, crucified, He paid back, as the Prophet says, that which He had not taken. He paid it back with as much rigour as if He had taken it under the most criminal circumstances. What, then! "The Just perisheth and no man layeth it to heart,"[105] and the thieves who have plundered His goods refuse to bear even a light punishment.

---

[103] Ps. 7:13-14
[104] Ps. 93:19
[105] Isa. 57:1

*Conclusion:* Novices should conclude from all that has been said, that they ought, in their own interest, to detest sincerely their past sins and endeavour to conceive, with the help of grace, a profound sorrow for them. Then, arming themselves with courage, let them impose strict laws on the body, so that having overcome the obstacles arising from their former offenses, they may hope after a favourable voyage to arrive safely at the port of salvation.

# VI. Abstinence and Sobriety

## 1. Nature and Excellence of Abstinence and Sobriety

In the chapters on chastity, poverty and penance, we have said much with regard to the acts proper to abstinence and sobriety. They would not require to be treated separately if gluttony were not such an insidious and troublesome enemy. We shall add a few remarks concerning these two virtues which are so closely connected with penance.

Abstinence and sobriety are the virtues which regulate the use of food and drink. They are parts of temperance, and have always been much recommended by the founders of monastic life.

It will be easy for us to understand the excellence of these virtues, so becoming to youth, if we consider that they make us like the angels by the superiority which they confer on the spirit; since by the continual vigilance which through them we exercise over ourselves, as Jesus Christ has counseled, we are preserved from the heaviness arising from the excessive use of meats and wine.[106]

Yes, to seek, at the expense of bodily strength, the food which sustains the spirit is to imitate the life of the angels.

Nothing can be more profitable than such efforts, for the nourishment of the soul is so much the more abundant in proportion as that of the body is more meagre. And as these two kinds of food exclude each other

---

[106] Cf. Luke 21:34

reciprocally, it would be an irreparable loss to pamper the body while starving the soul.[107]

Moreover, the pure pleasure given by spiritual food which makes itself felt in the depths of the heart, surpasses infinitely all the delights of the most exquisite meats and wines.

The most illustrious Saints and Fathers of the Old and New Testament have so perfectly practiced the virtues of abstinence and sobriety that one would think they were no longer made of flesh and blood. Yet, in their exhausted bodies they preserved an invincible strength, as their lives amply testify.

Let Novices tread in the footsteps of these great men and strive to emulate them, so that, free from the shackles of the flesh, they may apply themselves to the study and contemplation of Divine things which is the end of their holy vocation.

## II. Practice of Abstinence and Sobriety

It is necessary to remark that gluttony is exceedingly clever in seeking out what pleases it. First, it must have delicate dishes; if they are not to be had, it will choose the best in that which is served. If the things presented are equally good or mediocre, it compensates itself by quantity; if the quantity is small, it will vitiate this act, so necessary to life, by eating or drinking with undue slowness, or in some other way that gives pleasure to the palate.

For this reason Novices should make a resolution to take at meals, not what is most pleasing to the palate, but that which is best calculated to sustain nature; and to follow the practice of the saints, by avoiding all precipitation and fastidiousness, at the same time giving suitable nourishment to the soul by attending to the spiritual reading which is made in common.

But as concupiscence often feigns necessity, the Novice should be slow to yield to its demands unless experience proves them to be real. Not only Religious, but those who are aiming at perfection in their secular state, avoid eating outside the prescribed times.

---

[107] "If a man is sincere about fasting and is hungry, the enemies that trouble his soul will grow weak." Benedicta Ward, *The Desert Fathers,* Ch 4, #16. "Daniel said, 'If the body is strong, the soul weakens. If the body weakens, the soul is strong.' He also said, 'If the body is prosperous, the soul grows lean; if the body is lean, the soul grows prosperous.'" Ibid., Ch 10, #17, Pub.

## Interior Acts

O Jesus, model of temperance, I resolve to make use of food and drink only as far as it shall be necessary to give me strength for Thy service.

O most meek Lord, I renounce all the pleasures of the table.

God forbid that I should ever seek after things that are delicate and pleasing to the palate.

O God of all sweetness, I wish for love of Thee, that all I eat or drink may become bitter to my taste.

O most amiable Lord, I desire for love of Thee, to withdraw my heart from the things which are set before me at table and to attend to the reading.

I resolve, O Lord, to make my body suffer hunger and thirst for Thy sake.

O most clement God, would that at each repast the worst portion should fall to my lot.

May all my repasts, O most benign Jesus, be seasoned with the vinegar which Thou didst taste in Thy Passion.

These acts may be produced under various forms, but they should be made with great fervour and earnestness.

## Exterior Acts

We learn from the teaching of the ancient Fathers that it is necessary to use various devices to subdue gluttony; for in a matter of daily occurrence such as the nourishing of the body, it would be vain for anyone to believe that he is temperate who confines himself to interior acts. What sort of virtue would that be, I ask, which does not make use of the frequent opportunities that occur of practicing it?

Novices should not rest content with making pious reflections at the table on the sufferings, the gall and vinegar of Jesus Christ, but they ought to strive with still greater care to practice virtue while they are taking their repast. Thus, they will leave a portion of each dish for Jesus Christ Who was so poor; for love of Him they will often deprive themselves at table of something that is specially pleasing to the palate; they will use wine with great moderation; they will decide for themselves beforehand a certain quantity of food and drink to be taken; they will abstain on some days from savoury fruits that excite the appetite; they will, from time to time, make their food insipid by adding water to it, or bitter by mingling absinth with it; they will keep one foot raised from the ground at intervals, in order to deaden by the pain the pleasure the body receives from the nourishment.

These means, and many others which the desire of eternal salvation will suggest, should be practiced by each according to his capacity, in order to acquire the virtues of abstinence and sobriety; and no matter what difficulties he meets with, he should never abandon them, as the following reasons will show.

## III. Motives for Abstinence and Sobriety

*First Motive:* There are men who, like animals, seem to have no other care than that of treating their bodies well. If doctors prescribe for them a strict regime, they will practice it with wonderful exactness, in order to conserve or recover their health, which is comparatively of such little importance. Why, then, should the Servants of Jesus Christ be less careful to observe in the use of food the measure prescribed by the holy Fathers, in order to acquire or increase the health of the soul, and thus to arrive at the joys of eternal life.

*Second Motive:* Those who apply themselves assiduously to the study of human sciences and desire to become very proficient in them, hesitate not to lead a frugal life, and to endure patiently hunger and thirst, so much do they fear to clog the brain by self-indulgence. Why, then, should not the study of heavenly wisdom, which is not acquired without temperance, constrain us to renounce willingly the satisfaction of the palate?

*Third Motive:* It is natural to man to use his reason, and no one is so insane as not to prefer the loss of the eyes of the body to the use of his intellectual faculties. Hence a man ought to love naturally, and to exert himself with all his might to excel in, what will procure for him not an ordinary but a remarkably good understanding. Now, it is a fact that men devoted to the pleasures of the table become daily more dull and stupid; whilst, on the contrary, those who are temperate, having their minds free from obscure vapours, are always better disposed to apply themselves to the study and contemplation of Divine things.

*Fourth Motive:* Besides, what can be more shameful for a Religious, invited to the table of the Angels, than to love the husks of swine and attach his heart to them? By this means he makes himself not only the object of the Angels' contempt, but he also shows himself unworthy of the state he has chosen and provokes the indignation of those around him; for true Religious can have no respect for a man who is a slave to his appetite.

*Fifth Motive:* Furthermore, God Himself, notwithstanding all His goodness, sovereignly detests the glutton. This is exemplified in the punishment inflicted on the chosen people, when, after having "rained upon them flesh as dust; and feathered fowls like the sand of the sea," His anger was provoked, and: "As yet their meat was in their mouth; and the wrath of God came upon them, and He slew the fat ones among them, and brought down the chosen men of Israel."[108]

*Sixth Motive:* Greedy Religious certainly belong to the race of Esau, who sold his birthright for a mess of pottage. In choosing them preferably to thousands of others whom He left in the world, God adopted them, like the people of Israel, as His first-born; and they, unmindful of this sacred privilege, sell for a mean gratification of the palate, the presence of God, prayer, devotion, purity of heart and the other privileges of their birthright.

And indeed their advancement is so much the more to be despaired of, since they will not listen to the warnings of Superiors or heed the maxims of the spiritual life: for though they must of necessity assist at the common acts of the Community, it is as if they were not there, for their affections are not with God, but where concupiscence finds its delight.

Temperate Religious, on the contrary, make continual progress; nothing troubles them in their application to the acts destined for their advancement, and they come forth from them with renewed vigour. They are attentive, circumspect, affable, and make themselves all to all. They are especially distinguished for their purity; for abstinence is the promoter of chastity, as gluttony is the prolific source of impurity.

*Seventh Motive:* But what shall be said of the sweetness of the interior food which is the fruit of abstinence from what is exterior? Truly, it would seem as if men of temperate habits share in the privilege enjoyed by Our Lord, when, after His fast of forty days, "Angels came and ministered to Him."[109] For God is wont to replenish with Divine consolations those who for His love and service deny themselves the gross pleasures of the table.

*Eighth Motive:* For the rest, let us turn our eyes on Jesus Christ and His Immaculate Mother. Indeed, all is comprised in their example; their whole mortal life was but a continual practice of these virtues. Herein, they eclipsed the Apostles, of whom it is written that they rubbed the ears

---

[108] Ps. 77:27, 30-31
[109] Matt. 4:11

of corn between their hands when pressed by hunger,[110] and the Solitaries whose abstinence seemed miraculous. Yet, compared with our laxity, the self-denial of the Apostles and Solitaries is a prodigy.

*Conclusion:* Novices should endeavour then not to depart in anything from the rule of life approved by Jesus Christ, in order that, having their minds raised to God, they may preserve purity of soul and body, and advance with gigantic strides in the way of Christian perfection.

# VII. Humility

## I. Nature and Excellence of Humility

Nothing is more advantageous to those who sincerely repent of their sins and desire to appease the anger of God, than that profound humility taught by Jesus Christ. We may convince ourselves of this by many parables and events narrated in Holy Scripture.

Humility is a virtue which restrains the mind so as to hinder it from aspiring to things that are above it. Though it has its seat in the irascible part of the sensitive appetite, it is, however, a child of temperance. It is in itself a most illustrious virtue.

Indeed, there is no one but knows how sublime, how useful and sweet humility is. For if anyone is not perfectly acquainted with its Divine strength, the eulogies that have been pronounced on it by voice and pen since the foundation of the Church to this day, are so abundant, that the name of this virtue cannot fail to awaken in the minds of all men a high idea of its excellence.

It is a truly Christian virtue; this alone is a signal glory for it. No school of pagan philosophers has been able to attain its height. Only the school of Jesus Christ has taught this sublime science, which has transported to heaven men formerly wedded to earth.

It is fitting, then, that Novices should desire to know the beauty of so excellent a virtue; in order that, considering it attentively, they may love it more ardently, and by practicing it acquire immense riches.

---

[110] Cf. Luke 6:1

Undoubtedly, that must be a rare kind of beauty which can charm the heart of God, and sweetly incline Him to fulfill its desires. Now, the Holy Scriptures positively assure us that such a power is the property of humility. There never was a man, no matter how wicked he may have been, who sincerely humbled himself, who God did not instantly restore to His friendship and lift up from the dust. The sweet and consoling parable of the prodigal son is proof of this. He wasted all the goods he had received and returned sick, bruised and in rags; however, the abasement of his afflicted heart sufficed to turn to him the heart of his father. So is it with God and the sinner.

Assuredly, after spending an immense fortune of graces, what can be more advantageous to the poor wanderer than to gain in so short a time, by a single sigh, the Kingdom of Heaven, to which he had not dared to raise his eyes? Without this prize, "What shall it profit a man if he gain the whole world?"[111] No, since the beginning of the world men never discovered anything more profitable than deep and solid humility. It constrained a loving father to give his son shoes, a ring, fine clothes, rich ornaments, and to lavish on him more than he had possessed before his departure.

Then what rejoicings they had! The fatted calf was killed, a sumptuous repast was prepared, and sweet music provided for the guests. Indeed, words cannot sufficiently express the interior joys of the humble man. He strives to lower and abase himself to the very depths of hell on account of his numerous sins. What, then, must be his delight when he sees a God of all mercy run to him, embrace him, and tell him to have confidence!

Those who are familiar with Divine things well know that the consolations of God are inestimable; but when they inundate a heart that deems itself unworthy of them, they ravish it with admiration and it seems hardly capable of containing them.

Since then this sweetest of virtues is so fruitful, it is but just that Novices should allow themselves to be captivated by its charms and strive to acquire it at any cost. Let us now pass on to the acts proper to humility.

---

[111] Mark 8:36

## II. Practice of Humility

Let us consider that the measure of this abasement of mind in which humility consists, is the knowledge of one's own frailty; hence, this virtue requires two things, namely, a right understanding and a pure will.

Each one should humble himself by the consideration of his own frailty and especially the remembrance of his sins. He should also have more esteem for others than for himself, since he considers them less guilty than himself, or at least that they have profited more by the graces they have received.

However, he should not, on this account, think but little of the graces God has bestowed on him, but rather that they are gratuitous favours of which he is unworthy, and that He may take them away again on account of his ingratitude, or because they have been abused. Thus it is that the benefits of God weigh, in a sense, on the soul and abase it to the earth. If it examines them attentively it is overpowered and covered with confusion.

The Fathers distinguish in various ways different degrees of humility. For greater clearness we shall adopt the following division. First, as regards to the *matter*: We may submit to Superiors, to equals, to inferiors, or to all men, even the most unworthy. Here are four degrees by which we mount successively. The fourth is the most elevated of all.

But since this submission or abasement relates to the exercise by which we acquire humility rather than to the nature of the virtue itself, we will give another division. Secondly, with regard to the *form*: Herein the first degree is to believe others better than ourselves; the second, to wish that others may have the same opinion; the third, to wish that others may treat us as inferiors; the fourth, to bear patiently the contempt of others; the fifth, to receive contempt with joy and to love those who despise us.

This last degree is very sublime, and when the soul has arrived at it, we cannot imagine what an increase of Divine love it receives. Let us remark, however, that it may happen to the imperfect, and even to the newly-converted, owing to the interior consolation they experience, that they seem to love more ardently those who reprehend their faults. This disposition is not the humility which is proper to the advanced; it is only an image of it. Moreover, we know that it is natural to a man who is in joy, not to heed the affronts which irritate a heart that is plunged in grief.

## Interior Acts

My most meek Jesus, I confess before Thee that I am the vilest of men.

O most bountiful Lord, no one has ever been so ungrateful and unfaithful to Thee as I.

O God of mercy, the greatest libertines would have served Thee more faithfully than I, had they received the graces Thou hast lavished on me.

Alas! O Lord, I am always tending to earth and what is earthly; thus I am unworthy not only to enter heaven, but even to look up to it.

O my God, all living creatures draw near to Thee according to their capacity; I alone withdraw from Thee by the wickedness of my life.

Yes, O my Saviour, I am more hideous in Thy sight than a leper on account of the grievousness of my sins.

Indeed, O most loving Lord, I richly deserve to be thrown into a pit and separated from intercourse with other men, on account of the wickedness of my life.

Preserve me, O Lord, from wishing to walk in great matters, or in wonderful things above me.[112]

O God, sovereignly just, would that all men knew my baseness that they may despise me.

Grant, O Lord, that men may upbraid me with reproaches on account of my unworthiness, in order that I may be despised for love of Thee.

In eliciting these acts we should endeavour to conceive profound sentiments of contempt for ourselves, and a corresponding desire to be treated as we deserve by others.

## Exterior Acts

We must start with this principle that in the judgement of God and of the truly wise, the vilest things of this world—indigence, leprosy, opprobrium, capital punishment, and all that has ever been invented to degrade man—render him less worthy of contempt than the stain of a single sin. To enlightened minds this is as clear as the fact that two and two makes four. The result is that if God gives us grace to have a true knowledge of our own sins, we shall consider ourselves so contemptible that we will believe it only our due to be despised by others, and will think that those who make little

---

[112] Cf. Ps. 130:1

of us are on God's side. For the same reason we will blush for the honours that are done to us, looking upon ourselves as ragged lepers covered with a royal mantle.

Such are the sentiments Novices should strive to have. Then, with a strong conviction of their own lowliness, they will give themselves to the exterior practice of humility, by means of the following acts:—To tell their faults in the Refectory or at Chapter, in order to receive a correction; to fulfill, with the sanction of obedience, the meanest offices; to seek the lowest place when anything is being done in common; to salute respectfully those whom they meet; to listen with attention and docility to those who speak; not to contradict anyone; to yield at once when contradicted; to make much of what is said or done by others; when an occasion offers itself, to praise the actions of others; never to show a contemptuous spirit; to meet all with a serene countenance and a sweet condescension; to hide, as far as charity will permit, all that may win esteem for them; such as wit, noble lineage, science; to manifest whatever will lower them in the estimation of others, such as stupidity, incapacity, ignorance; to kneel down when speaking to the Superior or Novice-Master; to prostrate when praised or blamed. Those who are desirous of advancing will easily discover a variety of other similar practices.

Finally, let them not be deceived. If they find they cannot, without much pain and difficulty, produce these acts so contrary to nature, they should consider that the hour of battle has sounded, and that it is only after having overcome all such obstacles they will enjoy the peace of humility. What seems now so hard and painful in this warfare is the source of priceless merit. They should not, then, allow themselves to be discouraged on account of these continual struggles in the pursuit of so excellent a good. The reasons which follow will confirm what we have said.

## III. Motives for Humility

*First motive:* The more ambitious men are, the more they are seen cringing in royal courts, and multiplying in a thousand different ways the testimonies of their servile submission, in order to obtain the honours they desire. They know there is no surer means of attaining them. Why, then, should not those who aspire to eternal honours be more ardent in abasing themselves before others, since it is an oracle from the mouth of the God-man that "He that humbleth himself shall be exalted"?[113]

*Second Motive:* Let us consider for a moment avaricious men: Their ardent thirst for gold drives them from their country where they enjoyed considerable distinction, and conducts them to remote regions; there they suppress all pomp, reduce themselves to what is strictly necessary in food and clothing, and condemn themselves for many years perhaps to a sort of servitude and painful toil in order to become rich. Why, then, should not we, who are called by God in this land of exile to amass immense spiritual wealth, be humble of heart, and cast off all self-esteem, which is the direct and sure way to attain it?

*Third Motive:* It would ill befit a poor man to wear clothing embroidered with gold. Should he not blush to appear with it in public? What, then, is to be thought of a Religious who, making interior and exterior profession of despising the world, is not ashamed to lay aside the livery of humility and put on the pompous ornaments of pride? Is he not a monstrosity? Certainly a heart so debased by pride gives but little hope of perseverance.

*Fourth Motive:* Besides, there is no one such an enemy to self as not to wish to be loved by others. All men, indeed, desire to reign, and desire it in such a way that, as the proverb says, if one must sin, it is in order to reign. But they know that the most desirable and excellent reign is that which is exercised over hearts; for he who possesses hearts commands even kings. Since then, as daily experience teaches, humility is the assured means of making ourselves loved by others, and exercising over them a most agreeable kind of empire, how is it that the whole world does not apply itself to the practice of this virtue?

Several considerations may be added to the force of this motive. How does the humble heart act? Judging others to be better than itself, it believes that they should have the best of everything; regarding itself as worthy of contempt, it covets humiliations, inconveniences and sufferings. Thus it willingly takes what others dislike, and easily yields to them what they prefer. What misunderstanding, then, can come between it and others? In giving them the best and in reserving to itself the worst, does it not remove all cause of discord? And if union exists, the humble man must of necessity attract love, and consequently reign over hearts.

---

[113] Luke 14:11

*Fifth Motive:* It is not only the hearts of men that submit to his sway, but humanly speaking we may say the humble man has such power over the heart of God that he seems to be master of it. What is it to be master if not to constrain others to do our will? Now, God has such an affection for the humble that their desires seem to guide Him in the government of the universe. There are many striking examples to prove the truth of this.

What did He not do for David? "He took him from the flocks of sheep: He brought him from following the ewes great with young, to feed Jacob His servant, and Israel His inheritance."[114] And this David would one day cast off his kingly ornaments before the Ark of the Covenant, and say with a deep sentiment of humility: "Before the Lord Who chose me,... I will both play and make myself meaner than I have done; and I will be little in my own eyes."[115]

To come nearer to our own times, was it not in the body of St. Francis of Assisi, the humblest of men, that, by an act of love hitherto unheard of, He reproduced His adorable Wounds? This inestimable favour was the reward of humility.

If the thing were possible, we might pause here to describe the ineffable joys which God lavishes on humble souls, and to tell how He unites them to Himself, fills them with Himself, and fashions them to His own image.

*Sixth Motive:* But we must not by accumulating other reasons, turn away from the source of humility to draw from rivulets. His word has gone forth: "Learn of Me, because I am meek and humble of heart."[116] "Of Me", that is, of Him Who is best fitted to teach such a science, for being in the form of God He emptied Himself, taking the form of a servant.[117] Why, then, should not the servants elevate themselves, by the practice of humility, to a participation in the form of God?

Would that Novices were privileged to hear the words uttered by our Lord when seated after washing the feet of His Apostles: "Know you," said He, "what I have done to you? You call Me Master and Lord; and you say well; for so I am. If then I, being your Lord and Master, have washed your feet: you also ought to wash one another's feet. For I have given you an example, that as I have done to you, so you do also."[118]

---

[114] Ps. 77:70-71
[115] 2 Kings 6:21-22
[116] Matt. 11:29
[117] Cf. Phil 2:6-7
[118] John 13:12-15

*Seventh Motive:* But even if we had not this great Model, Whose excellence is infinite, the Daughter of Sion, the Virgin most prudent, should be a sufficient example for men who have retired to monasteries. All beautiful, and all amiable, the object of universal praise, she descended, by self-knowledge and self-abasement, to the deepest abyss of humility, as if she were unworthy to enjoy the light of day.

Humility is the great characteristic of her Firstborn Son, Whom she wrapped in swaddling clothes; such should also be the special trait of all those spiritual children whom her virginal heart afterwards begot. The One teaches humility, the others should learn to be humble of heart, in order to find rest to their weary souls. They are revived by the salutary perfume of her humility whilst occupied in seeking the eternal repose they hope to enjoy one day.

Such, also, is the mark of the inhabitants of the heavenly Jerusalem, whose names are written in the Book of Life. Whilst abjuring the pomp of proud Babylon and despising themselves, they have borne away by violence the kingdom that "suffereth violence."

*Conclusion:* Consequently, if Religious, who are the special children of the most pure and humble of Virgins, are to be worthy of such a Mother, like her, they must become humble. And although they strive to acquire all the virtues in their perfection, as they are bound to do, yet they should endeavour to distinguish themselves specially in humility, which is in itself a virtue so excellent, and the guardian of all the others. For this is the shortest way, as experience will teach them, to the enjoyment in this valley of tears of that "peace which surpasseth all understanding,"[119] a foretaste of eternal felicity.

# VIII. Meekness

## I. Its Nature and Excellence

Meekness, which ranks among the fruits of temperance, resides in the irascible part of the sensitive appetite; it is a virtue which governs anger, and its ordinary effect is to extinguish the ardour of that passion. It is then

---

[119] Phil. 4:7

worthy of the highest praise we can bestow upon it. It is the companion of humility, for Our Lord Jesus Christ recommended both these virtues at the same time when He said: "Learn of Me, because I am meek and humble of heart."[120]

As meekness keeps anger, the most ferocious of all the passions, in subjection to the precepts of reason, it seems to have naturally among the rest of the virtues a singular and most abundant sweetness, besides an infinity of other goods which it bestows upon man.

Indeed everyone knows that meek people are very agreeable to others; so far from wishing to wound anyone, they, on the contrary, receive without resistance the injuries done them, and show a smiling face even to those who offend them.

Not only do they willingly accept bad treatment, but, exposed to new outrages, they show no disposition to defend themselves, till at last they come to extinguish by the ineffable sweetness of their virtue the fire of anger in others.

This sufficiently demonstrates the nobility and beauty of Christian meekness. Whilst other men, abandoning reason descend to the nature of wild beasts, the meek remain unruffled, and partaking in some sort of immortality preserve themselves invulnerable in the midst of injuries.

It would also seem as if they were elevated above the common condition of men. The unfortunate events which most deeply agitate the human heart cannot touch them; it is as if they had already attained to the state of the blessed in heaven.

For as in the midst of the troubles produced in the inferior air by storms, tempests, whirlwinds, thunder and lightning, the superior region loses nothing of its calm serenity, so also the meek heart, elevated as it is above all the agitations of the world, preserves its tranquillity, since it is a stranger to earth's troubles and the fluctuation of human things.

From this we can also learn how profitable the virtue of meekness is, for it gives us a right to a magnificent inheritance which nothing can destroy, as it is written: "The meek shall inherit the land." And in order to remove all suspicion of warfare the Royal Prophet adds: "And they shall delight in abundance of peace."[121] What was said of the happy reign of Solomon the Peaceful is verified in the heart of the meek: no noise of war comes to trouble his interior.

---

[120] Matt. 11:29
[121] Ps. 36:11

This peace is not sterile; on the contrary, it brings forth the most abundant fruits of Divine consolations. For this reason it is said: "they shall delight in abundance of peace." Indeed it is wonderful how admirably meekness disposes the soul for divine consolations by removing all that can impede their tranquil enjoyment.

Let Novices then, in the hope of gaining such signal favours, devote themselves most assiduously to this virtue, and strive, as it behooves Religious, to reproduce in themselves by meekness the state of the blessed in heaven.

## II. Practice of Meekness

It is worthy of notice that among men there are some who are naturally prone to anger; and others, on the contrary, are less easily moved. This observation should be equally applied to the other virtues, especially to humility, of which we have treated in the preceding chapter. We know by daily experience that if certain men are puffed up with a sense of their own excellence others are but little touched by it.

The result is, that for beginners, the practice of each virtue will have merit in proportion to the repugnances of nature. Is it not a proof of greater generosity to devote oneself to the acquisition of that virtue which will entail the most violent conflict? We say for beginners, since in those who are already advanced it is clear that each virtue will be more perfect, when, after long struggles it enjoys repose, and has no longer to resist the attacks of temptation.

This consideration should cause Novices not to judge rashly of others, and not to think themselves better because they are free from temptations. For those who feel more inclined to anger, pride, or envy, and resist these passions, though they may now and then commit small faults, are in reality more advanced than persons who, not being subject to similar temptations, appear to have more virtue.

The degrees of meekness may be reduced in general to five; it is the same with the virtue of patience. 1. The person is moved by an offense received, but he represses with pain and sadness the movement of anger. 2. He is moved, but possesses himself in peace. 3. The victories already gained over anger enables him to remain quite unmoved. 4. He rejoices at the offense on account of the spiritual good to be derived from it. 5. He forgets himself so far as to conceive a deep sorrow and compassion for the evil his neighbour does himself by offending him. Aided by the consideration of these various degrees let each one examine and see what progress he has made in the virtue of meekness.

## Interior Acts

O my most meek Jesus, I firmly resolve, as often as I shall be offended, to remain meek as a lamb before his shearer.

O God of all sweetness, when I am hurt or unjustly treated, I desire, with Thy grace, to show a smiling countenance to those who cause me the pain.

O most amiable Lord, whenever I am maltreated or abused by an inferior, I will, for Thy sake, show him kindness.

O most clement Lord, grant that I may be never irritated with my neighbour, no matter what injury he does me.

O most meek son of God, whenever I am tried I shall rejoice in contradictions, "as one that hath found great spoils."[122]

O God of all goodness, whenever I am annoyed by anyone, I shall forget myself, and, for love of Thee, compassionate him.

These acts should come from the heart. We ought to practice them especially when we find that others show themselves hostile to us by contrary opinions, by words of censure or other like things. In circumstances of this kind acts of patience and meekness are more real. Such trials are frequent, and they nearly always occur without any fault on the part of those who make us submit to them. They are usually the result of thoughtlessness or of natural antipathy and God puts them in our way for the advancement of our souls in perfection.

## Exterior Acts

It is not enough for advancement in Christian perfection and the beauty of the House of God, that our heart be not inflamed with anger against him who has offended us, or that we rejoice at the spiritual good we derive from this outrage, or have compassion on him who has committed it. It is also necessary that these sentiments should not be so shut up in our hearts

---

[122] Ps. 118:162

that we show outwardly a "vinegar aspect," or appear to be only waiting for a favourable opportunity of resentment. This is a point in which many fail by imprudence.

What then is to be done? We must strive by our meekness to heal our neighbour's anger. For this end we should so compose our face and all the movements of our body that he who has offended us may be convinced there is no bitterness in our hearts. Thus—we should respond to him with the "mild answer" that "breaketh wrath;"[123] we should give him a modest and kindly smile; we should ask his pardon for our shortcomings promising to correct them; we should prostrate before him; if there is anything in our speech, walk, deportment or the rest of our exterior that displeases our neighbour we should carefully correct it. For the choice of these acts, and of many other similar ones, we should be careful to consult the particular dispositions of the person whom we are endeavouring to mollify.

## III. Motives for Meekness

Novices would certainly be wrong if they allowed themselves to be discouraged in the practice of this sweet virtue, as if it were too painful and temptations against it too numerous. It behooves them, on the contrary, to show all the more valour in proportion to the difficulties of the combat, and in the hope of obtaining a more advantageous peace. Here then are the reasons.

*First Motive:* Mutual offenses are of very frequent occurrence in the world. In courts especially, where the sentiment of honour is more keen, how often are not persons wounded by signs, words, or actions? However, the more a man is elevated in dignity and the greater thirst he has for honours and riches, the more also he learns to support with patience all that contradict him; since he does not wish to submit to the shame of appearing incapable of managing affairs that are subject to a thousand difficulties, or to expose himself to the risk of losing his position. Why then should not the Servants of God, who aspire to the goods and honours of eternity, labour to repress anger, to show benevolence and to be filled with kindly feelings towards their neighbours?

---

[123] Prov. 15:1

*Second Motive:* Ah! Since the glorious possession of the land of the living has been promised to the meek by these words of the Gospel: "Blessed are the meek for they shall possess the land,"[124] it would be a signal folly to fall back on account of the difficulties, and not endeavour to secure such immense wealth. For what happiness can they expect who do not strive to put themselves in a state that will fit them for the celestial inheritance?

*Third Motive:* But even if meekness gave no right to citizenship in the heavenly Jerusalem, the advantages which this virtue procures in the present life should determine us never to neglect the practice of it. Here is a convincing proof. All creatures love peace; even wild beasts seek it and delight in it. Lions, tigers, and bears never fight unless their peace is upset, that is, unless they are disturbed in the peaceful possession of their prey. It is the same with men who are still more wicked than beasts. What do pirates and assassins desire? What is the object of their robbery and murder, if not the peaceful possession of their spoils? Yes, the very demons themselves when they attack men to drag them into hell, burn with a desire to be satiated, if that were possible, with such cruel trophies, and this is the peace that is most pleasing to them. If then pirates, assassins, demons, and all beings whose portion is trouble and discord; seek so greedily for peace, those who are the children of God, and on whom this title imposes the duty of being peaceful, would give proof of their insanity if they did not strive with extreme care to obtain the peace attached to meekness—a peace which they can enjoy without the fury of combat or the odious fruits of revenge. Have not the most illustrious victories been gained by generals who have taken cities without bloodshed?

*Fourth Motive:* But what shall we say of the Divine joy which proceeds from the peace acquired by meekness? This peace, this calm serenity of heart, is like the mirror of a tranquil lake in which God contemplates Himself lovingly, and reproduces His celestial image; for meekness, more than all the other virtues, makes a man master of himself in a singular manner, and brings him an ever increasing satisfaction. The angry heart, on the contrary, a prey to trouble and agitation, intercepts or repels the Divine communications. Happy are we then if we are meek of heart. Bearing within us a mirror of paradise, we shall know heavenly things and this knowledge will fill us with delight.

---

[124] Matt. 5:4

*Fifth Motive:* But if we are not able to appreciate from this point of view things from on high, we may easily understand the excellence of meekness by consulting the impression produced on men by it. It would be impossible to tell with what sweetness and power it attracts hearts. As in the material order nature loves that which is soft to the touch and abhors that which is coarse, so in the moral order reason attaches itself to gentle spirits and withdraws from those that are choleric. This may be particularly remarked in assemblies of men. Some are inclined to get hot, they are shunned like prickly hedgehogs; others are gentle, and we would gladly have them always with us, live and negotiate with them.

*Sixth Motive:* But to elevate ourselves above this purely natural sphere, when we see that a man who has been provoked returns good for evil, and receives outrages with a kindly smile for the perpetrator, are we not moved to the very depths of our being, and constrained to admire the strength and sweetness of a virtue so worthy of being loved?

The Old Testament furnishes a beautiful example of this. It tells us that Saul, the unfortunate King of Israel, was seized with frequent attacks of frenzy, and that on two occasions when more than usually infuriated, he left the city with armed men in his train, to seek David among the steep rocks, accessible only to the wild goats. Now it happened that, the first time, David cut a piece of fringe off the King's mantle in a cave; and the second time, while the King slept, he carried away the regal lance and cup. He might easily have killed or wounded him, but he did him no harm. Saul was surprised, and, wicked as he was, could not help admiring such meek conduct.

On the first occasion after going out from the cave, when he recognized from afar the voice of David who showed him the fringe of his mantle, he was moved. The second time, having risen from his sleep, he heard David calling to him in the most affectionate terms, and saw him presenting the cup together with the lance which he might have used to kill him. Vanquished by such wonderful meekness, he shed copious tears, a sincere proof—not of his own virtue—but of David's. Here then was a heart harder than adamant, which had thirsted for the blood of his enemy, but now it is softened. The King weeps. He loves David, and disarmed by the simple force of his meekness, he returns to the city. How then will this virtue act on hearts that are not dominated by passion?

*Seventh Motive:* But why should we pause over examples which are far inferior to that given by the Word Made Flesh? This most gentle Son of God has not limited Himself to the counsel: "Learn of Me, for I am meek." His works, still more numerous than His words, have spoken more eloquently. Did He not allow Himself to be conducted to death as "a sheep that is led to the slaughter?"[125] When they struck Him, did He open His mouth to complain? Whilst His enemies, like furious bulls, surrounded Him to shed His innocent Blood, did He betray impatience even by a look? All this is truly inexpressible. Here are two examples of His wonderful meekness. A rough servant, instigated by satan, struck His Sacred Face, and Jesus merely said to him: "If I have spoken evil give testimony of the evil, but if well why strikest thou Me?"[126] A vile traitor, who once held an honoured place among His Apostles, gave Him a perfidious kiss in the Garden of Gethsemane, and Jesus inquired gently: "Friend, whereto art thou come?"[127] Ah, what a vast field is here opened up to our reflection! "He that can take, let him take it."[128]

*Eighth Motive:* For the rest, the meekness of the Blessed Virgin Mary is in a very special manner the appanage of every Religious Order. Now sheep do not beget wolves. Who ever heard of such a monstrous thing? Mary gave birth to the Lamb of God, and her children should be "lambs full of meekness that are carried to the sacrifice."[129] Those whom this Virgin, "gentlest of the gentle,"[130] has adopted as her own ought to be filled with her spirit.

*Ninth Motive:* Finally, to sum up all in a few words, among the most illustrious titles which meekness possesses; and which are capable of moving the hardest hearts to combat anger, are the three following. Meekness is at the same time a Virtue, a Fruit of the Holy Ghost, and a Beatitude. In other words, three sovereignly efficacious motives should urge us to be very fervent in our efforts to acquire meekness. It is, as we have seen, a sublime virtue; it is a fruit of charity, not of an ordinary but of a most exquisite charity, such as is proper to the Fruits of the Holy Ghost; and it is a beatitude containing the highest perfection, which corresponds with the Beatitudes extolled by Our Saviour on the Mount, as we shall show at greater length later on.

---

[125] Isa. 53:7
[126] John 18:23
[127] Matt. 26:50
[128] Matt. 19:12
[129] Cf. Jerem. 11:19
[130] Hymn of the Church.

This triple cord is not easily broken; indeed it breaks hearts harder than iron. It was by the weapon of meekness, by suffering and not by resisting, that a few men triumphed over the whole world and subjugated the Roman Empire—that empire of iron which had overturned all the kingdoms of the earth.

This admirable victory achieved by men who were as lambs among wolves, dazzled the eyes of the universe, and brought out in bold relief the spirit of their Divine Master Who had overcome the world, not by the sword, but by the wood of the Cross.

Such is the glory of the children of God: opposing to hearts harder than steel the meekness of Christ, giving anger time to consume itself and die out, they make a special conquest of those who had been their inveterate enemies.

*Conclusion:* Let Novices then make haste to carry off that celestial prize, and seek to obtain the victory over their neighbours by the spirit of meekness. Outwardly they bear the likeness of Jesus Christ; let their interior be free from all kinds of hardness and asperity. The arena is open; let them rush in, and with a peaceful heart and tranquil conscience, take possession of the inheritance reserved from all eternity for the children of God whose names are written in the Book of Life.

# IX. Patience

## I. Its Nature and Excellence

Acts of patience are usually confounded with acts of meekness. Indeed, we call those patient who remain calm in the midst of injuries, though we should rather call them meek. It is fitting then that like the other virtues we should give a distinct chapter on patience, that virtue so deserving of eternal praise, for it differs from meekness as to its nature and seat. Meekness governs anger in the irascible appetite, and patience moderates sadness in the concupiscible. The former is a child of temperance, the latter of fortitude.

Thus patience is a virtue which defends reason against the passion of sadness, and on this account it has its proper seat in the concupiscible appetite where this passion exercises its activity. Among the Christian virtues it is particularly praised by the Holy Fathers.

St. Paul signalizes it as the eldest daughter of Divine charity. Making out a list of the noble fruits of this virtue he says: "Charity is patient, is kind,[131] etc." Enlightened from on high, he finds no better way to praise charity than to attribute to it the merit of patience, as if this were the chief character of true charity and the infallible mark by which it may be recognized.

This is but just; for if the gold of charity is not submitted to the test of tribulation, in the endurance of which the exercise of patience consists, it does not at all merit its first title of glory; and it is this especially which manifests the nobility of the virtue of patience. For what can be grander than to furnish the first flower for the crown of this most excellent queen, charity, which is the life of the soul and its virtues?

But this is not all. Patience is still more sovereignly useful to charity; for the latter is not perfectly rich until by exercise of patience in warfare it has secured peace of heart. Job after his trials and St. Paul after his sufferings had certainly treasures which raised them as much above their former state as heaven is raised above the earth. Moreover, if such a truly Christian virtue is not exercised by trials, it degenerates and soon becomes indolent and dormant.

Thus God Who is, in His goodness, the protector and guardian of men, is wont to try by divers pains even those that are guiltless in His sight, in order to increase their eternal riches. Such is the chief way in which the Divine Wisdom has judged fit to procure and increase the happiness of man. He prefers that those whom He sovereignly loves should be tormented for a short time, rather than that they should be deprived of a greater right to the eternal inheritance.

Not content with permitting the demon and wicked men to try the just, He Himself, in His merciful designs, tries His most faithful friends. He oppresses them with all kinds of evils in order that they may acquire more precious and lasting goods. It was for this reason He tempted Abraham, the man whom He delighted to call His friend. He willed that one so dear to Him should be laden with more abundant riches.

Besides, the beauty and utility of this excellent virtue are a source of incredible delights to the heart; and words fail us to describe the extent of

---

[131] 1 Cor. 13:4

the joy arising from labours and pains endured with patience. Then the good conscience begets a firm hope with regard to the eternal recompense. From this comes an immense joy for the soul which dilates in some sort, and stretches out its arms to seize the heavenly goods. Herein there is a foretaste of the happiness of our fatherland.

Novices should then weigh well the excellence and fruitfulness of this virtue, and like avaricious merchants let their great endeavour be to multiply their rights to the kingdom of heaven, by their constancy in supporting the trials of life with true Christian patience.

## II. Practice of Patience

### Interior Acts

O most patient Jesus, I shall bear patiently for love of Thee, whatever falls to me through obedience.

O my most meek Jesus, if the austerity of the religious life seems hard to bear, nevertheless, I will willingly embrace it for Thee.

O most clement God, if temptations assail me I will oppose them with a strong heart.

Dearest Lord Jesus, if all hell should be let loose against me, I will endure the trial with constancy.

O God of all meekness, when sadness weighs me down, I will not let myself be overcome by it.

O my most amiable Jesus, when afflicted with maladies, I will bear them patiently for love of Thee.

O God of all sweetness, if my body were lacerated with scourges, my members cut to pieces, fire and other cruel tortures inflicted on me, I would endure all with constancy with the assistance of Thy grace.

O God, infinitely desirable, I wish to suffer for Thy sake with tranquillity all the contradictions and importunities that can befall me from men.

O most sweet Jesus, if Thou triest me by aridity, if Thou leavest me in prolonged desolation, I shall most willingly embrace all as long as Thou wilt.

These acts, most necessary and at the same time worthy of the Soldiers of Jesus Christ, should be produced very often, for there are many things that engender and increase sadness. Now the end of patience is to combat this passion and to hinder it from weighing down the soul by making it sleep on in a fatal lethargy.

## Exterior Acts

Let us suppose that an illness, a temptation, a fatiguing work, scruples, aridity, or some other trial has excited the passion of sadness. Now such is the weakness of human nature that immediately all joy is extinguished in the depths of the heart. The powers of soul and body, and all their faculties are benumbed by grief; and what Job experienced in himself happens to man: "I am become burdensome to myself."[132]

What will the patient Religious then do? He will wake up, and in order to preserve all the clearness of his reason he will repress melancholy by means of interior acts such as those we have indicated, uniting to them exterior efforts.

To this end, he will employ with profit the remedies we have pointed out in the first part for the cure of sadness,[133] and various other means which circumstances will suggest, in keeping with the nature of the evil.

We shall sum up all in a single maxim. When exercising the virtue of patience we should strive to preserve in the superior part at least, the same dispositions as in the time of joy and consolation, and to master the sensitive appetite, in order not to let ourselves be cast down.

This principle will enable Novices to discover an evil device of the devil. When he sees anyone a prey to some pain which requires the practice of patience, he is accustomed to insinuate maliciously into the soul a false attraction for interior things. The imperfection of the intelligence makes people regard this attraction as a sentiment of true devotion, whilst it is evidently but a movement of the passion of sadness excited by suffering. Hence cheerfulness is necessary, if we wish to derive from patience all the desirable profit. This has its foundation on the following reasons.

---

[132] Job 7:20
[133] See Part I., Ch IV.

# III. Motives for Patience

*First Motive:* No one has ever passed through this mortal life without being besieged by many evils; for although a man may escape certain calamities, he cannot avoid feeling the burden of mortality, and paying his tribute to death and sin. And if anyone seems to be exempt from this tribute, as a Prince who to all appearance looks to be quite happy, it is certain that he cannot long escape interior pains. In speaking thus we are below the reality, for men of this condition are much more tormented by sadness than the poor and common people. Important affairs which do not succeed according to their desires, injuries done to their honour or their fortune, hatreds, jealousies, worries, and various other evils afflict them incessantly. Since it is then true that all men subject to the law of mortality are compelled to endure many sufferings, for which they will have no reward, what can be more honourable and advantageous for those who are called to follow Jesus Christ than to endure adversity courageously, and to rejoice at the immense profit which proceeds from it?

*Second Motive:* We cannot doubt that those who became celebrated among the pagans, whether as soldiers or scholars, reaped their glory by the patience with which they endured public calamities or private pains. How many vigils, privations, bodily fatigues and sacrifices of health their solicitude for knowledge cost them! And to win victory on battlefields, how often have not men put up with bad roads, snowstorms, hunger, thirst, rain, blows, and wounds! Certainly it is wonderful that men, without any hope of enjoying heaven, should give proof of such incredible patience to obtain the perishable goods of this present life, whilst so many Servants of Jesus Christ, after having resolved to conquer the eternal kingdom, become so relaxed that they will not seize with eagerness the occasions which present themselves for the practice of patience.

*Third Motive:* Let us add this powerful consideration. God does not ask His servants to undertake such severe labours and sufferings as pagans, and even Christians, willingly undergo to gain frail earthly goods. They have not to encounter cruel wars, long voyages, the rigour of frost and snow, the assassin's sword, prolonged vigils, or any other similar evil. Quite the contrary. They are sheltered from domestic dissensions, bitter cares, indigence, chagrins, and other smarting pains which torture those who appear to enjoy delights in great cities. Can Religious, then, who aspire to eternal felicity refuse to exercise patience in little things, when the children of the world hesitate not to endure far greater sufferings to attain some miserable end?

*Fourth Motive:* But to consider the pains of life merely from the point of view suggested by human prudence, it is evident that one is guilty of an act of folly by manifesting impatience in adversities. For suffering increases by reason of the repugnance opposed to it, and the sadness we conceive ends by exhausting us; on the contrary, the patient heart sweetens in an admirable manner the bitterness of pains and contradictions, and makes them instruments of merit and titles of glory. To be convinced that it is really so, we have but to consider two men afflicted by the same evil, whether it be hunger, thirst, or something else. One endures his pain with patience,[134] and finds in the practice of virtue a remedy and consolation; the other suffers with impatience, and his agitation develops into rage.

*Fifth Motive:* Yet all this is but little; for if we turn our eyes towards heaven, we shall see that all the crowns of that happy kingdom are marked with the seal of patience. Who can tell the combats the Virgins had to sustain in order to preserve the beauty of their chastity; the labours which Doctors have undertaken to teach nations; the blows received by the Martyrs when they bore witness to Jesus Christ? How resplendent are those bodies covered with wounds! How beautiful these members torn by whips! How glorious these faces shriveled by toil and endurance! The virtue of patience adorns each phalanx of the city of God and magnifies the greatness of their eternal recompense.

*Sixth Motive:* In truth, since "the life of man upon earth is a warfare"[135] and all must of necessity suffer, it is astonishing that so many hearts are but little touched by the hope of the magnificent reward promised to those who suffer. Hence we can easily understand the salutary lesson contained

---

[134] "For a long time my place at meditation was near a Sister who fidgeted continually, either with her Rosary, or something else; possibly, as I am very quick of hearing, I alone heard her, but I cannot tell you how much it tried me. I should have liked to turn round, and by looking at the offender, make her stop the noise; but in my heart I knew that I ought to bear it tranquilly, both for the love of God and to avoid giving pain. So I kept quiet, but the effort cost me so much that sometimes I was bathed in perspiration, and my meditation consisted merely in suffering with patience. After a time I tried to endure it in peace and joy, at least deep down in my soul, and I strove to take actual pleasure in the disagreeable little noise. Instead of trying not to hear it, which was impossible, I set myself to listen, as though it had been some delightful music, and my meditation—which was not the "prayer of quiet"—was passed in offering this music to Our Lord." St. Thérèse of Lisieux, *Story of a Soul*, Ch 10, Pub.

[135] Job 7:1

in the Passion of Christ, by which He willed to stir us up from our lethargy: "He suffered for us, leaving us an example that we should follow in His footsteps."[136] Certainly, it was His infinite goodness and mercy which caused Him to rouse at such a cost the children of Adam from their fatal drowsiness. But let us try to develop this thought more fully.

*Seventh Motive:* Just judges are wont to condemn criminals to corporal punishment and to absolve the innocent, since pain is the consequence of crime. Therefore, every man who recognizes himself guilty of any fault is, in the judgement of God and men, worthy of chastisement. Now, as no one on earth is free from some stain of sin, not even an infant a day old, it is evident that no one can allege his innocence in order to dispense himself from suffering. If, then, every man is deserving of punishment, why, after having received the remission of eternal pain, should he not endure patiently a light trial imposed by Him Who is at once the most tender of Fathers and the most equitable of Judges? Why, he must have lost his mind who will not admit this consequence. Nevertheless, self-love causes us to fall into this insanity. It is so great in each one of us that it persuades us we should not submit to the chastisement which we have merited.

*Eighth Motive:* What, then, did the son of God, innocence itself, do? Not being liable to any pain he gave Himself up voluntarily to a cruel death, in order to persuade us that, far from regarding ourselves as dispensed from the law of chastisement, we should, on the contrary, seek to avoid eternal punishment by enduring temporal pain. This example is so truly admirable that it should overwhelm us with confusion. Indeed, it is wonderful that the whole world is not touched by it, and that it will not choose rather to be patient for a moment than to be impatient for all eternity.

*Ninth Motive:* But let us weigh well the importance of Our Lord's example. Is there anyone so devoid of heart and sense as to consider a God submitting to chastisement, accepting hunger, thirst, indigence, cold, heat, and other miseries of this mortal life, without conceiving a sentiment of compassion and a desire to walk in His footsteps? When David fled before Absalom, Ethai gave him a grand proof of fidelity. He did not wish to be separated from his King, and rejecting from afar the warning of David not to share his misfortunes but to return to Jerusalem and enjoy Absalom's favours, he protested with an oath that he would never abandon him.[137] Why, then, should not a Christian attach himself to his Chief? Why not

---
[136] Cf. 1 Pet. 2:21
[137] Cf. 2 Kings 15

swear fidelity to Him even unto death? Will the son of God be forsaken in the midst of His torments? Let others abandon Him; but this infamy is unworthy of the true Religious.

*Tenth Motive:* The Immaculate Virgin! She was innocent, and her purity was of more dazzling whiteness than the snow. However, she was not a stranger to the law of pain, and had an ardent desire to associate herself with her Son in His sorrows. Without this what was there in common between her celestial purity and such cruel torments? But it was fitting that the Mother should accord with her Son, her Model, in a perfect resemblance.

*Eleventh Motive:* This is also the reason why "all who will live godly in Jesus Christ"[138] place their glory in suffering, and fear nothing so much as to be left without it. How could a valiant soldier feel honoured by being shielded from blows, if he saw His King all covered with wounds?

*Twelfth Motive:* We have an illustrious example to animate us in the practice of patience.[139] During forty years St. Teresa passed no day without sorrow. She had to endure the attacks of men, the assaults of demons and rebuffs from God Himself; so that her life was a succession of almost incredible sufferings. Indeed, true Religious can not without dishonour show themselves unequal and adverse to pain.

It was for our instruction that God exercised St. Teresa so much, for no part of her escaped pain. Moreover, to arrive at the summit of sanctity it was fitting that she should climb the "purple steps"[140] of Solomon's throne, that is, the steep path of patience by which all the other imitators of Christ have mounted.

*Thirteenth Motive:* This is our wisdom, which procures for us all that is honourable and good, and makes us like those of whom the Church speaks in her canticles: "The strength of iron claws has been feeble against them; in tearing their flesh it has not been able to wrench from them the invincible courage which filled their hearts."[141]

---

[138] 2 Tim. 3:12

[139] "Let nothing disturb you. Let nothing frighten you. All things are passing away. God never changes. Patience obtains all things. Whoever has God lacks nothing. God alone suffices." *St. Teresa's Bookmark*, Pub.

[140] Cant. 3:10

[141] Hymn of First Vespers for Many Martyrs.

This is the noblest portion of the elect of God and the patrimony of Jesus Christ; for there is nothing so splendid in the Court of the Living God as the souls that are adorned with the ornament of patience.

*Conclusion:* Let Novices then, after having shaken off all sadness, and armed themselves with so many reasons and examples for the conquest of eternal glory, impress on their hearts as deeply as possible the maxim of St. Teresa: "To suffer or to die." For the labour and pain will soon pass away; and if for a little time "God hath tried them and found them worthy of Himself,"[142] they will rejoice in His presence, "As conquerors rejoice after taking a prey,"[143] at the expense of their blood. May they, after the example of the Apostle, St. Paul, "forget the things that are behind, and stretch forward,"[144] towards still more noble achievements.

# X. Modesty

Modesty, which has for its object the regulation of our exterior movements, seems to have its origin in the virtues we have already explained, but especially chastity, humility, meekness and patience. For this interior assemblage of good dispositions produces, as a fruit pleasing to the eye, the holy and worthy composition of all the exterior parts of man.

The functions of modesty are differently distinguished by pious authors; however, the best of them agree in saying that modesty comprises all that can fittingly serve to regulate the movements of the body and exterior things. For this reason we might, if it were necessary to speak of each point in particular, place here several things belonging to temperance which are in keeping with modesty. But these things are not, strictly speaking, virtues, and do not require a separate treatise. An example will make our meaning clear. Bashfulness is the ornament of youth; but bashfulness is not a virtue, it is a praiseworthy passion which may be defined: the fear of something shameful that might expose one to blame. Shame is another passion which is of the same nature as bashfulness; however, it differs from it in this, that is stops the dishonourable act, whilst bashfulness hides it.[145]

---

[142] Wis. 3:5
[143] Isa. 9:3
[144] Cf. Phil. 3:13
[145] Cf. St. Thomas Aquinas, *Sum. Theol.*, II-II, Q. 144.

It will suffice then, with regard to bashfulness, to impress on Novices to attach themselves seriously to the practice of true virtues. For if the love of virtue causes them to have a horror for the deformity of sin, bashfulness will be usefully excited when circumstances require it. But let them not forget that it is often set in motion in spite of us, and on account of the frailty of our nature, even for unreasonable things such as some corporal defect, ignorance, dullness. On these occasions the practice of humility will correct the movement of the sensitive appetite.

When this blush tinges the cheeks of modest young persons who have to go into the company of their seniors or to do anything in public, the Fathers praise and approve of it, for this timidity is the mark of a good education.

There is yet another kind of virtue which depends on temperance, and which consists of a certain spiritual luster shed upon our actions; it is called decorum or civility. There is no necessity to treat of it specially here, if we are determined to practice true virtues such as we have described in the chapters on humility and meekness; for these virtues will naturally produce beautiful and courteous actions. However, we shall give, according to the teaching of the holy Fathers, the rules to be followed in the composition of the exterior man if he wishes to be irreproachable in his manner.

## The Head

The Religious should be careful not to raise his head too high, or to go to the opposite extreme by letting it hang down, or yet again, by allowing it to drop towards the right or left. If, whilst he is walking, someone calls him from behind, he should turn, not the head alone, but the whole body; and this he should do composedly and without precipitation—a point which ought to be kept in mind whenever it is necessary to turn the head. There are some other details, but they will suggest themselves, if we remember what has been already said.

## The Arms

When something has to be done, the Religious should avoid all excess in the movements of the arms, there is no necessity to stretch them out immoderately, like an athlete who wishes to display his strength; neither is it becoming to work with a languid air, as if the task were a disagreeable one. In Choir the arms should be held on a level with the chest, so that the Breviary may be held with both hands. It would be unbecoming to let them droop lower, to hide one hand, or to do anything that savours of indolence. At mental prayer, in order to avoid languor, the great enemy of this holy exercise, the arms should be crossed, or the hands joined under the scapular. In the Refectory when the signal is given, the arms should not be stretched out with undue haste, for this would indicate a want of mortification. In other places, generally speaking, when the hands are at rest they should be held near the buckle of the cincture with the arms modestly composed.

## The Feet

The feet ought to be composed in uniformity unless some special ceremony requires that only one foot should be used. Religious should be careful never to cross the feet or legs when seated; and they should avoid everything that is unusual and unbecoming.

## The Whole Person

In walking attention must be paid to the carriage and movements. As to the former, the body should not be held too straight or too bent; and as to the latter, excessive haste or slowness are alike to be avoided. When seated, whether in Choir, Oratory, Refectory, Recreation Room, Cell, or elsewhere, the body should not be kept in a position that is bent, stiff, distorted, or that would savour in any way of indolence or affectation. At night the Religious should lie in bed as if he were in the coffin, and not allow any part of the body to remain uncovered. During the day whilst he is in the Cell, he should stand, kneel or sit without lying down; and the whole person should be so regulated that nothing can displease those who enter unexpectedly. In fine, Novices should carefully avoid everything which from its nature would be hurtful to their own eyes or those of others.

## The Body in its Relation with Others

When speaking with others, the Religious should neither approach too near nor remain too far away, but at a distance in keeping with the matter of which he treats. When walking in company with others, he should be careful not to inconvenience them by keeping ahead or lagging behind, delaying them, knocking against them, or wearying them in any way. When seated he should strive not to be disagreeable to others by sitting too near them, obstructing their view, hindering them from hearing the general conversation, or inconveniencing them in any other way. In every position of the body the garments should be so adjusted that they cause no embarrassment and leave nothing uncovered. Finally, not to give offense to our neighbour, we should attend to cleanliness in dress, cell, books and everything else.

## Modesty of our Actions With Regard to Others

When there is question of doing anything in common such as work or recreation, it is the duty of a good Religious to adapt his conduct and the motions of his body to the dispositions of others, so that he may not offend them either by hilarity and excessive laughter, or by his chagrin and sour looks. On this principle, he will carefully avoid the following faults:—To cry out or raise the voice too high; to speak too low or between the teeth; to open the mouth inordinately or make a disagreeable sound when obliged to yawn; to expectorate frequently; to walk too quickly or too slowly; to push another with the shoulder; to poke with the elbow; to touch the hands of others; to multiply words when relating anything; to show signs of contempt or disapprobation of what others do or say; to contradict or to act in an unseasonable manner; to meddle with the offices of others; to seek information about things that are not committed to his care. We might enumerate other faults of a like nature; but the Servants of God will easily find them out for themselves if they impress on their hearts this general advice: they should accomplish in a more holy manner all that modest and prudent seculars are wont to do for the observance of politeness. Thus, in so far as obedience will permit, the Religious will yield his place to others; he will rise when his elders approach him; he will uncover his head while speaking to his Seniors; he will offer his services to his Seniors who have something to carry; if at night he meets a Religious older than himself he will obtain a light for him if he requires it; and if it happen that he should meet the Superior he will take the candle from him with politeness and carry it before him; in fine, he will do many other things that courtesy will suggest.

Religious ought to be convinced that the practice of this politeness, which is the modesty of the Saints, is so necessary to conserve charity, peace, humility, and all the other virtues, that it is impossible without it, as wise and experienced men say, to arrive at true sanctity. On the other hand, where this politeness reigns, communities are an image of the celestial hierarchy, in which such perfect harmony exists.

For this reason Novices should endeavour, not only to avoid grave faults against modesty, but also to perfect themselves day by day in this courtesy which is so appropriate in the House of God. They shall attain this end if they are careful to reflect on and apply themselves to the practice of the means by which perfect modesty is acquired. Such are a simple and pleasing aspect; gentle and well-considered words; a moderate and sonorous tone of voice; agreeable answers; proofs of kindness given without affectation; condescension to others; moderate praise of their neighbour; the avoidance of all that can procure esteem for self; consideration for persons, times and things; thought beforehand as to what they shall say and the manner of saying it; and various other means which meek and humble minds will easily discover.

Religious who, as adopted children of the Blessed Virgin, are more obliged than others to the practice of courtesy, ought to perfect themselves therein in such a way that nothing may be wanting in this respect to the beauty of the Virgin's House.

Though we have treated of several notable points relating to modesty, we have purposely omitted two which are certainly the most important of all, one of which pertains to the manner of regulating the eyes and the other the tongue. Indeed, these are of such importance that they could not be conveniently mixed up with other subjects which do not require so much explanation; therefore, we shall devote the two following chapters to them.

# XI. Modesty of the Eyes

## I. Excellence of Modesty of the Eyes

Of all kinds of modesty, that which has for its object the government of the eyes has acquired by special right the name of modesty; since it is in the eyes, true mirrors of the soul, that this virtue shines with greater splendour. Hence adhering to the counsels of the holy Fathers who are our guides in this matter, we shall treat of it more fully.

It is not necessary to demonstrate how beautiful and becoming this virtue is, as it is a well-known fact that even those who do not understand it are won by its charms. The eyes, as daily experience proves, have marvelous power in improving the whole appearance of a man, and by the luster of their beauty seem to cover every defect. To be convinced of this we have only to consider that the natural beauty of the eyes suffices to make a face otherwise ugly appear handsome. Accordingly modesty of the eyes, which is a sort of spiritual beauty, is able to make a man even of lax life appear angelic in character and beauty.

On the other hand, the forgetfulness of this virtue produces such a bad effect on men otherwise well regulated in their conduct, that we are inclined to believe true virtue and the exercise of the presence of God are incompatible with this liberty of the eyes. This is a reproach which often comes from the lips of worldlings who like to make themselves censors of others.

But modesty of the eyes does not stop here. It is of the greatest utility in securing for a man interior peace, of which it is the fruitful source. For as it closes the door to a multitude of dangerous and hurtful images, it follows that the soul that is cruelly tormented by distractions withdrawing it reluctantly from Divine things, becomes again more closely united to God by the mortification of the sight than it was removed from Him by the sensible objects. We cannot allege a better proof of this truth than each one's own experience when he gives full liberty to his eyes.

When the doors are well closed we are saved from the noise of the street and the attacks of robbers. In like manner, when the eyes which are the windows of the soul are closed, the tumult of the world can have no access; and according to the language of Scripture death will not enter by our windows, and the mind shall be occupied by things of real importance.

But what shall we say of the interior spectacle offered by the soul when it has the courage to refuse the sight of these material things? Let us remember the woman who, by the advice of the prophet Eliseus, borrowed a great number of empty vessels from her neighbours, closed her door, and filled them to overflowing with oil. When the liquid flowed so abundantly and continuously from a little phial, she tasted in the interior of her house a pleasure which would have been wanting to her in the public places. Thus it is with him who, docile to the advice of the holy Fathers, recollects himself, and carefully closes all the openings of the senses. He tastes ineffable delights, when he sees the "oil of joy" inundate all his faculties.

Novices, then, who are called to the enjoyment of Divine consolations, should willingly support the privation of the sight of present things, since it is rewarded so liberally.

## II. Practice of Modesty of the Eyes

We must here remark that the sense of sight, the most perfect of all exterior senses, is also the most active and lively; and that for this reason it requires a far greater vigilance to keep it under control.

We should also bear in mind that the practice of custody of the eyes is a most fruitful source of merit. Under this head, though the acts of the other virtues, for example, of humility and meekness, are higher and more difficult, however, as the occasions of practicing these acts come rarely whilst the eyes meet with very numerous occasions, it results that, all things considered, so far as the acquisition of merit is concerned, this modesty of the eyes yields not to any of the nobler virtues and perhaps is equal to several of them together. The same may be said of silence.

Here is the reason which we advance in support of our view. The more perfect a Religious is, the less he is exposed to suffer on the part of his Brothers in Religion. For all are bound to be meek, humble, burning with charity, and consummate in other virtues, by the practice of which they carefully avoid all that can give pain to their neighbour. Superiors themselves, finding hardly anything to reprove in their subjects, for whom they have a sincere affection, treat them with much gentleness, and strive to console rather than try them. Thus we know that Religious rarely have to support very grave pains; for we do not consider as such the pains inseparable from the common life. We must, then, conclude that the abundant merits which they acquire have their source in the efforts which each one makes, through love of God, to contradict his natural inclinations, and to repress his senses.

## Interior Acts

O most modest Jesus, I make a firm resolution for love of Thee, to turn away my eyes from all unnecessary things.

O most gentle Lord, I no longer desire to behold any of the beauties of this earth.

O most loving God, for love of Thee, I renounce all pleasure, however great it may be, that the sight of creatures can procure me.

O my God, never let me look at anything through curiosity.

O Lord God, in order to merit the sight of Thee one day, I desire to see nothing here below of all that we are permitted to see.

O God of all sweetness, I resolve not to look deliberately on anything which might prevent me from thinking on Thee.

I would prefer, O Lord, to have my eyes plucked out rather than even once abuse them by offending Thee.

O my most desirable Lord, "turn away my eyes that they may not behold vanity."[146]

These acts are extremely useful if they are united to exterior acts.

## Exterior Acts

It should be noted that in this work we do not follow, when treating of acts, scholastic rigor; but that by *acts* we also understand omissions. This is particularly the case concerning modesty and silence. However, when exterior bad acts are omitted, acts truly good are produced in the interior. Indeed, if the eyes abstain from looking on something, it is because reason makes a law for them by an interior act truly and properly so called.

Then, concerning the eyes, the practice of exterior acts consists in this, that, when occasions present themselves, the mind commands the eyes not to look, or to cease looking. Let us apply this principle to our kind of life.

A Religious, passing through the dormitory, hears another coughing, opening his cell, speaking or walking; at once curiosity impels him to turn and find out whence the noise comes. But reason steps in, constraining

---

[146] Ps. 118:37

him to cast on God the interior eyes in order to repress the exterior. He will then say: Lord, I desire to see nothing save that which will conduct me to Thee.

The Religious should follow this practice faithfully in the following circumstances:—When walking; when they enter the Choir, the Oratory, the Refectory, the Recreation Room; when occupied at some work, such as sweeping, washing the dishes, carrying a burden; and in general, whenever necessity or utility does not call for the use of the eyes.

We say *necessity* or *utility*, for in serving Mass or in the Refectory, or at any other duty, it is not well to restrain the eyes wholly; but, without giving them too much liberty, we should attend carefully to what is wanting and what is superfluous, and consider the other circumstances of place, persons and functions.

It is unbecoming to look fixedly in the face at those to whom we speak, especially if they be Superiors. Indeed, it is a kind of audacity which is contrary to the spirit of our state. The look, which is the interpreter of the heart, ought to breathe both gravity and gaiety, but in a measure which excludes license and vulgarity.

But particular care must be taken that modesty of the eyes is observed in the exercises which are performed in common or in public. Thus, while in Choir, it would be very improper to keep gazing at the opposite side, or to watch those who come in or go out; in Refectory, to fix our eyes on those who enter, are leaving, or are seated at other tables; at Processions, or during the singing of the *Salve Regina*, and in general, at any ceremony in the Church, to look from side to side.

Now, the best means of overcoming all difficulties to be met with in practicing the virtue of modesty is a great attention to the presence of God. When the eye of the soul is fixed on heaven we shall not be moved to occupy ourselves with earthly things.

As the sight is an extremely prompt and subtle sense, it will also be very useful to have some sign, such as a little cord attached to the arm, to aid the memory and be a continual reminder to practice modesty of the eyes. We shall find out and make use of many other means if we weigh well the following considerations.

## III. Motives for Modesty of the Eyes

*First Motive:* Modesty occupies a high rank among the instructions proper to infancy and youth, and it is particularly recommended to pupils by their tutors, for it is considered a dishonourable and rude thing to give too much liberty to the eyes. There is not in the whole universe a nation, however alien to the faith of Christ, which, merely be the aid of natural reason, does not acknowledge and commend the beauty of this virtue. We find proof of this in the histories of Japan and China. Is it not just, then, that modesty should be sincerely and generously practiced by those who are trained for the celestial court and earnestly pursue its treasures?

*Second Motive:* Besides, as far as we are concerned, it is certain that the sights to be seen in religious houses are not of a nature to procure great delectation for us. There are no plays or other fantastic representations performed in monasteries to amuse us by their variety and novelty. We see only poor men in coarse garments, bare walls, unadorned ceilings, and other such things; and although these may have some beauty no doubt, yet it suffices to have seen them two or three times. Why, then, shall we not sacrifice such a vain and unreasonable pleasure in view of the precious goods of the soul?

*Third motive:* We know that God created man righteous, but that man, contradicting the designs of God, has plunged himself into an infinite labyrinth of trifles. For God wished man to go to heaven straight without going out of his path in search of foolish things[147]. Since then monasteries aim at re-establishing this ancient rectitude, what folly it would be to abuse them by acting in them as if they were theaters, and launching ourselves by the liberty we give our eyes into an inextricable maze of worldly affairs!

*Fourth Motive:* Indeed, we all know that too much liberty of the eyes exposes men to dangerous occasions of evil in which they too frequently fall. Witness Dina, daughter of Jacob, who lost her honour on account of her curiosity to see the city of Sichem; David whose sad fall was due to the covetous looks which he cast upon Bethsabee; the old men of Babylon whose unhappy fate was the result of the cupidity with which they regarded the chaste Susanna.

*Fifth Movie:* Innumerable other examples might be brought forward to prove this. But we do not require them, as each of us knows by experience

---

[147] "Vanity of vanities, and all is vanity." Ecc. 1:2, Pub.

the injuries he has suffered from unguarded looks. It is not only the negligent who fall, as sometimes it happens to those even who have applied themselves to a strict guard over the eyes. Such was the young man of whom St. Augustine speaks in the book of his Confessions. For a long time he had resisted the entreaties of his friends who wished him to assist at the combats of the gladiators; in the end, overcome by their importunities, he consented, but he resolved to keep his eyes closed in order not to see the representation. At first all went well; but hearing the wild cries in the amphitheater, curiosity overcame him, he opened his eyes, looked, and at once the fatal seed was sown in his heart. He returned to his dwelling a far worse man than when he left it. What, then, will be the fate of those who willingly yield, and eagerly seek after that which can satisfy their curiosity?

*Sixth Motive:* It is certain that all which perfect Religious have gained by prayer, austerity of life, frequent admonitions and other exercises, may be easily lost by too great a liberty of the eyes. Even if they were to consume themselves with labour in the Convent for a hundred years, they would never become spiritual men while this fault remained uncorrected. Hence they should never forget the prudent counsel contained in these words of Job: "I made a covenant with my eyes that I would not so much as think on a virgin."[148] This form of speech appears to be incorrect; for he made a compact not to think, and that compact was made not with his intellect but with his eyes. Yet in reality there is great force in the expression, for he who does not wish to think evil should make a compact with his eyes, that is to say, he must close the doors through which the bad thoughts enter.

*Seventh Motive:* Our Lord and Saviour Jesus Christ is the most perfect Model of modesty; indeed, He excelled in the practice of this virtue for our instruction. The holy Fathers remark that the Evangelists in their writings seem to rank it among the most striking works of the Redeemer. They have thus expressed themselves: "Jesus lifting up His eyes to Heaven," "raising His eyes to His Apostles," "having lifted up His eyes." This manner of speech indicates that though Jesus had nothing to fear, He did not, however, give unrestrained liberty to His eyes. All Christians ought to follow His example; Religious at least are bound very strictly to do so.

*Eighth Motive:* What shall we say of the Blessed Virgin Mary, who was assuredly the most faithful imitator of her Son? We represent her to ourselves as a maiden of ravishing beauty, enveloped by modesty, and

---

[148] Job 31:1

keeping her eyes cast down. Such are, to the minds of all Christians, the traits proper to the Immaculate Virgin.

*Conclusion:* Hence, those who delight in being called her children should strive to adorn themselves with this beautiful virtue of modesty, and to uphold everywhere by its practice their honour as children of Mary. Let them remember, too, that in recompense for their fidelity they will have, among the joys of the celestial Home, the happiness of contemplating the Body of Jesus Christ and that of His most holy Mother, both sovereignly beautiful and shining with ineffable splendour.

# XII. Silence

## I. Excellence of the Virtue of Silence

"If any man," says St. James, "thinks himself to be religious, not bridling his tongue, but deceiving his own heart, this man's religion is vain."[149]

These are certainly very serious words; for the Apostle seems to say that though a person might practice all the other virtues in an eminent degree, yet if he did not govern his tongue he would be but a vain man, and like one deprived of the true faith.

Herein we see a proof of the great merit of silence, which may be called the modesty of the tongue; for if liberty of the tongue has such an effect on men, as to make them as if they had no religion, silence raises them to true sanctity.

In the very name of silence there is something so holy, peaceful and profound that it seems to draw us to recollection. The beauty of this virtue is so perfect that it can be said of it, that it is the special ornament of Convents, both of men and women. Thoughtful people who visit them remark it, and return to their homes quite penetrated with the sanctity of silence.

It has a certain resemblance to Divine contemplation and the rapture of the soul. It teaches "without noise of words" things above the understanding of the world; and though all men do not penetrate this mute language,

---

[149] James 1:26

all, however, admire it. This observation alone would serve to show the excellence of the virtue of silence.

But it is also very fruitful and very useful. For it produces as many good fruits, and acquires as many advantages, as it retrenches superfluous words. It has besides, as experience teaches, the singular privilege of making us speak well, and of procuring peace and tranquillity of heart.

The most eloquent tongue cannot express the sweetness of the secret communications between God and the soul that has ceased to converse with men. The solitude in which He caresses the heart is full of sweetness, for a single word of His gives it more consolation than all the eloquence of the world could confer in ten centuries.

Silence is the road of solitude, by which the soul that is athirst for God is withdrawn from the noise of the world, and conducted into a well assured peace. Then are realized the words of the Prophet Osee, speaking in the person of God: "I will allure her, and will lead her into the wilderness; and I will speak to her heart."[150] As if this God of love would say: she desires not the food of men; she tastes not the cup of their consolations; she has a horror of sinners who would wish to draw her by "words sweeter than milk," and she has not consented to them; for this reason "I will allure her." Then, explaining what this allurement means, He adds: "I will speak to her heart." That is, I will console her, and substitute Divine words for human words.

Novices, then, who have left the world, and retired into solitude in order to lend the ear of their hearts to God, should apply themselves with all their strength to the cultivation of silence, and desire only to hear the words of God. Let us consider the acts which serve to control the tongue.

## II. Practice of the Virtue of Silence

The tongue is a kind of savage beast, and, as St. James teaches, "no man can tame it."[151] The evils it begets are grave and numerous. It resembles by its vivacity a torrent which nothing can stop. Once set in motion, it breaks all bounds of modesty: "Behold how small a fire kindleth a great wood."[152]

---

[150] Osee 2:14
[151] James 3:8
[152] James 3:5

This is why the ancient Fathers have placed silence among the first and most important precepts of the monastic life; they have celebrated its praises in the highest terms. One could not, without having read their writings, imagine that silence is of such sovereign importance. This virtue seems to pertain, not to the heart, but to the lips, and in some sort to the exterior man; however, though its object is to govern the lips, it penetrates to the heart and exercises there its action.

The holy Fathers also regarding silence as sovereignly necessary to acquire Divine union and to preserve us from sin, as well as to avoid giving scandal to our neighbour, have recommended it with so much earnestness that they would seem, on this point, to have gone beyond the bounds of reason. Indeed, though the virtue of silence does not suppress all words, but only those that are detrimental, that is, those which are neither necessary nor useful; yet, these ancient ascetics had this matter so much at heart, that they would even retrench useful words in the young. Has not St. Vincent Ferrer counseled us in certain cases to make use of signs instead of words?

It was after having well examined the things by the light of faith and reason that these men led by the Holy Spirit prescribed with a superior prudence the rule of silence. For, considering on the one side, that it is sometimes necessary to speak, and on the other, that they themselves with all their love for silence have often fallen when speaking into light faults which they dreaded more than death, they have come to the conclusion, seeing the natural frailty of man, that it is better to sin through want of words than through excess. The want of words wounds more rarely and more lightly. The excess thereof, on the contrary, wounds more frequently and more deeply, since it is at the same time hurtful to our neighbour.

For this reason the custom has been introduced into some Religious Orders never to speak without permission of the Superior, save to give the mutual salutations, and to ask and answer some necessary questions; and again, during the time of great silence not to give the salutations; and, for the rest, when necessity requires it, to use little notes.

We see, then, that it is more conformable to the teaching of the holy Fathers, and to the spirit of Religious Institutes, to incline towards excessive silence rather than to liberty of the tongue; and experience itself proves that in acting otherwise one will end by not even remaining within the limits of the virtue. However, as there are cases when it is necessary to speak, we should be careful, through respect for silence, to do so in a low tone and as briefly as possible. Let us now indicate the interior acts of the virtue of silence.

## Interior Acts

O my most modest Jesus, "set a watch before my mouth, and a door round about my lips."[153]

O most meek Lord, for love of Thee, I am resolved to abstain from every idle and unnecessary word.

If I were called upon to die in order to preserve the silence prescribed by my rule, I wish, O my God, for Thy sake, to do so.

I will at once abstain from pronouncing a word, as soon as I notice that it is idle, no matter what it costs me.

No, my God, never will I open my mouth when my conscience upbraids me for doing so.

When others tempt me to speak, and human reasons urge me to do so, I will look rather to God, Who wishes me to be silent.

O my God, I would prefer to lose the use of speech rather than pronounce a single word that would displease Thee.

We should produce these acts when, in certain circumstances, God inspires interiorly the practice of silence, though men may counsel exteriorly the contrary. We will now proceed to the exterior acts, that is, the occasions of practicing silence exteriorly.

## Exterior Acts

First of all we must make a remark very appropriate to our subject. Novices should not consult the feeling of others when there is question of practicing virtue. Let them recall the words of St. Paul: "If I yet pleased men, I should not be the servant of Christ."[154] They should then strive to regulate all their actions by obedience, and if God, perchance, should allow anyone to be offended thereby, let them bear it patiently without altering their conduct.

Now in order to explain what is more difficult to understand by that which is more easy, I shall suppose that a Novice meets one of the senior Religious. They give the mutual salute, but the Religious stops to ask the Novice if he is well. This question may indeed be asked without

---

[153] Ps. 140:3
[154] Gal. 1:10

imperfection, but as it seems unnecessary, the Novice may respond to it by a smiling face and a sign of gratitude, at the same time keeping firm interiorly and producing an act of silence in this fashion or in some other: Lord, I prefer to converse with Thee rather than with men.

Then if the Religious persists, let the Novice, if he cannot conveniently get away, continue to show signs of benevolence; but if he can, let him withdraw joyfully and give thanks to God for having observed silence.

He who is thus inflamed with zeal of silence and gains many victories over himself, may be convinced that his conduct is pleasing to God, and extremely useful even to those who seem desirous of drawing him into conversation; and he can rest assured that he augments considerably the beauty of the House of God.

But we ought to be victorious not alone on such occasions, but even under severer tests. For it often happens that juniors are tried by their seniors for the sake of their advancement, and in order to prove their constancy, fidelity, knowledge of spiritual things, and discernment of true virtue from that which is virtue only in name.

All this goes to show the gross error those Religious commit who, in the absence of the Superior, begin to talk as soon as they are invited to do so. Indeed, they are far removed from the true path of virtue, and greatly injure themselves, their neighbor, and the beauty of the House of God. Novices should then conquer their tongues, and render themselves worthy, by silence, of hearing the words of God rather than those of men.

## III. MOTIVES FOR THE VIRTUE OF SILENCE

*First Motive*: No man, however alien he may be to the law of Christ, has ever maturely considered the dangers of the tongue without fearing it as a deadly instrument. The writings of pagan authors give proof of this. As a matter of fact, one can hardly enumerate not only the sins, but the kinds of sins which have their origin in the tongue; such are detractions, murmurs, lawsuits, quarrels, disputes, falsehoods, perjuries, blasphemies, and other terrible sins. Furthermore, the tongue adds to the malice of certain sins, by affirming, denying, defending, dissimulating, or exciting. How, then, can negligence in controlling the tongue be allied with a true desire of advancing in virtue? Does he not condemn himself out of his own mouth who makes profession of tending towards perfection while giving full liberty to his tongue?

*Second Motive*: But if the evils engendered by the tongue are great and multiplied, the goods produced by silence are very numerous and of exceeding value. Is it not true that a man of silence is regarded by other men as a tower of strength wherein wisdom abides? Is it not true that it suffices to be silent to gain the reputation of a prudent man? May we not say that, without science, the silent are counted learned, and without experience they are regarded prudent? Or, as the Scriptures have it: "Even a fool, if he will hold his peace, shall be counted wise."[155]

On the other hand, it is equally certain that a man, however learned he may be, cannot speak long without committing many errors. For it requires extreme circumspection to speak rightly, and, all things considered, it is much easier to keep silence than to speak without fault. How, then, can a Religious who has neither knowledge nor experience expect to converse with safety, since even the wise and prudent cannot do so without falling?

*Third Motive*: Worldly people who seek for some dignity employ with great care the means best calculated to attain their end. If silence can favour it, as is frequently the case, they abstain rigorously from speaking on certain matters. Now, the end of the Religious life is Divine union, and the most assured means of acquiring it is silence. What, then, can be more just than to apply ourselves to it with constancy, in order to make ourselves worthy of that glorious prerogative?

For this reason the ancient Fathers who have laid the foundations of the monastic life have shown extreme severity on the subject of governing the tongue, in order that they might not be turned by it from the great end which they proposed to themselves. They loved solitude only in order to unite themselves to God, and they shunned the company of men, since they feared the tongue and the evils that flow from it. A single example will suffice to convince us of this. Witness that of St. John the Baptist, so illustrious in the eyes of the Holy Church. If, then, Religious aspire to the same end as these great men, they cannot without extreme temerity give a loose rein to their tongues.

*Fourth Motive:* But among all the examples and motives which should urge us to the practice of silence, we cannot consider without amazement the prodigies wrought by our Lord by His silence. He was the Word of

---

[155] Prov. 17:28

God; nothing but what was good could proceed from His mouth, and yet He remained silent for thirty years, and consecrated only three years to the exercise of preaching. Can we imagine a greater marvel than this? In truth, all that sacred and profane writers have ever said on the value of moderation in speech pales before the sublimity of this example, more astonishing in itself than many miracles. Let us pause here, and strive to penetrate its full meaning.

If the Son of God came on this earth to fill the world with the knowledge of His heavenly Father, and to dispel the darkness of hereditary ignorance which blinded the whole human race, why did He keep silence? Was it that men had no need of being instructed? Had they not called on the Holy One with all their hearts to "rend the Heavens and come down?"[156] "That He might instruct His princes as Himself, and teach His ancients wisdom."[157]

*Fifth Motive:* But this is not all. It is a recognized fact that the most perfect practice of silence is when one keeps silent in presence of a grave danger or of a serious injury. For when no difficulties are encountered the practice of virtue has nothing heroic in it. Now Jesus, the Divine Lamb, "was dumb before His shearer, and opened not His mouth."[158] Isaias predicted this, and the Evangelists have expressly recorded it. What was it that our Lord herein wished to make us understand?

Dragged before Herod, and questioned with much curiosity, He kept a profound silence, whilst the seniors of the city obstinately accused Him. The Son of God could assuredly have given some satisfaction to this vain king, and thereby obtained His release. But He kept silence, and this caused Him to be despised and turned to derision. Is there not a great lesson hidden herein?

And what took place before Pilate? We will not speak of the infamous and cruel preference given to Barabbas, a preference which the Divine Word could have so easily set aside by uttering words that would have softened those hard hearts, and set off His innocence in contrast to the wickedness of him to whom He was compared. But let us further consider the scene in which furious men, urged on by the devil, importune Pilate with rage, and heap up lies to ruin the Saviour. Still Jesus is silent, and no effort of the Governor can wrench a word from Him. In the face of such a

---

[156] Cf. Isa. 64:1
[157] Ps. 104:22
[158] Cf. Isa. 53:7

spectacle who will not be filled with astonishment, and desire to know the meaning of this sublime silence?

A momentous affair was here at stake. The life of the Word Incarnate was unjustly and cruelly menaced. It behoved the whole human race, and especially this city of Jerusalem, so long cherished by God, to know the truth about the Messias; and yet this Messias remained silent when questioned. When asked even what is truth, He was still silent. Why, then, should not the Religious who give full liberty to their tongues blush and fear the judgement of the Son of God?

*Sixth Motive:* We may well apply to this subject the words addressed to Jesus by the Samaritan woman: "The well is deep, and we have nothing wherein to draw,"[159] the hidden water of this silence. We are forced to admire that which we see without knowing the cause. But woe to the Religious who does not admire a prodigy capable of moving the very pagans. For when the Son of God held His peace it was with such dignity, and in so extraordinary a manner, that "the Governor wondered exceedingly."[160] Assuredly, if a wicked man like Pilate was struck with admiration at the silence of Jesus, why should not Religious be still more amazed at it?

*Conclusion:* But this admiration should impel them to seek the cause of the prodigy which strikes them, and if their search should have no other result it will at least convince them that silence ought to be scrupulously observed by the disciples of Jesus Christ. If silence had not been useful to men He would doubtless have preached for a longer time. Since He chose to remain in silence during so many years, we must be convinced that this silence contributed as much as His preaching to our salvation and perfection. Would it not then be an atrocious crime to reject the silence of Jesus and not to imitate it, if it be sinful to reject His words and not to keep them?

Let Novices weigh well these reasons drawn from the example of Our Divine Saviour, and by the imitation of His adorable silence seek after a true knowledge of the words of life.

---

[159] Cf. John 4:11
[160] Matt. 27:14

# XIII. Gratitude

## I. Nature and Excellence of Gratitude

Certainly there can be nothing more beneficial to us than to seek out and get rid of all that distracts our souls from their attention to God. Now, modesty and silence do this by suppressing the idle use of the senses. But as we are indebted to the goodness of God for so many and such signal favours, we should gather in, as it were, all the powers of our soul and unite them interiorly in order to thank Him fittingly for His benefits.

And as Religious have been enriched with the choicest graces, they are bound to give themselves with greater fervour to the practice of this most sweet virtue of gratitude, which, alas! is but too much forgotten by many.

Now, gratitude is a virtue subordinate to justice, which engenders in us with regard to our benefactors a particular sentiment of affection, and which leads us to return thanks to them, as far as we are able, when an occasion arises.

How shall we describe the beauty of this virtue, so full of sweetness in its character? It speaks so well for itself that there is no necessity to enter into explanations. Indeed, all know that grateful men have a particular power of winning hearts; whilst, on the contrary, the ungrateful repulse others.

Gratitude is also of the greatest utility, for everyone loves to do good to those who are grateful, and we know from daily experience that "gratitude for past favours is the surest means of obtaining new ones."

It is also a source of joy to the benefactor and to the recipient of his favours, uniting them by mutual love and an exchange of kind sentiments.

All this is admitted as true by every nation, and is taught us by the light of natural reason itself. But if we raise ourselves to the supernatural order of grace, these truths shine with greater splendour, and gratitude appears to us more beautiful, useful and agreeable. Indeed, we cannot sufficiently admire the extent to which Divine grace perfects natural gratitude by making us more grateful for the higher and more desirable benefits we have received.

For is it not a benefit much more worthy of gratitude to be born to God than to be born to the world? If, then, as history relates, the pagans believed themselves obliged to celebrate their birthdays by great acts of thanksgiving, what should not the children of God do who are born for heaven?

Now, if all creatures ought, according to the measure of their power, to exercise this virtue, Religious who have received with their holy vocation far more considerable benefits, are bound to love most ardently and to practice most faithfully gratitude, which is the most precious ornament of their hearts.

## II. Practice of Gratitude

It is not enough for grateful souls to experience the sentiment of gratitude interiorly, they must also express it exteriorly by works.

Now, the sentiment is developed and increased by interior acts; and as these acts are always in our power we should produce them very frequently. As to exterior acts, we have not always the opportunity of practicing them, or the power to do so. Furthermore, when there is question of God, as we have nothing to give Him which is not already His, we have no other means of testifying our gratitude than to use for the purpose the benefits He has bestowed on us.

### Interior Acts

O God of all sweetness, I am truly grateful for the innumerable benefits, natural and supernatural, which Thou hast bestowed on me.

O most merciful Lord, how can I repay Thee for the benefits of creation, conservation, redemption, justification, preservation from evils and so many helps and inspirations.

O my most loving Lord, how shall I return thanks for Thy goodness in having preserved me from so many offenses which I might have committed? I have received as many benefits from Thee as Thou hast removed occasions of sin from me.

O my God, so full of goodness, how shall I thank Thee for the good thoughts, words and actions I have entertained and performed by Thy aid? Indeed, I could not have a good thought but for Thee.

O my God, I deserve to be now burning in hell for my offenses, but Thy mercy has saved me; how shall I ever repay Thee?

My most liberal Lord, Thou hast bestowed on me the right to an eternal inheritance; I hope to possess it one day. How shall I thank Thee?

O most bountiful God, Thou hast given me the Sacraments, Thy holy word, counsels, consolations and innumerable other graces which facilitate my spiritual progress. How shall I respond to such love?

O Lord, I return Thee this heart which Thou hast given me; I offer Thee my life; I sacrifice my entire being to Thy honour.

O my most amiable God, if I had at my disposal the hearts of all the Angels, Saints, and creatures that are pleasing to Thee in the whole world, but especially the Hearts of Thy Divine Son and His holy Mother, I would gladly offer them to Thee with profound sentiments of gratitude.

O my God, I offer Thee in return for Thy benefits, Jesus Christ, my Redeemer, the most holy Virgin, His Mother, all the hierarchies of Angels and all the blessed. May they aid me to manifest my gratitude to Thee!

We see clearly that acts of this kind may be produced in different ways, and are well calculated to excite the affections of the heart.

## Exterior Acts

Our Lord Jesus Christ was wont, even in the most trifling things, to render profound thanks to His Eternal Father. Not only at the great miracle of the raising of Lazarus, but also when He multiplied bread, the Gospel relates that lifting up His eyes to heaven He gave thanks to His Father.

It is also a very ancient and general custom among all nations to return thanks for benefits received. But Religious should go yet further in the practice of gratitude. They should not limit themselves to thanking God with sentiments of lively gratitude for all that they receive in the way of clothing, food, and other common necessaries; they ought also to strive to animate with this virtue all their exterior actions, by performing them as debts of gratitude which they must pay to God. In other words, the remembrance of the great benefits the Lord has bestowed on them should so penetrate them that they will perform each work with the intention of testifying a very special gratitude to Him.

And when on solemn feasts they celebrate the signal benefits of the Redemption and salvation of the world, they should be careful to give themselves up at the same time to interior and exterior acts of gratitude by offering to God prayers, communions, disciplines, and other practices authorized by the Superior. It is simply inconceivable to what extent all this serves to nourish devotion.

## III. Motives for Gratitude.

*First Motive:* Even the most savage animals are sensible to the benefits bestowed on them, and testify exteriorly the gratitude with which they are animated. Several touching anecdotes are related in proof of this. For example, what a spectacle was that of the lion whose roaring had spread terror all around him, and who, in his combat with a monstrous serpent, was aided by a man! Having gained the victory, thanks to this help, he fawned on his benefactor, and followed him about like a dog. This took place some time ago in Upper Africa on the coast of the Mediterranean.

But who could ever believe, unless he saw it with his own eyes, the manner in which dogs show their gratitude? Neither the chain nor the lash can take out of them their fidelity to their friends, and when separated from their masters they manifest great sadness and even refuse to eat.

St. Ambrose relates something still more prodigious. A dog was seen to follow his master's funeral bier, to lie down on his grave, and manifest by piteous howlings his sorrow for his benefactor.

Assuredly, if lions and dogs, to say nothing of other animals, go so far in their gratitude to those who have done good to them, it is but reasonable that Christians and especially Religious, who have sworn allegiance to their Divine Benefactor and Master, should give true signs of a spirit of thankfulness.

*Second Motive:* Nature itself has a horror of ingratitude and teaches us by example to practice gratitude. Ungrateful hearts repulse their benefactors, and exhaust as it were the source of goodness, just as the earth which remains sterile after careful cultivation drives away the tiller in despair.

*Third Motive:* Would you like to know the effects produced on men in olden times by such considerations? They despised the world and founded Monastic Institutes. Like avaricious merchants who strive to enrich themselves in order that they may pay their debts, they passed their days and nights in spiritual exercises; so much were they penetrated with the thought of God's goodness. Indeed, these benefits they had received from Him seemed to press on them as a heavy burden.

*Fourth Motive:* Let us now apply this to ourselves. If a man knows for certain that by his sins he has deserved eternal fire, and that it is due to the pure mercy of God he is not already burning there. Nay, that this Divine Master invites him to the heavenly Banquet, and he may lawfully believe he will enjoy it one day. Can this man forget all these benefits, and do no more to testify his gratitude than if they were merely proper or natural goods? Indeed, if for this one benefit of being delivered from hell, God demanded him to serve Him as a slave in painful toil for all eternity, without promising any recompense, would He not still act very liberally and mercifully towards him? For what are those painful labours in comparison with eternal fire? Yet God is not content with saving him from everlasting punishment, He has also deigned to promise the glory of paradise to those who shall bear His light yoke here on earth.

*Fifth Motive:* Who could ever have been able, if it had not been Divinely revealed, to hope or imagine that God would deliver, in order to redeem a vile slave of sin and the devil, His only Son, the Lord of all things, and sovereignly worthy of honour and glory, to a frightful death, and to the most cruel and ignominious torments? Now, this great benefit which comprises the Incarnation, life, passion, and death of Jesus Christ, belongs to each man in particular, as if he alone were in the world, since Jesus Christ offered Himself wholly for each. Could a heart of stone be insensible of such love?

*Sixth Motive:* What shall we say of the food given to the children of God? Let us here ponder the words of Jeremias: "How is it the gold becomes dim, the finest colour is changed, the stones of the sanctuary are scattered in the top of every street?"[161] Never, since the beginning of the world, could anyone have conceived a benefit such as that which the infinite love of God has prepared for us in the Eucharistic Banquet. Nevertheless, instead of burning as they ought with love and gratitude, Christians are blind, and change the brilliant gold of their hearts into a dark and repulsive metal. Those who should be, as it were, living stones of the noblest and inmost part of the sanctuary, that is, of the House of God, now run through the streets and public places to occupy themselves with worldly affairs. Why is this? How can they forget the benefits of God, so great, so numerous, so calculated to bring about the conversion of souls?

---

[161] Lam. 4:1

*Seventh Motive:* If we see some people filled with interior goods they owe them to gratitude. For the more this virtue is practiced, the more it dilates the heart and renders it capable of containing spiritual treasures. Such was David, who, without neglecting the care of his kingdom, employed a great part of his life celebrating, by his chants and Sacred Writings, the benefits of God. One should be blind, indeed, not to recognize this truth in reading the Psalms. And it was for this reason that he was so happy, and so filled with heavenly wisdom.

Such also was St. Paul, who, on the one hand, felt profoundly convinced that all he was he was by grace, and, on the other hand, preserved ever in his heart a lively and ardent gratitude to Jesus Christ, his Master. Thus, he enriched himself with treasures of grace, and attained to the highest heaven.

*Conclusion:* Novices then should not content themselves with common gratitude which ordinarily grows cold. They ought to engrave on their hearts one that is more intimate, noble, and useful; and they should be careful to give it more vigour day by day by means of oft' repeated aspirations. Then the God of all goodness, Who incessantly seeks occasions of bestowing His benefits, will fill their hearts, opened wide by gratitude, with the most abundant and excellent gifts.

# XIV. Magnanimity

## I. Nature and Excellence of Magnanimity

He who recognizes that he is indebted to God for signal benefits should undertake great things to testify, as far as he can, his gratitude. Hence it is that magnanimity is a virtue proper to those on whom God has lavished great favours. Now, it cannot be doubted that Religious belong to this category.

Magnanimity is a virtue which carries the soul to that which is great; for it is one of the companions of fortitude, whose property it is to perform magnificent actions. It is seated in the irascible part of the sensitive appetite. The matter of this virtue is honour or glory: not that it seeks glory as its end, for glory is as nothing in its eyes; but it proposes to itself great works worthy of honour, and for this reason it adds to all the virtues something distinct which adorns and embellishes them.

Like the general of an army covered with a heavenly armor, it runs through the different legions of the Living God, that is, the virtues, in order to mark them out for exploits, for magnanimity is not content with an ordinary glory.

Thus, the beauty of this virtue, truly worthy of the Soldiers of Christ, is so admirable that its very name evokes esteem. It seeks greatness in works done for God. It impels the heart to advance in perfection, and has a horror of all relaxation or backsliding.

Who is there, then, who will not be attracted by the charms of this virtue, since there is no one who does not love greatness?

Moreover, this resolution of undertaking great things is sovereignly advantageous. It is certain that he who aspires to a very high dignity will take more pains than a man who is content with a lesser position. And if he does not attain the goal of his ambition, he will obtain the reward of his efforts.[162]

It happens thus at least in our efforts to acquire Christian perfection. He who proposes nothing less to himself than to walk in the footsteps of the great saints honoured by the Church, even if he attains not this lofty end, will arrive at least, thanks to magnanimity, at an eminent degree of sanctity. On the contrary, he who, hiding his want of courage under a false humility, is not generous in his designs, will make but little progress in the Religious life. Daily experience provides this.

It is then certain that magnanimous hearts acquire great riches, but these riches do not engender any care; indeed, they are a source of marvelous joy. What is more pleasing than to be endowed with this generosity of heart which despises trivial things, counts as nothing labours and fatigues, advances towards heaven and sees itself the object of God's choicest favours? Is it not natural for a man to rejoice in the possession of a rich patrimony, a magnificent inheritance, an elevated dignity, or other similar things? Let us add that souls adorned with this virtue, become in some sort divine by their resemblance to the Divinity, and are ardently cherished by God, Who fills them with a heavenly joy.

---

[162] "The zeal of a Carmelite ought to embrace the whole world." St. Thérèse of Lisieux, *Story of a Soul*, Ch 11.

Novices, then, since they are called to great things, should have a marked predilection for this virtue. In order to win the palm, they should enter on the Religious life with generous hearts.

## II. Practice of Magnanimity

### Interior Acts

O my God, Who are sovereignly perfect, to Whom I cannot attain without a generous resolution, I desire to obtain the virtues of the Apostles.

O omnipotent God, strengthen me by Thy grace, since I desire for love of Thee to perform heroic acts of virtue.

I despise, O Lord, all the honours of this world, and I trample on all its pomps, in order to raise myself above it to Thee.

O most powerful God, I wish I had at my disposal all the glory of the world, not to enjoy it, but to reject it with contempt, for love of Thee.

I desire, O Lord, to have the patience of Job, the love of St. Paul, the sorrow of St. Mary Magdalen, and the purity of the holy Angels.

Would, O Lord, that I might find an occasion of suffering martyrdom for Thee.

O God of all sweetness, each time I shall meet anything difficult in the practice of virtue, I will run to embrace it in order to fight for Thee.

No, O Lord, I will never be discouraged in the pursuit of Christian perfection.

"I will meditate on Thy Commandments; and I will consider Thy ways. I will think of Thy justifications; I will not forget Thy words."[163]

These acts elevate the heart and strengthen it against trials; but in order to be real they must be joined to exterior acts.

### Exterior Acts

A practice very familiar to magnanimous souls is to endeavour to equal those whom they see to be the most advanced in the Community.[164]

---

[163] Ps. 118:15-16

[164] "As the busy bee flies to all the flowers, and sucks from each its purest juice with which to form honey, so should a religious soul observe the virtues of others, and learn, for instance,

For example, if they perceive that a Religious is eminent in the exercise of modesty or silence, they will not rest until they have attained the same degree of perfection. As we have already remarked in the chapter on obedience, there are certain great works which the Superiors, who are guided by prudence and Christian charity, assign only to those that dare to undertake them, and demand permission to do so. Such are prolonged fasts, extraordinary vigils, very sharp chains, rough hair-cloth, missions in far-off lands, opportunities of martyrdom, and other like things.

The virtue of magnanimity undertakes these works, and relying on the help of God demands them of the Superior. This holy audacity brings about a marvelous progress, for it makes known to the Superior the spiritual strength of his subjects. Thus, he can make use of them for great things when an occasion presents itself, or, if he thinks well of it, grant what they ask.

Novices should aspire to this perfection if they wish to acquire merits of real value. But, lest it may appear too difficult, let them attentively consider the following reasons.

## III. Motives for Magnanimity

*First Motive:* Ancient history teaches us that the most illustrious among the pagans acquired their renown by aspiring to great things. The example of Alexander the Great is sufficiently known. This king, destined to be insignificant for all eternity, acquired among men an imposing surname. What was the true source of his greatness? How did he attain it? By keeping his mind fixed on great things, and not contenting himself with the possession of one nation only. Yet, after all, what did he gain but a trifle? What, then, should not those undertake and carry out, who desire to be great for all eternity?

*Second Motive:* We shall find, to the shame of our cowardice, many other similar facts. Thus, the most flourishing condition of the Lacedemonians was developed by the magnanimity, not only of their men, but also of their women. For it is well known that both sexes counted as nothing life or worldly honour when there was question of practicing virtue.

---

modesty from one, science from another, and obedience from a third; in a word, he should take from each one that which he perceives to be most perfect, and copy it in his own person.—St. Antony." St. Francis de Sales, *Month of Mary*, 2nd day, Pub.

*Third Motive:* It was the same with the Romans who extended their dominions to the ends of the earth. Was it not by magnanimity that they subdued all nations? By proposing to themselves a great end, they succeeded to the height of their desires. But these Lacedemonians and Romans, and many others like them, being strangers to the faith of Jesus Christ, were doomed to perdition and the object of eternal opprobrium. Why, then, should not those who hope to reign eternally with God, strive to make light of little things and to make heroic efforts to arrive at so great a happiness?

*Fourth Motive:* All that we have said of pagans is certainly nothing in comparison with the exploits of the Soldiers of Jesus Christ. For it is unquestionably more glorious to conquer oneself than to overturn material ramparts. Now, we all know the marvelous things related, under this head, of the Martyrs, Confessors and Virgins. They showed an invincible constancy in presence of the evils which menaced them; they trampled the world under their feet; they were victorious over the flesh.

Hence, they have acquired an immortal name, not only before God, but also before men, even those who put them to death. As to the Church, she records the names and sings aloud the praises of those among her children who were not content with mediocre virtue, whilst she makes no commemoration of the lukewarm whom, on account of their feeble merits, she considers unworthy of public praise.

This is what we see in our days. Apart from some men and women illustrious by their sanctity, whom the Church intends to place upon her calendar, she is silent about others, since they have displayed but little valour in the spiritual combat, and have done practically nothing to advance the glory of Our Lord Jesus Christ.

*Fifth Motive:* Magnanimity will urge us, not by a vain desire of glory which would be unworthy of a magnanimous heart, but in view of that sanctity which the Servants of Jesus Christ ought to seek, to imitate the illustrious examples of the Saints, especially of those who have lived in these latter times. Such examples are as powerful voices to stimulate our courage, and incessantly impel us to advance. Now, if we are not determined to advance, how great is the evil we shall cause!

It is beyond doubt that indolent Religious are a burden to themselves, and a scandal to others. Since they fear pain, things seem more difficult to them than they are in reality, and they are fond of seeking dispensations. Those who are cast in a more courageous mould are justly disturbed by such conduct. Then one of two things take place; either they disapprove of their conduct, or yielding to temptation, approve of it and stop short in their good undertakings. Nothing is more prejudicial to the general good.

*Sixth Motive:* Here there is something which appears strange. All those who renounce the world in spirit and in truth, conceive, in the beginning, high ideas of sanctity. All even endeavour to accomplish great deeds. Yet, many in the course of time are seen to degenerate and to content themselves with a mediocre virtue.

If magnificent rewards were not promised to our efforts, if we did not expect, as the prize of our combats and victories, the abundance of all that the human heart can desire, there might be some semblance of reason for tepidity in the service of God. But no, His promises are so vast and gracious that they seem capable of raising the dead, and making them begin again a life of hard labour. How, then, are the hands of Christ's Soldiers feeble, their knees weak?[165]

*Seventh Motive:* And if the promised rewards make but little impression because they have for their object future goods, let us at least consider that without magnanimity it is impossible to sustain with advantage the incessant combats to which our implacable enemies subject us. Is it not astonishing to see in this matter the "children of the world wiser in their generation than the children of the Light"?[166] The Hebrews had begun to act with magnanimity when, at the arrival of the Ark, or rather of God Himself, in their camp, they set up a clamour with which the earth resounded. However, the Philistines, arming themselves with courage against the fear inspired by this presence of God, and by the formidable cry which they had just heard, exhorted one another by saying: "Take courage and behave like men, ye Philistines: lest you come to be servants to the Hebrews."[167] If, then, these reprobates pushed magnanimity, or rather audacity, so far as to rise against God, why should the chosen people, whose camp is honoured by His presence, lose courage and let themselves be overcome by the Philistines?

*Eighth Motive:* St. Paul furnishes another example: "Forgetting the things that are behind, and stretching forth myself to those that are before, I press towards the mark, to the prize of the supernal vocation of God in

---

[165] Cf. Isa. 35:3
[166] Luke 16:8
[167] 1 Kings 4:9

Christ Jesus."[168] It is after this manner that, among the different divisions of the Church, the Religious Orders especially have learned to combat.

*Ninth Motive:* But without going too far to seek, we have a most remarkable example in the person of St. Teresa of Avila. Although we all know it, yet it is to be feared we do not sufficiently consider it. For among all her sublime virtues, magnanimity shines with the greatest splendour.

If it is the property of this virtue to despise what is mean and to undertake what is great; what is there that is little about St. Teresa? What great things has she not undertaken? In a woman's body she carried a man's heart; and this heart embraced the whole universe. Who ever heard before her time of a woman founding or reforming an Order of men, a woman preoccupied with the salvation of infidels, directing towards that end her aspirations and her works? Such things are hardly expected from the most courageous men. How, then, has a woman, crushed by maladies, exposed to a thousand persecutions, confronted by obstacles humanly speaking insurmountable, "hoped against hope," and triumphed over all, contrary to the expectation of all? The best answer that can be given is that nothing resists magnanimity.

*Conclusion:* Then even "if armies in camp should stand together against them," Novices should imitate the noble example of this illustrious Virgin. They should hold it for certain, that, in the practice of the virtues, trivial things are not enough. They should habituate themselves to fight generously against the assaults of evil habits and all the enemies of their salvation. And turning their aspirations wholly towards the celestial land, they should not hesitate, if an occasion were to present itself, to shed their blood gladly for its attainment.[169]

---

[168] Phil. 3:13-14

[169] "Strive like strong men until you die in the attempt, for you are here for nothing else than to strive." St. Teresa of Avila, *Way of Perfection*, Ch. 20. "The spirit of the Crusader burns within me, and I long to die on the field of battle in defense of Holy Church." St. Thérèse of Lisieux, *Story of a Soul*, Ch 11, Pub.

# XV. Diligence

## I. Nature and Excellence of Diligence

Without diligence, which is also called solicitude, we are not only incapable of doing great things, which belongs to the virtue of magnanimity of which we have already treated, but we cannot produce anything of good.

Diligence is the care one takes to do things promptly. It depends on prudence, and is the only virtue we have taken in this category, since the treatise on prudence has but little application for Novices. All their prudence resides solely in their Master, and they could not without fault exercise it for themselves. As the act proper to prudence is the command, the use of this prudence is as foreign to inferiors as is the power to command.

However, if any function of prudence applies to them it would be that which belongs to the superior part of man, which has for its object the regulation of the inferior part by the light of reason conformable to the Divine precepts. Yet, it is not permitted them to use it without the control of the Novice Master.

True prudence then on the part of inferiors consists in obedience. As long as they are obedient they will never act imprudently, for they are then following with certainty the direction of God Himself.

As to diligence, which is the companion of obedience and of all the other virtues, it is recommended to all Christians, and especially to the young, as a mode of action necessary in the service of God, by which one makes great progress in the school of the virtues.

Promptitude imprints on the soul a wonderful facility for the practice of acts of virtue, and renders it like to the Angelic spirits who fly with extreme rapidity to accomplish all that is ordered them, according to this passage of Scripture: "Thou Who makest Thy Angels spirits; and Thy ministers a burning fire."[170] These expressions indicate the extraordinary promptitude with which the Angels accomplish the will of God.

Hereby we see that diligence is an angelic virtue, and that its effect is to reproduce in Convents the eagerness and alacrity with which the heavenly spirits execute the orders of God. This virtue is then very beautiful, since it

---

[170] Ps. 103:4

in some sort frees man from the weight of the flesh, and enrolls him among the Angels.

One loses nothing by this transformation; on the contrary, this virtue alone considerably augments the merits of all the others, since it causes their acts to be produced with all the strength and perfection of which they are capable. It is also a wonderful thing that, of two Religious who perform the same acts, and apply themselves thereto during the same space of time, one will be ten times more holy than the other, solely because of the higher degree of his diligence. We should pay attention to this point; it will greatly increase our courage.

Further, promptitude and heavenly agility will be a fruitful source of consolations; for virtue practiced expeditiously engenders joy, and God, Who, according to the Apostle, "loveth a cheerful giver,"[171] sheds on him, even here below, the sweetest and most abundant blessings.

To speak the language of men, we may truly say that this most liberal King takes a singular delight in the virtue of diligence, just as the general of an army, who, seeing his soldiers acquit themselves well, rejoices exceedingly, and is thereby disposed to bestow favours on them. And as negligent souls, like masses of lead, drag on with their work slowly and regretfully, and are distressing to the eye of God, so joyous and quick souls are extremely agreeable to Him and provoke His generosity.

Novices then should practice diligence, and endeavour by overcoming the indolence of the flesh to make themselves pleasing to God in the combat. This one advice contains for them the whole prudence of the just.

## II. Practice of Diligence

### Interior Acts

O my most amiable God, I am resolved to apply myself diligently, during my whole life, to the works that please Thee.

O most sweet Lord, "I will rejoice as a giant to run the way."[172]

O most clement God, I will be generous in overcoming sleep, sloth, and all that can retard my progress.

---

[171] 2 Cor. 9:7
[172] Cf. Ps. 18:6

O my most desirable Lord, I will endeavour to arrive first at office, prayer, instructions, and all the other exercises of the community.

My God, for Thy sake, I will not delay a single moment when the signal is given.

O God of all goodness, I will pay, for Thy sake, the greatest attention to all the exercises, such as the Divine Office, prayer, and other acts performed in common.

O Lord, I will not allow heat or cold to make me languid or tepid in Thy service.

My God, I will be vigilant and prompt in fulfilling every duty of obedience and all the other virtues.

## Exterior Acts

It is evident that the opportunities for practicing diligence are well-nigh innumerable. It is astonishing to see how often negligence glides into our works, and diminishes or even ruins their merit. Thus, it is necessary to fight this enemy bravely.

Exterior acts of diligence may be practiced everywhere. For example: when the signal for Matins is given, one should rise, or rather jump out of bed with great promptitude, and pay no attention to the flesh, whatever pretext it may put forward; during prayer, one should banish all languor and softness, regulating the senses and members; during sermons or exhortations, one must pay great attention to what is being said, avoiding all unnecessary movement of the body or distractions of the mind; when walking, standing or sitting, one must not show any sign of weariness or lassitude; when working, one must pay serious attention to his task; when serving at Mass, all inopportune devotions must be set aside in order that the whole mind may be given to the present duty. Thus, in a variety of circumstances, we should act in such a way that the mind and body may concur together, so that nothing may be wanting to the perfection of the work.

Such is the doctrine of the Saints. Undoubtedly, it is severe to nature; but how much it ennobles us! How great are the advantages it procures for us! Do they not compensate us for the pain it gives?

## III. Motives for Diligence

*First Motive:* We speak of the pains that must be taken. But in truth, there is little pain or fatigue if we do not give way to carelessness. Let us take, for example, the recitation of the Divine Office. Willing or not willing, we must recite it. Now is it not more painful to spend an entire hour in the weariness which negligence engenders at almost every verse, than to overcome this torpor by earnest elevations of the heart, and thus employ the time in watchfulness and fervour?

Moreover, our merit is diminished or lost by voluntary distractions, whilst it is augmented by diligence. It is then wiser to overcome idleness.

*Second Motive:* It is truly a matter of regret to see the Servants of Jesus Christ conduct themselves so carelessly in His service when "The children of Agar also that search after the wisdom that is of the earth, the merchants of Merrha and of Theman; and the tellers of fables and searchers of prudence and understanding: That hoard-up silver and gold, wherein men trust, and there is no end of their getting,"[173] are so diligent and full of solicitude.

*Third Motive:* With what diligence do not merchants, business men, sailors and artisans work to procure the necessaries of the present life! They spend sleepless nights, and complain that the sun does not rise soon enough. How often do they not endure physical pain rather than interrupt their work and see their profits stopped!

*Fourth Motive:* Anxiety is the portion of covetous men. They might live quietly by their own firesides, for the present life affords simple joys at little expense. But since they desire to become richer, they willingly sacrifice their repose, and expose themselves to innumerable dangers and fatigues.

If, then, we wish to make ourselves acquainted with the true state of things, we shall find that men are all on fire to gain perishable goods, and that the affair of their salvation is the only thing about which they are negligent. We see this more clearly when we consider the conversations and daily occupations of men.

*Fifth Motive:* If anyone wishes to obtain a favour from a king, he must secure mediators and take other necessary steps. He is not dismayed at the prospect of a long journey, or the various other inconveniences that may

---

[173] Baruch 3:23, 18

arise; he is ready to endure all to attain his end. But, alas! the "ways of Sion mourn because there are none that come to the solemn feast."[174]

*Sixth Motive:* However, all that we could say on this subject would be little compared with the incredible solicitude of men for the sordid goods of this life. The less that remains of the journey, the more provision they make for it. Old men are a proof of this. What they amassed in youth should suffice for the little time they have to live, but the nearer they approach the term, the more avaricious they become. This was the error of him to whom it was said: "Thou fool, this night do they require thy soul of thee."[175]

*Seventh Motive:* Ah! why do not the Servants of Jesus Christ, seeing under their eyes so many prodigious examples to reproach their sloth, "hasten," according to the advice of the Apostle, "to enter into eternal rest"?[176] If so many hundreds of years ago diligence was, in the judgment of St. Paul, of such great necessity that he said: "It is now the hour for us to rise from sleep: for now our salvation is nearer than when we believed,"[177] what shall we think *now*, when we are closer to the end of the world, and each one of us is advancing towards the term of his life? Is it not true that great diligence is necessary, and that for us too, the hour is already come to rise from sleep?

*Eighth Motive:* But whatever may be said of the end of the world and of each particular man, it is certain that, as far as Christian perfection is concerned, there remains for us a long career to be fulfilled. If others do not think so, we at least should always remember what the Angel said to St. Elias: "Arise, eat; for thou hast yet a great way to go"[178] If, then, we are called to run this way, how is it that we are not more fervent and diligent?

*Ninth Motive:* "We all die," said the woman whose wisdom is praised in the Scriptures, "and like waters that return no more we fall down into the earth."[179] All of us, whether we wish it or not, march on quickly to a death which is, in one sense, uncertain, but very near. Now, there are some men who, seeing that life is so short and full of trouble, give all their energies to the pursuit of riches and pleasures, and mutually excite one another by saying: "Come, therefore, and let us enjoy the good things that are

---

[174] Lamen. 1:4
[175] Luke 12:20
[176] Cf. Heb. 4:11
[177] Romans 13:11
[178] 3 Kings 19:7
[179] 2 Kings 14:14

present, and let us speedily use the creatures as in youth."[180] Others, far less numerous, say: Let us fast and pray lest we be suddenly overtaken by death, and vainly seek for time to repent. Of these two classes, Religious should choose what their conscience shall dictate to them.

*Conclusion:* But what can be the choice of the holy nation, the purchased people of the Son of God, of those whom God has willed particularly to be His, of Jacob whom He has taken for His inheritance?[181] If they choose diligence, is it not to run where they shall rejoice, "as conquerors after taking a prey?"[182] Let the feet of others be "swift to shed blood"[183]; for our part, let us hasten in emulation to "remove out of the midst of Babylon,"[184] to climb with the rapidity of a hart the fertile slopes of the mountain of God.[185]

Certainly he who has once got a knowledge of the Land of the Living will work day and night to attain it. Like the valiant woman, he "has tasted and seen that his traffic is good; his lamp shall not be put out in the night."[186] All these considerations should excite Novices to banish sloth and quicken their pace on the path which they have chosen.

# XVI. Perseverance

## I. Its Nature and Excellence

The Eternal Truth has pronounced this oracle: "He that shall persevere unto the end, he shall be saved";[187] as if our Lord would say: it is of little consequence to begin well, to practice virtue for a long time, and to apply ourselves diligently to it, unless we continue thus until death.

Perseverance is then the crown of the entire edifice, and for this reason it is but just that we should end the treatise on the virtues with it.

---

[180] Wis. 2:6
[181] Cf. Deut. 32
[182] Isa. 9:3
[183] Ps. 13:3
[184] Jerem. 50:8
[185] Cf. Ps. 67:16
[186] Prov. 31:18
[187] Matt. 10:22

Perseverance is a virtue by which we are firmly resolved to persist in good until the end. It is characterized by courage, for it is a daughter of fortitude. It combats time, the rock on which the human heart is so often broken.

It has for its ally constancy, which arms itself against everything that can oppose perseverance. But all those who have acquired this virtue do not persist in good until the end of their lives, since, through their own fault, they do not obtain the great *gift* of perseverance, which depends on the help and protection of God. It must be recognized, however, that the *virtue* of perseverance is extremely calculated to dispose us for the gift; for it assists man, with God's grace, to do what lies in his power; and if he does so, his final perseverance will depend on God alone.

The description we have given will suffice to make known to us the dignity of this generous virtue of perseverance, which advances by desire from the beginning of the Christian's career, travels to the end of the way of perfection, and vows to God eternal fidelity. All this is truly sublime and quite worthy of God Himself.

A virtue so vigorous excludes all vacillation, since it has always before its eyes to encourage it the victory and the palm. Such a thought is well calculated to make us love it.

Without it we lose all that we had acquired; with it, on the contrary, we amass rich treasures of merit in the eternal dwellings, "where neither rust nor moth doth consume, and where thieves do not break through nor steal."[188] Fatal accidents to which we are exposed so long as perseverance has not planted in heaven our victorious standard.

What shall we say of the joys engendered by this virtue? Nothing can be compared to their strength and sweetness. It is not only at the end of life that perseverance rejoices the soul, but by the firmness of its resolution it is already an ineffable consolation for man during the voyage, and while he is yet far from port. For it strongly excites hope, and like a fountain of living water which sweetly pours out its stream on the earth, it begets abundant delights, as if the victory were already gained.

There is nothing astonishing in this. Indeed, if the most infamous sinner, after having been purified in the Sacrament of Penance, which has healed his wounds and restored him to health, rejoices because he is in a state that permits him to hope for eternal salvation, how much greater

---

[188] Matt. 6:20

ought to be the joy of him who, having been already for a long time in God's grace, is enriched with many merits, and has every reason to believe that by the firmness of his perseverance he will maintain himself thus to the end?

Moreover, there are many examples to prove this. God, Who is infinitely good, waits not for the end of their course to lavish on those who have long persisted in His service, the wine of consolation which rejoices, and the bread of children which fortifies.

Thus, Novices should strive to adorn themselves with this virtue, which will preserve them from all dangers, and to strengthen themselves more and more every day by making frequent acts of it.

## II. Practice of Perseverance

It will not be necessary to treat of the exterior acts of this virtue, since the chief work of perseverance consists in fortifying the soul in order to establish it in good, and in such a manner that this stability becomes uniform and unvarying, save for obstacles which are surmounted by constancy. It will then suffice to say that when anything vexatious, painful, or difficult, in a word, any obstacle presents itself, the acts to be produced in order to overcome it will be acts of constancy. But whenever we require to strengthen the soul in good, and to help it to keep to its resolution of continuing therein, we should make acts of perseverance. Consequently, whether obstacles really exist, or we fear they may present themselves, we can practice the following interior acts:

O my God, I am firmly resolved to serve Thee even unto death.

My most faithful Lord, if I had to labour in this troublesome life for a thousand years, I would not abandon my purpose of being faithful to Thee.

O most merciful God, grant that no adversity may change my dispositions in Thy regard.

O most amiable Lord, rather let me perish by fire than abandon Thee.

Were I to be overwhelmed by all the miseries of this life, yet I would never abandon my vocation.

Let me die rather than be separated from Thee.

There is no joy equal to that of belonging to Thee, O Lord; then, I wish to be Thine for ever.

Even to my last breath nothing shall ever separate me from Thee.

Acts of this kind are always useful, but when the temptations are violent, and human reasons or the appearance of virtue try to shake us, they become quite necessary. Thus, Novices, in time of peace, should prepare themselves for war, in order that they may not be taken by surprise and overcome.

## III. Motives for Perseverance

*First Motive:* It may be said that this virtue is too difficult, but do men of the world allow themselves to be deterred from their enterprises by the difficulties which they encounter? Ah! How many, distinguished by birth and knowledge, worthy of all honour, have passed twenty, thirty, or more years in the courts of Princes and Kings, and after having grown grey in pursuing their favours, have ended by being disappointed in their hopes, or at best received but a poor recompense! How many are there, who, by attaching themselves to the service of God, would become great saints, and be enriched with eternal riches, but who, alas, die even before the Princes in whom they have placed all their expectations, and lose their souls for ever! How much more easy, sweet and advantageous it is to persevere in the Religious life, and to pass thence after a short interval to the immortal crown!

*Second Motive:* Now, as regards the dangers to be feared from the duration of time, from the enemies of our salvation, and from our own frailty. Have numerous shipwrecks at sea and the loss of riches hindered from returning to the Indies those whom God preserved in the midst of such catastrophes? Is it not an admirable thing to see with what audacity they face the ocean, without allowing themselves to be discouraged by all they have suffered? And even after having escaped two or three times from shipwreck, they never dream of embracing another kind of life, but persist invincibly in their designs.

*Third Motive:* Their fool-hardy conduct is a lesson for us. For, if they are happy enough to escape death three of four times, it often happens in the end that a tempest assails them and the avenging wave swallows them up at the very moment when, sufficiently enriched, they think of putting an end to their voyages and returning to the domestic hearth, there to taste the sweetness of repose. Is it not infinitely more worthy and secure to follow a route in which there is no fear of shipwreck, however bitter its trials may be?

## Moral Virtues

*Fourth Motive:* The deformity of the contrary vice shows the beauty of the virtue of perseverance. It happens, indeed, by a just judgement of Providence, that among all faults, inconstancy appears so odious that even those who are least virtuous themselves can scarcely endure it. This is why, when a Religious announces his vocation, those who have known him mock and say: "This man began to build, and was not able to finish."[189]

*Fifth Motive:* Inconstancy is not only an ugly defect, it is also the cause of fatal injuries. This is true even in what concerns the search after temporal goods. Indeed, we shall hardly find one in a thousand who, quitting a kind of life which he had undertaken by wise advice, will succeed in any other. God wishes to make known to us by this the injury those inflict on themselves, who, after having been called by Him, renounce their engagements. Unfortunate beings! What will become of them? One day Jesus Christ, our salvation and our life, said to His Apostles: "Will you also go away?" St. Peter, as if wounded by the question, answered: "To whom shall we go? Thou hast the words of eternal life."[190] Indeed, no one can withdraw from life unless to go to death.

*Sixth Motive:* Do we not see with sorrow that those whom God has rejected, since they were unworthy of their vocation, and wished to leave, are covered, as it were, by the shadow of death? We are not permitted to waste too many tears over their unhappy lot. Remember what God said to Samuel: "How long wilt thou mourn for Saul, whom I have rejected"?[191] We should then have more joy for those that are substituted than sorrow for those who lost their dignity, as in the case of David and Saul.

*Seventh Motive:* Indeed, it is vain for us to strive to express adequately the power, dignity, and immense advantages of perseverance, for all these things shall only be known at the end of life. But what shall be the greatness of the joy that will inundate at the moment of death the heart of the faithful Soldier of Jesus Christ? He has dwelt for many years hidden in the depths of the Cloister. He has had numerous and violent combats with the princes of darkness. At that supreme hour, throwing a look on the past, he sees that he has gained victories without number, and that he has remained firm in God's service. Then, without doubt, shall he "see and abound, and his heart shall wonder and be enlarged"[192] when the day of glory begins

---

[189] Luke 14:30
[190] John 6:68-69
[191] 1 Kings 16:1
[192] Cf. Isa. 60:5

to dawn, and he will receive, as the prize of his perseverance, an immortal crown, and a robe of dazzling whiteness.

Then, shall he "leap as a hart"[193]—he, who, overwhelmed with labours, had formerly appeared lame and, as it were, unable to move a single step. Then the tongue of the dumb that was tied by past sorrows shall be loosed; the soul which was dry and parched with thirst by the abandonment of God, the source of life, shall be changed into ponds and fountains of water; for it will be so inundated with Divine consolation that the words of Isaias may be applied to it: "The land that was desolate and impassable shall be glad, and the wilderness shall rejoice."[194]

*Conclusion:* What shall pass in the heart of him who has faithfully practiced the virtue of perseverance, when Jesus Christ, like a resplendent sun, shall unveil His face to him, and invite him to the incomparable delights of the Eternal Nuptials, saying: "Come, my well-beloved soul, whom I have chosen, and I shall establish in you My throne"?[195] Is it possible that perseverance, otherwise so sweet in the Religious life, shall be so gloriously crowned?[196] Does not an end so magnificent deserve that we should greedily drink, even to the dregs, the chalice of all earth's bitterness, in order to obtain it? Thus, Novices should endeavour, from their first entrance into the Religious life, to impress profoundly on their minds the thought of the glorious term where their labours shall end, in order that they may arm themselves against all kinds of obstacles, and so obtain the crown of immortality, the object of their desires.[197]

---

[193] Cf. Isa. 35:6-7
[194] Isa. 35:1
[195] Little Office of the Blessed Virgin.
[196] "Are we thinking of the good God, of our salvation, of our soul? O my children, what folly is the world! We come into it, we go out of it, without knowing why. The good God places us in it to serve Him, to try if we will love Him and be faithful to His Law; and after this short moment of trial, He promises us a recompense. Is it not just that He should reward the faithful servant and punish the wicked one? Should the Trappist, who has passed his life in lamenting and weeping over his sins, be treated the same as the bad Christian, who has lived in abundance in the midst of all the enjoyments of life? No; certainly not. We are on earth not to enjoy its pleasures, but to labor for our salvation." St. John Vianney, *Catechism*, Ch. 2, Pub.
[197] "As I say, it is most important–all-important, indeed–that they should begin well by making an earnest and most determined resolve not to halt until they reach their goal, whatever may come, whatever may happen to them, however hard they may have to labour, whoever may complain of them, whether they reach their goal or die on the road or have no heart to confront the trials which they meet, whether the very world dissolves before them." St. Teresa of Avila, *Way of Perfection*, Ch 21, Pub.

# III

# VICES

## I. CAPITAL VICES

### I. GENERAL REMARKS

Though in our treatise on the virtues we have furnished suitable arms for overcoming the opposite vices, yet it will be useful for us to treat here collectively the principal vices, so that Novices may find it more convenient in studying them and comparing them with the virtues, and thus be better able to know and conquer them.

However, since in speaking of the virtues it was necessary to mention the vices also, and show their hideousness and the method to be followed in eradicating them, we shall content ourselves here with an exposition of them that is short and appropriate to Religious. This explanation will give us a knowledge of the vices as the treatise on the virtues has indicated the remedies for them.

### II. PRIDE

Among the vices, pride, which is their king, holds the first rank. It is a disordered appetite for the excellence to which honour and respect are due. For pride seeks not every kind of excellence, but only that which others honour. It is always seated in the irascible part of the sensitive appetite, and in the will, in so far as this latter corresponds to the inclination of the irascible appetite.

The holy Fathers employ the word *pride* in three different senses. First, they understand by it the propensity to elevate oneself, which, since original sin, is natural to man, because of the utter corruption of his being. Under this head, pride is the root of all sin, since the inferior part of man, having no longer the curb of original *justice*, is, as we too often experience, like a wild beast carried away by the violence of his instincts to all kinds of excess.

Secondly, by pride is understood revolt against authority, or, in other words, an irregular appetite for preeminence in all things. In this sense, pride is a general sin which allies itself with all the other sins.

Thirdly, as we have already said, pride is a disordered appetite for the excellence to which honour is due, and in this sense it is one of the seven capital vices.

It is of this kind of pride that we are going to speak. Let us remark in the beginning that, as the definition indicates, it is in the nature of this vice to attribute to ourselves things greater than we possess. For, as on the one hand, the appetite for excellence dominates the heart, and on the other, the intelligence naturally follows the affections, and, consequently, gives ready credence to what the will desires with ardour, it happens that the proud believe great things of themselves, and think they have a right to the homage of others.

Such is the source from which all the wickedness of this vice proceeds, and especially these four kinds of pride mentioned by the holy Fathers: 1. To esteem as coming from ourselves the good which we possess. 2. To believe we have received it from on high in consideration of our own merits. 3. To boast of what we have not. 4. To despise others and desire to appear as if we alone were good.

Indeed, presupposing this irregular esteem, by which man raises himself in his thoughts above what he is, it follows that he everywhere seeks excellence, that is to say, the things by which he may appear more worthy of honour. Now, it is more honourable to have of ourselves as the Divinity, the good which we possess, than to hold it from another; more honourable to have received an account of our own merits than to have received gratuitously; more honourable to have than not to have; and, lastly more honourable to appear to possess some good in a more excellent manner than others.

From the same source also proceed these twelve kinds of pride pointed out by the Saints, and opposed to the twelve degrees of humility:[198] curiosity, opposed to the practice of always keeping our eyes lowered to the earth; levity of mind, which makes us speak with ostentation, opposed to silence; silly mirth, opposed to moderate joy, which does not indulge in loud laughter; boasting,[199] opposed to the reserve which keeps us from speaking until we are questioned; singularity, opposed to the keeping of the common rule; arrogance, opposed to the habit of believing and admitting that we are the vilest of all; presumption, opposed to the practice of thinking that we are useless and incapable; defense of our faults, opposed to the humble confession of our shortcomings; sham confession, by which we seek to avoid bearing the penalty due to our faults, opposed to patience in pains and trials; rebellion, opposed to obedience; liberty, opposed to the renouncement of our own will; the habit of sin, opposed to the fear of God.

Let us here make an important remark with regard to what has been said, which particularly relates to Religious. It is that pride is excited not only by important things, but also by trifles. Thus, for example, the defense of our faults, which constitutes the eighth degree of pride, will have no place among us, thanks to God, for grievous sins; but there is cause to fear that it may with regard to light faults. Likewise, it is not to be presumed that a Religious, succumbing to the fourth kind of pride, will desire to eclipse others by any irregularity which will lead him to commit a mortal offense against God; but he should be vigilant not to wish or seek it in little things. Assuredly, if a Religious sees that he speaks more eloquently than others, that he reads, writes, or chants better, that he imbibes spiritual doctrine more easily, and acquits himself more exactly of the various duties confided to him, he will be exposed to frequent temptations, and perhaps he will desire that others should recognize his merits, and on this account render homage to him.

These miseries, and many other very hurtful ones, proceed from the disordered appetite for excellence. Novices will preserve themselves from them if they consider well and put in practice the counsels we have given in the chapter on humility. Then what we have here said of pride, its degrees and nature, will help them to discern the various characteristics of pride and humility, in order that they may avoid the one and embrace the other.

---

[198] See *The Steps of Humility and Pride* by St. Bernard of Clairvaux, Pub.
[199] St. Bernard lists "Boasting and too much talking." Ibid., Pub.

There are, as everyone knows, three remedies for pride: the consideration of our own frailty; the consideration of the greatness of God; and the consideration of the imperfection of the good that is in us. Books of piety foster this triple consideration.

## III. Vainglory

Vainglory constitutes a capital vice, and is nothing else than an irregular appetite of unstable glory, that is, that glory which has its source and splendour in the knowledge others have of us.

Glory is an effect of honour. When anyone is honoured and praised, others conceive a good opinion of him. Thus, glory has been defined as "an illustrious and honourable renown." Consequently, vainglory, which aspires inordinately to this distinction, is an empty vice, as its name indicates; and though it appears to have in view something grand, it is simply baseness. It is opposed to the virtue of magnanimity, which makes no account of the praise of men.

Vainglory seems to be a development of pride. The proud desire to excel, in order that others may honour them; and he who is athirst for vainglory desires also to shine. He wishes that, by reason of the honour which is rendered to him, others may have exalted ideas of his merits, and conceive an honourable opinion of him.

This poisonous mother begets seven treacherous children: boasting, the presumption of novelties, hypocrisy, obstinacy, discord, contention, and disobedience.

Indeed, the end of vainglory is to show our own excellence. This can be done in two ways: First, directly, as when anyone wishes to exalt himself by words, which is boasting; or by words and acts; then, if those are such as provoke astonishment, it is the presumption of novelties; if they are false, it is hypocrisy. Secondly, indirectly, as when a person manifests his superiority in an indirect manner, by desiring not to appear inferior to others; and this may take place in four ways. First, as to intelligence, in refusing to abandon his opinion to follow a better counsel; this is called obstinacy. Secondly, as to the will, in not wishing to yield for the sake of peace; this is called discord. Thirdly, in words, by disputing noisily; this is called contention. Fourthly, in actions, by refusing to execute the order of a Superior; this is called disobedience.

With regard to vainglory and its progeny, we shall make the same remark that we made with regard to pride: it is that they display their fury in very light matters. Indeed, the Religious a prey to vainglory, not wishing to appear inferior to others, is determined on all occasions to yield to those only who are of his own mind, and hence, he falls into the abyss of discord and contention[200]. For, and it is a thing worthy of remark, anger only engenders discord and contention when vainglory is in play.

To guard against these cruel beasts and many others, Novices should apply themselves to the study of humility, which rejects glory, and magnanimity, which makes small account of it, and they should practice the acts of these two virtues as we have indicated.

## IV. Envy

Envy, which manifestly comes from vainglory, is a sadness experienced at the good of our neighbour considered as a drawback to our own good. It is a very pernicious vice, being directly opposed to charity. According to the Fathers, it has for its offspring hatred, slander, detraction, joy at our neighbour's adversity, and affliction in his prosperity.

This is easily understood, for if a man greedy of vainglory, imagines himself to be eclipsed by another, he begins to hate him, and seeks to diminish this glory which clouds his own. If he does it in secret by malevolent insinuations, it is slander; if he does it openly, it is detraction. Then, if he succeeds, he rejoices at the trouble he brings on others; if he succeeds not, he grows sad at their well-being.

Indeed, it is certain that persons consecrated to God are tempted to envy for very trivial things. Let us suppose, for example, the case of two Religious, one of whom surpasses the other in amiability, good manners, or it matters not what quality, save that it is a thing of little importance. His

---

[200] "Among the proud there are always contentions." Prov. 13:10. "Now the works of the flesh are manifest, which are fornication, uncleanness, immodesty, luxury, idolatry, witchcrafts, enmities, contentions, emulations, wraths, quarrels, dissensions, sects, envies, murders, drunkenness, revellings, and such like. Of the which I foretell you, as I have foretold to you, that they who do such things shall not obtain the kingdom of God. But the fruit of the Spirit is, charity, joy, peace, patience, benignity, goodness, longanimity, mildness, faith, modesty, continency, chastity. Against such there is no law. And they that are Christ's, have crucified their flesh, with the vices and concupiscences." Gal 5:19-24, Pub.

companion is inclined to feel disturbed. On the other hand, if the former should fail in some point, the latter is tempted to rejoice. We all know by experience that this often happens in little things, but we would call special attention to the fact that envy is not so easily excited against those who are Seniors. Thus, a young Novice will not be tempted to envy an old Religious, with regard to prudence, reputation, or things of this kind, but it will easily slip in when there is question of companions whom the Superior seems to prefer.

These fatal germs of envy may be destroyed by a careful observance of the advice given in the chapter on charity.

## V. Gluttony

Gluttony is an inordinate appetite for eating and drinking. The Fathers point out five kinds of gluttony indicated by the following adverbs: sumptuously, fastidiously, excessively, hastily, eagerly. They assign it a corresponding number of daughters: silly joy, buffoonery, uncleanliness, garrulity, and feebleness of mind.[201]

The glutton wishes for rare viands, this is sumptuousness; for meats delicately prepared, this is fastidiousness; in great quantity, this is excess; then he anticipates the reasonable time, which is haste; and he eats greedily, which is eagerness.

Hence, proceed foolish mirth, on account of the disorder into which gluttony throws the sensitive appetite, by lulling to sleep the vigilance of reason; buffoonery, that is, all sorts of gestures which provoke laughter, and which man, in this state, has not strength to restrain; uncleanliness, by a natural consequence follows self-indulgence; garrulity, or a multiplicity of useless words; feebleness of mind, because of the chemicals that obscure the brain.

Gluttony is altogether an animal vice which Novices ought to hold in abhorrence. For the remedies to be employed against it, we must go back to the chapter on abstinence and sobriety.

---

[201] There are five forms of gluttony: "Hastily, sumptuously, too much, greedily, daintily." St. Thomas Aquinas, *Sum. Theol.*, II-II, Q. 148, Art. 4., Pub.

## VI. Avarice

Avarice is the immoderate desire of earthly goods. This word, like those of cupidity and covetousness, is taken in three senses. First, for concupiscence, which is one of the effects of the original fall; under this head avarice is the root of all sin. Secondly, the immoderate desire of possessing anything whatsoever; and in this sense it enters into the nature of all sin. Thirdly, for the desire of riches, and it is then a capital vice.

There are seven kinds of avarice: parsimony, tenacity, difficulty in giving, unjust gain, usury, larceny, and gambling.

Of the last four, we have nothing to say, since they are alien to the Cloister. As to the other three, they are often enough a cause of temptation to the Servants of Jesus Christ. This happens when they set their hearts on things which they are allowed to use, as if they were the owners. If those whose duty it is to distribute give little, it is parsimony; if they give nothing, it is tenacity; if they distribute with reluctance, it is difficulty in giving. It is truly wonderful how avarice insinuates itself into the offices and cells of Religious.

Avarice has seven daughters: obduracy, violence, deceit, anxiety, fraud, perjury, and treachery

Indeed, the avaricious harden themselves and become inaccessible to the sentiment of mercy. To acquire goods they use violence; they deceive by their words; they are eager and anxious in their desires; they cheat in their actions; they perjure themselves; and when an occasion presents itself they shrink not from treachery, like Judas who betrayed his Master through love of gain, and so many others who have abandoned the faith.

Of this wicked progeny, anxiety most frequently glides among Religious. Contrary to the counsel of Jesus Christ, they distract their minds from the thought of heaven, as if they were obliged, like people in the world, to take thought of food and raiment. Far better would it be for them to obey the words of the Master: "Be not solicitous, therefore, saying: 'What shall we eat, or what shall we drink?'"[202] It will be well to refer to what we have said on poverty, which is the mortal enemy of avarice.

---

[202] Matt. 6:31

## VII. ANGER

Anger is an inordinate appetite for vengeance. There are three kinds of anger, or in other words, among irascible people, some are hasty or passionate, these are too easily and quickly irritated for every light cause; others are bitter, they brood a long time over the injury received; and others again are hard to please, and will only be appeased by vengeance. The holy Fathers say that anger has six children: conflict, inflation of mind, injury, clamour, indignation, and blasphemy. With the exception of the first and the last, all these have frequent access to Religious houses, even those of strict observance, and are excited by mere trifles. Indeed, it requires but a light fault to provoke some persons to indignation, that is, contempt for those who have offended them, to clamour, or elevation of the voice, to inflation of mind, which fills the head with thoughts of revenge, and to injury, when one breaks out into disagreeable words against his neighbour.

This vice is very unworthy of the Servants of Jesus Christ. It is the same with the passion of anger, whose acts give birth to the vice itself. For both there are efficacious remedies given in the chapters of the first and second parts, which treat of anger and meekness.[203]

## VIII. LUST

Lust is an appetite for the pleasures of the flesh. This vice is certainly very degrading. The holy Fathers say that it gives birth to eight daughters which are: blindness of spirit, rashness, precipitation, inconstancy, selfishness, hatred of God, love of the present life, and horror of the future life. They indicate five degrees of it, namely, the look, the thought, delectation, consent, and the exterior act. If we consider words as exterior acts, there are four kinds, namely, shameful words, light pleasantries, voluptuous words, and foolish words. There is no vice which so lowers the intelligence of man as lust.

We have said so much, in order that Novices may thank God for having preserved them from these evils, and that they may avoid with the greatest care everything in the remotest degree relating to this vice. Since they are children of Mary, the very name of such a monstrous vice ought to inspire

---

[203] Cf. P. I., Ch. VI., and P. II., S. II., Ch. VIII.

them with horror and disgust. In the chapter on chastity they will find all the arms necessary for triumphing over it.

## IX. SLOTH

Sloth, considered as a capital vice, is the weariness or sadness which some experience of Divine or spiritual things; when the weariness relates to other than Divine things, it is a common passion. The holy Fathers assign to it six daughters, which are: malice, or aversion for spiritual goods; rancour, or indignation against those who would excite love for those spiritual goods; despair with regard to Divine goods; pusillanimity in seeking for them; laxity in the fulfillment of precepts; and levity of mind regarding unlawful things.

Sloth also gives birth to many other faults of the same kind, such as bitterness, idleness, drowsiness, importunity of thoughts, curiosity, talkativeness, restlessness of body, instability.

All these evils are extremely hurtful to spiritual advancement, and are found but too frequently in houses that have become relaxed. Novices shall preserve themselves from the vice of sloth by generously observing the advice contained in the chapter on diligence.

It will be remarked that we have indicated eight capital vices. Ordinarily seven only are given, the holy Fathers counting pride and vainglory as one, or leaving out one or the other of them.

What we have said of the capital vices is certainly little when we consider the extent of the subject. But it will suffice to show Novices how numerous are the enemies they must combat, and how much it behooves them to apply themselves seriously to the practice of the virtues, and to be courageous in the warfare to which they are exposed on every side.

The words of Baruch apply well to our subject: "Hear, O Israel, the commandments of life: give ear that thou mayst learn wisdom. How happeneth it, O Israel, that thou art in thy enemies land?... Thou hast forsaken the fountain of wisdom; for if thou hadst walked in the way of God, thou hadst surely dwelt in peace for ever"[204] It is as if he said the earth is filled with so many enemies because we have all strayed like

---

[204] Baruch 3:9-10, 12-13

wandering sheep, and have furnished weapons to those who would hinder our salvation.

For this reason we should apply to ourselves the commandment given by David: "He commanded that they should teach the children of Juda the use of the bow, as it is written in the book of the just."[205] Novices are of the number of those just who learn from their tender years the art of making war. They should then exercise themselves in the use of arms.

Undoubtedly, if they were to contend unarmed or alone with so many enemies, they could never hope to conquer. But they have the invincible arms of the virtues, and they are conducted by a wise and courageous General, even Jesus Christ Our Lord, Who, as David sings, "Binds their kings with fetters, and their nobles with manacles of iron."[206]

In the following chapter we shall point out to Novices the method they should make use of in overcoming the capital vices which are as so many monsters, in controlling the passions of which we have already treated in the first part, and in acquiring the virtues which was the principal object of the second part of these Instructions.

## II. Important Remarks on the Virtues and Vices

We reserve for the treatise on Prayer, as the proper place, the virtues which relate to the Divine worship.

It will be necessary to make a general remark here on the virtues and vices. A sin of theft, for example, if committed with the intention of raising ourselves above others, becomes also an act of pride; if committed for the sake of feasting and carousing, it will be an act of gluttony and drunkenness as well; and for each guilty end the thief has in view in his larceny, it becomes a special and distinct sin. In the same manner, an act of virtue, the serving of Mass, for instance, if done in order to obey a Superior, is an act of obedience; if done to please God, it will be an act of Divine love; if done through a desire to be useful to others, it is an act of charity; if to obtain heaven, it is an act of hope; if in satisfaction for our sins, it is an act of penance. Thus every good act will become a special act of virtue for each

---

[205] 2 Kings 1:18
[206] Ps. 149:8

good end proposed to ourselves in executing it. Novices should endeavour to reduce this great principle to practice.[207]

It is no light thing, then, that an act, which in itself is only susceptible of one kind of merit, may become by the intention of him who performs it, ten times more meritorious.

At the end of the first part[208] we have given advice well worthy of attention concerning the manner of acquiring virtues and overcoming vices and passions. It will be profitable to return to it here; for though we have indicated the best means, yet what we have said is hardly sufficient to smooth the way entirely, and to bring each one to his end according to his particular dispositions.

Indeed, some are troubled by one passion, others by another. In like manner some are attracted to one virtue, others to another. This is a fact which all the Fathers recognize, and which experience teaches. It is evident, then, that if a man is prone to anger and but little troubled by lust, he ought to give more attention to the practice of meekness than chastity. If he is tempted to pride, and but little moved by anger, he should apply himself with greater care to humility than to meekness. Thus in general, for a particular malady, a particular remedy must be applied.[209]

Further, we must bear in mind the weakness of the human mind. When anyone sees himself a prey to some spiritual ailment, it is well, in order to assure success, to concentrate nearly all his powers on that one point alone; that is, to apply himself particularly to the practice of one particular virtue. It is evident that when the powers, already feeble in themselves, are divided yet more, they produce no good result; like dogs that pursue several hares in the same chase, they catch nothing.

However, what we have said must not be understood in this sense, that when anyone is tormented by some particular passion he is obliged

---

[207] "For our actions to be meritorious it is enough, according to many theologians, that they be inspired by any supernatural motive: fear, hope or love. It is true that St. Thomas requires that our actions be at least virtually under the influence of charity through a preceding act of love, the influence of which still endures. He adds, however, that this condition is fulfilled in all those that perform any lawful action whilst in the state of grace: 'For those in the state of grace every act is meritorious or demeritorious.'" Fr. Adolphe Tanquerey, *The Spiritual Life*, P. I., Ch. II., Art. II., §II., II., I., C., II., (#241), Pub.

[208] See P. I., Ch. VII.

[209] "Let the examples of the Saints, and our meditations and prayers on the Life and Passion of Christ (so needful in every spiritual exercise), be all applied principally to the virtue which we have made it our task to practice." Fr. Lorenzo Scupoli, *The Spiritual Combat*, Ch 35, Pub.

to combat it by the practice of one virtue, and by the extirpation of the vice opposed to this virtue, without further occupying himself with the other passions, vices or virtues. What we mean is this, that while he pays the greater part of his attention to the thing most needed, he should not forget the practice of the rest when occasions present themselves. Now, in Religious Communities such occasions are daily and numerous, especially on account of the custom that prevails of assigning a virtue for each week, another for each month, and a third for each year.

The following comparison will make our idea clear; it is taken from the studies of Theology, law and medicine. The Theologian, for example, makes profession of knowing God and Divine things. To advance in this science he applies himself to it with the greatest ardour. But if in reading, writing, or discussing he meets matters concerning jurisprudence or medicine, he willingly makes himself acquainted with them, especially if they have any bearing, analogy, or connection with Theology. Thus, when we have once recognized the necessity of a virtue, or remarked the attacks of a vice or passion, we should courageously turn our efforts to this particular point, as if it were our profession. But at the same time we should not neglect to apply ourselves willingly, though not so earnestly, to the other virtues, on account of the close connection that exists between them, and to combat with vigilance the other vices and passions.

Such is the shortest and most advantageous way as we shall demonstrate. The greatest Theologians agree in saying that all the virtues, especially when they have attained their proper perfection, are connected.[210] They say that it is impossible for a man given, for instance, to the exercise of meekness, to apply himself to the exercise of this virtue without at the same time becoming chaste, strong, magnanimous, humble, sober, just, prudent, victorious over all vices, and master of all his passions. Here is the reason: there is no meekness without prudence; and there is no prudence without justice, chastity, and humility; since prudence cannot be unjust,

---

[210] "Of these eight faults then, although they are different in their origin and in their way of affecting us, yet the six former; viz., gluttony, fornication, covetousness, anger, dejection, accidie, have a sort of connection with each other, and are, so to speak, linked together in a chain, so that any excess of the one forms a starting point for the next. For from superfluity of gluttony fornication is sure to spring, and from fornication covetousness, from covetousness anger, from anger, dejection, and from dejection, accidie. And so we must fight against them in the same way, and with the same methods: and having overcome one, we ought always to enter the lists against the next." John Cassian, *Conferences*, Conf. 5, Ch 10, Pub.

intemperate, or proud. For prudence prescribes to the virtues, conforming to right reason, the means proper to attain the end which the virtues, on their side, propose to it. Hence the vices being eliminated, and the passions subjugated, a spiritual edifice is raised, the parts of which are composed of the different virtues.

If, then, one cannot perfectly acquire a particular virtue without at the same time acquiring all the others and making conquest of his vices and passions, is it not evident that he will arrive more quickly and efficaciously at perfection by applying himself with ardour to a single virtue than by pursuing several with a less fervent zeal? As we have said, the strength of man is but meagre. So far is he from being able to accomplish at the same time several difficult enterprises, that he can hardly succeed with one. Is it not better, then, to attack a particular point, which will serve as a first link to draw the entire chain in its wake?

It is certain that, when the powers are concentrated on one object alone they act more energetically. Thus, for example, the soul applied to humility will produce acts of humility more fervently than if its activity were divided amongst several virtues. Now, if this be true, it will certainly acquire humility more promptly. But it will not acquire humility alone; it will acquire all the other virtues more quickly with it. And as one cannot arrive at the perfection of all the virtues without overcoming all the passions, it follows that by the same act greater perfection will be acquired.

Let us add to this that when, as we have already remarked, each one has well weighed and compared his dispositions and needs, his choice of a virtue must be prudent and entirely conformable to the spiritual state in which he finds himself.

The lives of the Saints furnish us with abundant proofs that those who have been distinguished for sanctity, first concentrated all their energies on some one particular virtue, and then applied themselves in a special manner to the acquisition of it as the great affair of their lives. Some selected humility, others obedience or meekness, or one of the other virtues. It was by this means that they succeeded in acquiring all. Moreover, it is considered by all nations a more glorious thing to excel in one art than to attain mediocrity in several. Indeed, it is better to be an excellent artist than to be one and the same time an imperfect painter, musician, surgeon, and writer. Now, if this be true of the arts, which are not intimately connected with one another, what will it be with regard to the virtues, of which one is never acquired without the others coming in its train?

But let us show by an example that not only does a single virtue acquired in its perfection hold all the others united and enchained to it, but also that, in the efforts that are made to acquire it, all the other virtues are increased in us in proportion as that one is increased, and all the passions are subdued and the vices eradicated.

## Example of the Virtue of Meekness

A Religious learning from experience that he is subject to anger knows that this is the passion especially he ought to mortify, and that among all the virtues, meekness is the one he needs most. After having conferred with his Master, he makes a firm resolution to begin the warfare.

Animating his hope and confiding solely in the Divine goodness, he reads the chapter on meekness, and resolves to produce very often, and with great care, the acts indicated therein, to conquer anger, and to acquire the opposite virtue.

He prays frequently; with the sanction of his Superior, he undertakes disciplines and fasts; he often receives the Sacraments. In all these and other like things, he should show an unshaken constancy, and make a firm resolution to die rather than abandon his design; for it is here, above all, that he needs perseverance and magnanimity. Afterwards, he examines where, when, and why his anger is provoked. Then, when occasions arise, he acts in the following manner.

Let us suppose that he has been wounded by the words of another Religious, and this unjustly, without necessity, in an unbecoming manner. Immediately the passion of anger, like a wild beast rushing from his den, burns to return evil for evil. But at the same time, the young champion of meekness produces an act of reason, and he commands himself by saying: You should not be angry; be not excited. This order, which arms the understanding, is an act proper to prudence. However, anger is not yet fully appeased, but urges to revenge. The Religious on his part persists and says: Revenge is not permitted. Here the will detests vengeance; this is an act of the virtue of justice, opposed to the punishment inflicted by private authority, and this act of justice arms the will. But anger is still awake, for the concupiscible appetite enters into sadness, it seems to it too painful to endure the affront. It desires, then, to taste the joy of driving away sadness by giving itself up to revenge. Then the Religious, using the authority of reason, chooses to endure the sadness rather than answer harshly. This is an act of the virtue of temperance by which the concupiscible appetite is held in check. Anger continues to burn: and the Religious, opposing to its fury the authority of reason, elicits an act of constancy. He chooses to overcome this difficulty rather than be wanting in meekness towards his neighbour. This is an act which depends on the virtue of fortitude, and which rules the irascible appetite. In fine, the virtue of meekness, which has its seat in the irascible appetite, remains mistress of the situation, and anger is vanquished and suppressed. It will be seen by this example that the virtues, even before they are acquired, and during their attainment, are closely united, and that, by the same effort, the opposite vices are repulsed, and the passions subjugated.

But let us show this more clearly still, and demonstrate a principle more efficacious even than that which we have already pointed out. The Religious whom we have supposed to be applying himself to the virtue of meekness, feels the blood boiling in his veins, and his heart agitated in divers ways, yet he knows that it is more conformable to reason to keep silent, and to show a serene countenance. It is quite certain that to practice the virtue of which he has made choice he has the concurrence not only of the acquired virtues but also of the infused. And here is the proof of what we advance.

One of the first instructions we have given the Novices for the formation of the Religious spirit consists in teaching them to refer the acts of the acquired virtues to the end of the infused, and especially the Theological virtues. This we have clearly pointed out in the first chapter on the moral virtues in general,[211] taking temperance as an example; and in the beginning of this chapter by the instance of a single act referred to several good ends. Consequently, if the Religious may, on an occasion of practicing meekness, exercise acts of the infused virtues, why should not he do so? We will now prove that it is quite possible for him to exercise such acts.

An offense has been committed against someone. Faith teaches him that revenge is displeasing to Our Lord Jesus Christ. Enlightened by this teaching, the person offended makes an act of faith, and declares that vengeance is unworthy of a Christian; hope affirms that in overcoming this obstacle he makes a step towards the sovereign Good; charity tells him that his neighbour ought to be loved, even when he acts badly; prudence

---

[211] See P. II., S. II., Ch. I.

assures him that this offense is a favourable occasion of gaining a beautiful crown; justice warns him that he should render to each one his due, and that, consequently, he should not take vengeance, since God has said: "Revenge is mine, and I will repay";[212] modesty suggests that he should not expose himself to the hideous deformity of outward anger; humility urges him to abase himself beneath others, and to abstain from resisting them; temperance instructs him to refrain from unlawful pleasures, and, as a matter of course, that of revenge; magnanimity proclaims that he ought to act with gentleness, especially in difficult occasions. Thus, the acts of the different virtues unite; for it is by all the movements of the virtues indicated above that meekness may be exercised in our supposed case, and that the contrary vices and passions may be resisted.

It is quite true that all the acts mentioned here will not, perhaps, be entirely and under every aspect proper to these different virtues. But this matters little, since it is not necessary to have, according to the language of the schools, anything so rigorously formal.[213] Even if it were necessary, occasions would not be wanting to produce acts truly proper to the different virtues, as we may convince ourselves by the following reason.

He who, being prone to anger, has determined to acquire meekness, will perhaps feel irritated about his food; in this case he will properly practice abstinence and sobriety; sometimes on account of being contemned he will have an opportunity of practicing humility; sometimes, because of pains and labours, he will practice patience; sometimes, because of an aversion he feels towards someone, he will practice charity; again, on account of the difficulties he encounters in the spiritual life he will get an occasion of practicing constancy, and so in many circumstances which it would take too long to enumerate. In conclusion, even if it were impossible to find such direct applications, the reason given before from the mutual connection of the virtues is quite sufficient.

---

[212] Rom. 12:19

[213] "It is, therefore, useful in performing our actions to propose to ourselves several supernatural motives. We must, however, avoid all excess and preoccupation in seeking to multiply intentions, for this would disturb the soul. The prudent way is to make use of the intentions that suggest themselves more or less spontaneously and to subordinate them to that of divine charity. In this manner we shall increase our merits without losing our peace of soul." Fr. Adolphe Tanquerey, *The Spiritual Life,* P. I., Ch. II., Art. II., §II., II., I., C., (#239). Pub.

Novices should seriously reflect on all these instructions, and, with the aid of their Master, put them so well into practice that they may in a short time arrive at the summit of Christian perfection.

# IV

# The Gifts and Fruits of the Holy Ghost

## I. The Seven Gifts of the Holy Ghost

### 1. Their Nature and Excellence

After having treated of the virtues as far as the object we had in view requires, we shall speak in the two following chapters of the gifts of the Holy Ghost, the fruits and beatitudes, in order that Novices may learn to appreciate the goods lavished on them by God, be encouraged to advance, and have a salutary fear of losing such priceless treasures. The present chapter will be devoted to the gifts of the Holy Ghost.

It was not enough for man to be adorned and enriched with the Theological virtues and the moral virtues, both infused and acquired. For owing to his great weakness and absolute inability to make use of such high virtues, there was still something wanting to him which the Gifts of the Holy Ghost efficaciously supply.

These gifts are called habits, which give to man the perfections necessary for following the movements and inspirations of the Holy Ghost; just as the virtues are habits which give to man the perfections requisite for following promptly the dictates of reason.

The gifts have a higher dignity than the virtues, except the Theological virtues. Herein lies the reason. The Theological virtues surpass the gifts, since they unite the soul to God; but the gifts surpass the moral virtues, because they dispose the soul to seek God as its end; while the moral virtues perfect the soul with regard to the end.

These heavenly gifts are seven in number, namely: wisdom, understanding, counsel, fortitude, knowledge, piety, and the fear of the Lord. Wisdom, understanding, counsel and knowledge have their seat in the intellect; piety resides in the will; fear, according to St. Thomas, has its seat in the concupiscible appetite; and, lastly, fortitude, which is in the irascible appetite. Thus, all the powers of man, which are perfected by the virtues, are still further disposed for action by the Gifts of the Holy Ghost.

We will illustrate this by a comparison. When a chariot is furnished with wheels, it is ready to be moved, but unless it is well-oiled, the horses will draw it with difficulty. The virtues are as spiritual wheels, which enable man to move; but he will go at a lagging pace if he does not receive the unction of "the oil of gladness."[214] According to the words of the Prophet, we are right in attributing this unction to the Holy Spirit: "The Spirit of the Lord is upon me, because the Lord hath anointed me."[215] Let us now explain the properties of each of these gifts.

## II. Properties of the Gifts of the Holy Ghost

Understanding perfects the speculative reason for the perception of Divine truths; the gift of counsel perfects the practical reason. But after having perceived Divine truths, man ought to be able to judge them in a Divine manner. The speculative reason receives from wisdom the perfection necessary for this, and the practical reason receives it from knowledge. So much for what concerns the intellect. The gift of piety perfects the will. Fear of God gives to the concupiscible appetite the perfection necessary to keep it from yielding to the attraction of inordinate pleasure. Fortitude perfects the irascible appetite against the apprehension of perils.

The gift of understanding, added to the light of faith, makes the human intellect conceive the truths revealed by God more easily than it could by faith alone. The gift of counsel teaches us in a more certain manner how we ought to act. Wisdom and knowledge make us judge of things, the former by Divine standards, the latter by human, but always under the

---

[214] Ps. 44:8
[215] Isa. 61:1

impulse of the Holy Ghost. Piety acts on the will, and disposes it to run promptly and with a filial affection towards God as towards a Father, and to honour lovingly all that belongs to God, such as the Saints, the Holy Scriptures, the poor. Fear has for its object inordinate pleasures; it separates from them the concupiscible appetite in a special manner, through respect for God. Fortitude Divinely strengthens the irascible appetite against all that it ought to fear.

## III. Acts Proper to the Gifts of the Holy Ghost

The acts exclusively proper to the gifts of the Holy Ghost are not so common as to render it easy to furnish many examples of them. They cannot always be judged by the ordinary rules of morals. When men who are eminent in sanctity do certain extraordinary actions which cannot be imitated without rashness, Theologians attribute them to the gifts and particular movement of the Holy Ghost. The Scriptures relate many wonderful things accomplished by the Saints under the impulse and direction of the Holy Ghost. Without His gifts, they would never have been able to do the like.

Thus, when the children of Israel had come to the shores of the Red Sea, and Moses, by God's order, had divided the waters, Aminadab, excited by the gift of fortitude, sprang into the passage formed by the miraculously suspended waves, when the others trembled to do so.[216] Samson, sustained by the same gift, shook the pillars of the temple of the Philistines.[217] David tried his strength with the lion, the bear, and the Philistine, Goliath.[218] Many others among the Jews executed great deeds under a similar impulse of the Holy Spirit. The history of the Church also offers several very remarkable examples, amongst which we must undoubtedly rank what is related of those who, of themselves, and by a particular movement of the Spirit of God, cast themselves into the flames, or exposed themselves to the teeth of wild beasts.

The gifts of wisdom and knowledge, which help us, by a special influence of the Holy Spirit, to judge justly, directed, it is commonly believed, Solomon in the famous judgement when he ordered the child which two women disputed to be divided in two to find out the true

---

[216] Cf. Exodus 14:21
[217] Cf. Judges 16:30
[218] Cf. 1 Kings

mother. Indeed, he could not act so wisely without a special light of the Holy Ghost, especially as, according to the opinion of several of the Fathers, he was then only twelve years old.[219] The boy, Daniel, likewise by the influence of the same Spirit, when Susanna was delivered up to death, judged the two elders, her false accusers, with a wisdom which astonished all the people.[220]

We may justly attribute to the gift of counsel the conduct of those celebrated Saints who have pretended to be foolish or ignorant. Such were the illustrious philosopher Alexander, the Charcoal-burner, and Saint Alexis of Rome. Perfect renouncement of the world and contempt of its riches, its honours and its pleasures must also be attributed to the gift of counsel.

Under the influence of the gift of fear, the Saints have performed prodigies in the practice of chastity either by flying dangerous occasions of that virtue, or braving them victoriously. By the fear of God they triumphed over all the movements of concupiscence.

To the gift of piety, which makes us treat with God as with a loving Father, and inspires us with an affectionate respect for the Saints and all that relates to the Divine worship, we may attribute several extraordinary deeds in the lives of the Saints which had their source in these pious sentiments; as, for example, when coming out of their retreats, they launched maledictions on tyrants, and fought for the defense of holy images and other sacred objects.

We have said so much to make it clear to Novices that men who are docile to the Divine inspirations do many things which to carnal eyes seem blameworthy, or at least unworthy of praise. It is well to know that these extraordinary things may be not only good, but excellent. This pure and simple manner of judging others is most becoming to Religious, and highly useful for preserving peace of heart and fostering fraternal charity.

The fruit that Novices ought to derive from this instruction on the gifts is to hold themselves in readiness until the Holy Ghost gives them a particular impulse. When favoured with the Divine unction, they should not cross their arms idly, but by the practice of good works, dispose themselves to receive from Him a swift movement towards good.

We especially recommend them to preserve the fear of God, and labour to increase it in themselves by means of meditation. They have come to the Cloister to acquire wisdom. Now, the fear of God is the beginning of

---
[219] Cf. 3 Kings 3
[220] Cf. Dan. 13

wisdom, and if they do not foster this salutary fear, though they may live bodily in a Monastery, so far shall they be from advancing in the true path of sanctity, that they will never make even a beginning.

In order to increase in themselves this salutary fear, they will impress deeply on their minds, from the first, the four last things, but especially the thought of death, judgment, and hell. For this end they will assiduously read the meditations which treat of these great truths. Not having yet arrived at that state in which they can be conducted by pure love, they would grossly deceive themselves by wishing to rise at once to higher things without passing by the way of fear.

## II. The Fruits of the Holy Ghost and the Beatitudes

### I. Fruits

God Who, in His goodness, perfects man in all his parts by the habits of the virtues and gifts, in order to make the road easy for him which leads to heaven, is wont also to sweeten the fatigues of this exile, and to recompense his generous efforts by raising him to a degree of perfection which may be said to come near the beatitude of heaven.

Indeed, under the influence of the habits of the virtues and gifts, men given to Divine things produce a host of acts filled with sweetness for the human heart. Now, these acts are called fruits, by a comparison with natural fruits which contain all the sweetness of the plants. These fruits are twelve in number: charity, joy, peace, patience, goodness, longanimity, benignity, meekness, faith, modesty, continence, and chastity. It is the nature of fruit to be the term or something final in its kind, and to enclose in itself delicious flavours. These two conditions are found in the twelve fruits which we have enumerated; one example will suffice to prove it.

Charity, the first of these fruits, is nothing else but an act of the habit of charity. This act is love which has something final in it, since it is to this that the habit tends, and at the same time it has something of great sweetness, on account of a movement of the Holy Ghost Who sheds in the heart the savour of love.

The same may be said in due proportion of the other fruits. Meekness, chastity, or any other virtue produces what is called the fruit of the Holy Ghost, when, under the impulse of the Holy Spirit, it gives birth to an excellent and delectable act.[221]

## II. Beatitudes

The Beatitudes, besides possessing a delectable savour, have a perfection still more elevated than the fruits, and, consequently, approach nearer to the state of the heavenly country. This is why they are attributed rather to the gifts than to the virtues, whilst it is the contrary with the fruits. And as the beatitudes are final and delectable acts, containing in themselves all the excellence of the fruits, each beatitude may be called a fruit, but all the fruits cannot be called beatitudes. There are eight beatitudes: poverty of spirit, meekness, affliction manifested by tears, hunger for justice, mercy, purity, peace, and patience under persecution. Let us give an example.

Our Lord said: "Blessed are the poor in spirit: Blessed are the meek."[222] First there is question of an act of humility; then an act of meekness. In calling blessed those who exercise them, Our Lord, as several of the holy Fathers say, wished to indicate a beginning, in the present life, of future beatitude. Indeed, those who serve God with their whole hearts arrive at such a high degree of humility and meekness, that they may be regarded as possessing the kingdom of heaven with poverty of spirit, and the land of the living with meekness. These acts are excellent, filled with a heavenly sweetness, and shining with the brightness of Christian perfection.

Among the beatitudes we must refer to Divine contemplation, which belongs to purity of heart. It is an act of the understanding attentively gazing on Divine truths and suspended by admiration. This act is produced by the gift of wisdom, the most excellent of all the gifts. It is a most pure knowledge

---

[221] "Another time I was working in the laundry, and the Sister opposite, while washing handkerchiefs, repeatedly splashed me with dirty water. My first impulse was to draw back and wipe my face, to show the offender I should be glad if she would behave more quietly; but the next minute I thought how foolish it was to refuse the treasures God offered me so generously, and I refrained from betraying my annoyance. On the contrary, I made such efforts to welcome the shower of dirty water, that at the end of half an hour I had taken quite a fancy to this novel kind of aspersion, and I resolved to come as often as I could to the happy spot where such treasures were freely bestowed." St. Thérèse of Lisieux, *Story of a Soul,* Ch. 10, Pub.

[222] Matt. 5:3-4

of God, accompanied by an ineffable sweetness; so that contemplation is a faithful image of the true and celestial beatitude. We shall say nothing of it here, since the matter is above the capacity of Novices, who, nevertheless, should excite in themselves the desire to attain it.

Let them know, then, that this ineffable good is granted in this land of exile to those who fight valiantly. The very thought will animate them for the combat, and make them aspire with all the ardour of their hearts to the delights of contemplation.

It would seem that Our Lord, on the one hand, and the Apostle Saint Paul on the other, did not wish to enumerate all the beatitudes and fruits of the Holy Ghost, but only the most excellent of these acts to which the others can be referred. This remark will help to make clear several passages of Holy Scripture, in which the beatitudes and fruits of the Holy Spirit are exalted through other acts besides those mentioned above.

Besides the virtues, gifts, beatitudes, and fruits, God also grants to men, even to sinners, graces which Theologians call *gratis datae*. These are the gift of prophecy, the gift of tongues, the grace of healing. But as these favours relate to the good of our neighbour, and not to our own personal sanctification, with which we are at present concerned, we shall not treat of them here.

# PART III
# The Study of Prayer

# I

# Prayer in General

The virtue of Religion, which is the noblest of all the moral virtues, produces several acts, both interior and exterior. The interior acts are Prayer and Devotion. Of these we will speak first.

Religion is a virtue which has its seat in the will, and renders to God the worship and honour that is due to Him. Now prayer, which is an act of this virtue, is an elevation of the soul to God. In it the will acts on the understanding, and impels it to honour God.

We can easily form an idea of the dignity of prayer by considering the source from which it emanates. For, if the virtue of Religion holds the first rank among all the moral virtues, it is clear that prayer, which is an act of it, surpasses in excellence the acts of the other virtues. And although it is not a Theological act, yet it relates to God as to its end in a more elevated way than any other act.

Moreover, this elevation of soul, which, according to all the Saints, constitutes prayer, also demonstrates its sublimity.[223] For it indicates that a soul given to prayer devotes all its energies to advance towards God, and cannot bear to be occupied with creatures.

Indeed, if we are to judge of it by what takes place among men, prayer must have an incomparable nobility. For, if it is considered such a great honour to have habitual relations with a king or an emperor of the earth that men esteem it more than riches and the advantages and pleasures they

---

[223] "With me prayer is an uplifting of the heart; a glance towards heaven; a cry of gratitude and love, uttered equally in sorrow and in joy. In a word, it is something noble, supernatural, which expands my soul and unites it to God." St. Thérèse of Lisieux, *Story of a Soul*, Ch 10, Pub.

procure, as daily experience proves, what a signal honour must it not be for man to converse familiarly with God, as he does in prayer!

Prayer is the hinge on which turns everything that is admirable in the lives of all the holy Fathers. It is the exercise to which they applied themselves with the greatest ardour. For the sake of it, they buried themselves in deserts and concealed themselves in caves. The love of it made them refuse dignities. Finally, it is the strong and savoury food with which they nourished their souls.

And, indeed, we speak now, not alone of the Saints of the New Law whom Jesus Christ Himself instructed by His example—by spending whole nights in prayer, or retiring to the desert for forty days, or consecrating thirty years of His life at Nazareth to the silent contemplation of His heavenly Father—for the Saints of the Old Law also were most exact and constant in this holy exercise. Witness, for example, Abraham traversing the desert, Moses conducting his flocks through the solitary plains, Elias and Eliseus inhabiting the lonely clefts of Mount Carmel.

These men of renown, having rejected every other care save that of God alone, seem to have thus lived in such forgetfulness of themselves that their spirits, transformed as it were unto God by prayer, dwelt in their bodies, as if these bodies had become strangers to them.

Such is the virtue of prayer. But it has been manifested even in a more striking manner in the New Law. We know what happened to the Master of Divine Wisdom, the Son of God Himself, when He was at prayer on Mount Thabor: "The shape of His countenance was altered."[224] Now, the same prodigy seems to be renewed in men devoted to prayer, since they draw from their frequent colloquies with God a Divine brightness, and as if elevated to a higher region, exhibit to the eyes of others a noble appearance which inspires respect.

Prayer, indeed, is something very sublime; as soon as it takes possession of a heart, it begets therein an immense hope of felicity. For it is certain, on the one hand, that the goods which make a man happy can only come to him from God; and on the other, that God although predisposed to grant them, wishes that we should ask them of Him. Consequently, to form a firm resolution of giving oneself to prayer is to find the right road to happiness. Indeed, it is to begin favourably to travel on it.

---

[224] Luke 9:29

Hence it is, that the enemy of our salvation multiplies his artifices and attacks against those who devote themselves to this holy exercise, in order to turn them from it altogether, or at least make them indifferent in the practice of it. He knows well that those souls who are constant in prayer, inflict heavy losses on him, by the Divine light which they shed around them, and the holy emulation which they provoke.

The fear of those snares of the demon caused Saint Teresa, that accomplished mistress in the art of prayer, to exhort us earnestly to remain firm in our resolution to practice it.[225] For she was convinced that it is impossible for anyone who is devoted to this salutary exercise not to make great progress in perfection.

And not, indeed, without reason; for souls who are overwhelmed with spiritual difficulties derive from prayer fresh strength, by which they become more courageous in subduing their passions and acquiring the virtues. Although they may go to prayer weak and helpless, they will come forth from it full of spiritual energy and armed for the conflict. We have an admirable example of this in Our Lord Jesus Christ, Who advanced resolutely to meet His enemies after His prayer in the Garden of Olives.

Prayer gives to the heart of man a magnanimity that strengthens it, which is nothing else than the power of God instilled, as it were, into the soul. Nothing can revive man's courage like the helping hand of God. Now, he is sure to find this adorable hand always stretched out to aid him in the place destined for prayer.

But what shall we say of the interior consolations, the knowledge of heavenly things, the contempt of the world, the peace of heart, and all the other appendages of the Divine affiliation which are the fruits of prayer? Indeed, all that could be said on the matter by the most gifted orators of the world falls far short of what the true Servants of God have experienced in the practice of prayer.

---

[225] "A second reason why we should be resolute is that this will give the devil less opportunity to tempt us. He is very much afraid of resolute souls, knowing by experience that they inflict great injury upon him, and, when he plans to do them harm, he only profits them and others and is himself the loser. We must not become unwatchful, or count upon this, for we have to do with treacherous folk, who are great cowards and dare not attack the wary, but, if they see we are careless, will work us great harm. And if they know anyone to be changeable, and not resolute in doing what is good and firmly determined to persevere, they will not leave him alone either by night or by day and will suggest to him endless misgivings and difficulties. This I know very well by experience and so I have been able to tell you about it: I am sure that none of us realize its great importance." St. Teresa of Avila, *Way of Perfection*, Ch. 23, Pub.

For all these reasons, then, Novices should strive to be very assiduous in the exercise of prayer. Let them take care not to extinguish, like degenerate children, the glory of their holy Parents, so illustrious by their constant communication with God. What pretext can they allege, since their mode of life, which reflects the spirit of their ancestors, tells them they should aspire after constant union with God by means of prayer?

Indeed, it would seem that God requires of us in this matter what the most illustrious contemplatives have accomplished during their whole lives, namely, that we consecrate to prayer all the time that remains after fulfilling the necessary duties of the present life. And, in truth, it is this that exalts our state so highly, for it is its chief ornament.

What, I ask, could be more glorious for us than to be devoted to God after the manner of the celestial spirits, who form the highest of the angelic hierarchies, and as seraphim on earth to keep ourselves continually before the face of the Lord, so that nothing save necessity can distract us from this noble occupation?

Hence it is, even at the present time, that all those amongst us who have proved faithful to their vocation, have acquired wonderful experience in the art of prayer, and fulfilled all the acts proper to their state in a very perfect and meritorious manner. It is, indeed, an honourable and useful thing for us to walk in their footsteps.

For what are all the acts of our Religious life in themselves, abstracted from the elevation of the soul to God, but dead bodies, as it were, stretched on the earth, and incapable of any generous movement? Now, when the spirit of life which is attracted from the Divine heights by prayer begins to breathe in them, immediately they come to life, give glory to God, and obtain honour and merit for him who prays.

For all these reasons, then, Novices should apply themselves diligently to the study of prayer and be zealous in practicing it, so that nothing may be wanting to them in this respect for procuring every species of good.[226]

Let them read attentively and learn perfectly the following abridgment of prayer in which we have gathered together the teaching of the holy Fathers on the subject. By the aid of it they will be able to make a beginning, and this method will serve them until they shall be conducted by the Holy Spirit, Who cannot be bound by any fixed rules.

---

[226] "All the Saints have become Saints by mental prayer." St. Alphonsus Liguori, *Prayer the Great Means of Salvation and of Perfection*, P. 3, Ch. 2, Pub.

# II

# Summary of the Practice of Prayer

## 1. Advantages and Facility of Prayer

The love of the things of this earth is the source of all evil.[227] It proceeds from ignorance of better things, namely, such as are eternal.[228] For a soul that is well instructed in the knowledge of Divine things cannot lower itself to the vileness of temporal things which are only passing. This baneful ignorance proceeds from want of due consideration; "With desolation is all the land made desolate; because there is none that considereth in the heart."[229] For it is certain that the Divine light never fails those who earnestly seek after a knowledge of heavenly things.[230]

The three sorts of goods that captivate the heart of man are found abundantly in the celestial exercise of prayer. The useful, since it exempts

---

[227] "You cannot serve God and mammon." Matt. 6:24, Pub.

[228] "Let our thoughts always be fixed upon what endures, and not trouble themselves with earthly things which do not endure even for a lifetime… O my Lord, if we had a real knowledge of Thee, we should make not the slightest account of anything, since Thou givest so much to those who will set their whole trust on Thee. Believe me, friends, it is a great thing to realize the truth of this so that we may see how deceptive are earthly things and favours when they deflect the soul in any way from its course and hinder it from entering within itself." St. Teresa of Avila, *Way of Perfection*, Ch 29, Pub.

[229] Jer. 12:11

[230] "You shall seek me, and shall find me: when you shall seek me with all your heart." Jer 29:13, Pub.

223

him from the need of many things which would seem to be indispensable. Men given to prayer are less troubled than others by hunger, thirst, cold and heat, and consequently are extremely moderate in the use of food and clothing. The honourable, for prayer begets an intimate familiarity with God. And finally, the agreeable, since in prayer one tastes the ineffable and chaste delights of paradise.

Moreover, this exercise is easy and within the reach of all, even the dullest intellects. Its germ is implanted in our nature like the germ of the other virtues of which we make acts by a natural instinct, at least imperfectly. And what is more, the breath of Divine grace, which is never wanting, inspires its practice ordinarily in simple and illiterate souls. No one, then, can lawfully excuse himself under the plea of difficulty in the matter, as the following reason will prove.

There is no one so stupid as not to be able to think when surrounded by dangers and calamities, that God, Who is everywhere present, can deliver him from these evils, and, with this belief, implore Him to avert them and desire to enter into His friendship. Now, this is nothing else than to pray, according to the definition of prayer given by the holy Fathers, who say that it is "an elevation of the soul to God."

## II. Parts of Prayer

Prayer is composed of three parts: the preparation, the body of the prayer, and the conclusion. The preparation is of two kind, remote and proximate, and includes the reading. The body of the prayer is made up of acts of the intellect and the will. The conclusion comprises the thanksgiving, oblation and petition.

## III. Preparation

*Remote:* The remote preparation consists in avoiding the occasions of distraction, and the renunciation of all inordinate solicitude about things.

*Proximate:* The proximate preparation consists in a twofold consideration. First, the consideration of the Divine Majesty, which begets sentiments of reverence for the greatness of God, and love for His goodness. Indeed, the heart is deeply moved when we reflect that the Divine Majesty deigns to allow us to converse with Him. Secondly, the consideration of our own vileness which begets a sentiment of humility.[231] A man considers himself the more abject in proportion as the person with whom he converses is illustrious. Moreover, as there is nothing more contemptible than sin, he is filled with shame and confusion at the sight of his own guilt. He then detests his faults, and from the abyss of his own nothingness he comes to hold an audience with God, like the poor publican in the Gospel with downcast eyes and accusing himself. Thus, he begins his prayer on the foundation of humility.

*Reading:* The reading may be made either before or after the *proximate* preparation, for it is not necessary to observe any particular order with it. It should be suited to the end one has in view, that is, calculated to move the heart, such as is generally found in pious books of meditation. The reading should be made slowly, with great reflection, and not for the purpose of learning, but to increase our love for God.[232] When any thought strikes us and makes an impression on the soul, we should cease to read in order to penetrate and consider it attentively. For the end of meditation is to excite the affections, and by the affections to inflame the will.[233] Indeed, this

---

[231] "When you speak, as it is right for you to do, with so great a Lord, it is well that you should think of Who it is that you are addressing, and what you yourself are…" St. Teresa of Avila, *Way of Perfection*, Ch 22. "The most familiar meditation which the seraphic St. Francis was in the habit of making was this, first he elevated his thoughts to God and then turned them towards himself: 'My God,' he would exclaim, 'Who art Thou? and who am I?' And raising his thoughts first to the greatness and infinite goodness of God he would then descend to consider his own misery and vileness. And thus ascending and descending this scale of thought from the greatness of God down to his own nothingness the seraphic Saint would pass whole nights in meditation, practicing in this exercise a real, true, sublime and profound humility, like the Angels seen by Jacob in his sleep on that ladder of mystical perfection 'ascending and descending by it.' (Gen. 28:12)" Fr. Cajetan Bergamo, *Humility of Heart*, #66, Pub.

[232] "It should be known that the purpose of discursive meditation on divine subjects is the acquisition of some knowledge and love of God. Each time individuals procure through meditation some of this knowledge and love they do so by an act. Many acts, in no matter what area, will engender a habit. Similarly, through many particular acts of this loving knowledge a person reaches the point at which a habit is formed in the soul." St. John of the Cross, *Ascent of Mount Carmel*, Book 2, Ch 14, Pub.

[233] "The important thing is not to think much, but to love much; do, then, whatever most arouses you to love. Perhaps we do not know what love is: it would not surprise me a great deal to learn this, for love consists, not in the extent of our happiness, but in the firmness of our determination to try to please God in everything, and to endeavour, in all possible ways, not to offend Him, and to pray Him ever to advance the honour and glory of His Son and the growth of the Catholic Church. Those are the signs of love; do not imagine that the important thing

advice ought to be always observed in reading if we wish to derive fruit from it.

## IV. BODY OF THE PRAYER

*Intellect:* Meditation is nothing else than a process of reasoning on the part of the intellect by which it impels the will to good, or turns it away from evil. By it the intellect maturely weighs the reading that has been made with a view to prayer. It digests it as food which nourishes and fortifies the will. For this reason, meditation ought to be regulated as a work of the will, that is, it should be used as a means by which the will may attach itself to good. One ought to avoid with equal care making it either too long or too short, but should subordinate it entirely to the particular needs of the heart, so that when the will becomes inflamed it may be interrupted, and resumed again when that ardour cools down.

*Will:* More time and attention should be given to eliciting affections than to the meditation. This is so true that, generally speaking, the more concise and short the meditation is the more excellent the prayer will be, on account of the numerous affections with which it is enriched.

*Two Methods:* Meditation is made in two ways: either on sensible things which the mind may represent to itself under corporeal images, such as the circumstances of Our Lord's Passion; or on intellectual subjects, such as the goodness or beauty of God. Although the latter may also be conceived under corporeal images, it is not however strictly necessary, for in this kind of meditation nearly everything is done by the understanding without the help of the imagination. According to these two methods of meditation, we distinguish two kinds of the presence of God: one imaginary, according to the former, and the other intellectual according to the latter. The presence of God is the application of the mind and heart to God and Divine things conceived either in an imaginary or intellectual way.

*Important Counsels:* I. We should represent to ourselves the things on which we meditate as very near or within us, in order to avoid distraction of the mind.[234]

---

is never to be thinking of anything else and that if your mind becomes slightly distracted all is lost." St. Teresa of Avila, *Interior Castle*, Fourth Mansions, Ch 1, Pub.

[234] "The whole mischief comes from our not really grasping the fact that He is near us, and imagining Him far away—so far, that we shall have to go to Heaven in order to find Him...

It is not necessary to fix the imagination too attentively on the images which it forms, lest we fall into an illusion by taking for truth what is only imaginary.

We ought to be moderate in our reflection, and give ourselves up more to affections of the heart.

The will should be used with moderation and kept from all excess. It should never seek by excessive efforts which fatigue the head, to press out sentiments of devotion like wine from a wine-press. When God sends consolation it should avoid too much elation and agitation, but rather accustom itself to enjoy its happiness with tranquility.

We should pay great attention to the matter of the meditation; yet we ought to use moderation, especially in the beginning, when the mind must not be over-exerted, but we should rather wait until it is lifted up by the impulse of grace during the prayer.

We must not stop at every spiritual sweetness that presents itself, but should continue our prayer, that the heart may receive abundantly the celestial dew which refreshes it; for a little spark of devotion easily flies away and is lost.

When the Spirit breathes, no matter where it occurs, we should seize if possible the inspiration, which is like the whistle of a shepherd calling his sheep to pasture, and apply ourselves to prayer. Acting on this principle, should it happen that we feel ourselves attracted to other subjects, different from what we have prepared for meditation, and of which perhaps we had not even a thought, we should allow ourselves to be conducted by the Divine attraction.

When the will begins to be inflamed we should cease reasoning in order to develop the affections.

If the affections become too ardent, it would be well at times to divert them, and attach ourselves to other thoughts which will make less

---

The great thing I should like to teach you is that, in order to accustom ourselves gradually to giving our minds confidence, so that we may readily understand what we are saying, and with Whom we are speaking, we must recollect our outward senses, take charge of them ourselves and give them something which will occupy them. It is in this way that we have Heaven within ourselves since the Lord of Heaven is there. If once we accustom ourselves to being glad that there is no need to raise our voices in order to speak to Him, since His Majesty will make us conscious that He is there, we shall be able to say the Paternoster and whatever other prayers we like with great peace of mind, and the Lord Himself will help us not to grow tired." St. Teresa of Avila, *Way of Perfection*, Ch. 29, Pub.

impression on the will, in order to preserve the heart and give it a little repose.

We should not credit too easily all the images that come before our minds whilst thinking; for the same image, that of Our Lord for instance, may be the work of God, or of the devil, or of our own imagination; hence we need enlightened counsel to decide in the matter.

There are some who need very little meditation, on account of the virtuous habits and facility in prayer they have already acquired, by which the will is convinced and always well disposed; or it may be from the excessive sensibility of their natural disposition, which is an ordinary defect of soft natures. Great attention should be paid to this difference.

Others possess great power of imagination. They can represent a thing in such a way that every outline and even the minutest details of the body appear as if actually living. Such souls are exposed to the danger of illusions; they should often take counsel, and correct their imaginations.

Some again can hardly represent anything by the imagination; aridity is usually their portion. If these can, at least imperfectly, make some use of the imagination it will be sufficient, as it is not necessary that they should have very exact and vivid images. Let them not, until after some time, take subjects of prayer that are purely intellectual. But if their imagination is quite sterile they may, with the advice of their Master, apply themselves to intellectual meditation and the presence of God.

All, generally speaking, but especially those who are gifted with a lively imagination, should avoid multiplicity of details. Thus for example, one ought not to occupy himself in analyzing the image which he has formed of Our Lord, so as to adore at each affection, or at each act which he makes during prayer of the recitation of the Divine Office, the hands, feet, or sacred side. Such efforts would be very hurtful to the head, and soon render it incapable of continuing the prayer. It is more useful and prudent to embrace with a single gaze, and in a general manner, the whole person of Our Lord Jesus Christ.

Those who are much subject to distractions should take care to avoid all occasions of levity in looks or words, during the time which precedes the hours of prayer, and ought to desire no other science than that of Jesus Christ. If in spite of those precautions, they do not succeed in recollecting themselves, let them endeavour during the prayer to drive away all importunate thoughts. But if the distractions still continue, they should take some vocal prayer, for example, the *Our Father* or one of the *Psalms*, and recite it interiorly if they are making their prayer in common with others, or pronounce the words if they are praying alone, pausing at each for a short meditation.[235] Finally, if notwithstanding all, the wandering thoughts continue to disturb them, they can use, instead of prayer, spiritual reading accompanied with reflections.

No fixed rule can be laid down with regard to the matter of prayer or meditation. Let each one choose that which will be most useful to him. But as this will depend on particular dispositions, and the Divine attraction, it is well, before deciding, to take counsel with an experienced guide.

The advice we have given on the manner of meditating ought to be used by Novices only in accordance with the direction of their Master. If such direction is necessary for them in all things, it is chiefly so with regard to the practice of prayer, in which so many dangers are encountered. Hence, whenever anything extraordinary or doubtful occurs, they should at once consult the oracle of obedience, in order to avoid acting rashly.

## V. Conclusion

*Thanksgiving*:[236] When the meditation is ended and we understand better the greatness of the benefits of God, which we reflected on during the prayer, it is only natural that we should pass on to the thanksgiving; as for example, if we have meditated on the Crucifixion of Our Lord Jesus Christ, we naturally feel sentiments of gratitude to Him when we remember that it

---

[235] "Soon after we have begun to force ourselves to remain near the Lord, He will give us indications by which we may understand that, though we have had to say the Paternoster many times, He heard us the first time. For He loves to save us worry; and, even though we may take a whole hour over saying it once, if we can realize that we are with Him, and what it is we are asking Him, and how willing He is, like any father, to grant it to us, and how He loves to be with us, and comfort us, He has no wish for us to tire our brains by a great deal of talking. For love of the Lord, then, sisters, accustom yourselves to saying the Paternoster in this recollected way, and before long you will see how you gain by doing so. It is a method of prayer which establishes habits that prevent the soul from going astray and the faculties from becoming restless. This you will find out in time: I only beg you to test it, even at the cost of a little trouble, which always results when we try to form a new habit." St. Teresa of Avila, *Way of Perfection*, Ch. 29. "Sometimes when I am in such a state of spiritual dryness that not a single good thought occurs to me, I say very slowly the 'Our Father' or the 'Hail Mary,' and these prayers suffice to take me out of myself, and wonderfully refresh me." St. Thérèse of Lisieux, *Story of a Soul*, Ch. 10, Pub.

[236] These following acts may also be used with profit in the body of the prayer.

was by it we were redeemed. Now, to the special benefit in the consideration of which we have been actually occupied during the meditation, we should add all the other benefits, both general and particular, we have received since our creation, briefly recalling them all to mind. In order to render Him fitting thanks for such boundless favours, we shall desire to possess all the hearts that are pleasing to God in heaven and on earth, so as to be able to offer to our most gracious God the immense gratitude of all these hearts, enclosed as it were in one heart at the same time. We shall desire also to have the Immaculate Heart of the most Blessed Virgin, and what is a thousand times more, the Sacred Heart of Our Lord Jesus Christ, in order to intensify the ardour of that gratitude with which we desire to be inflamed.

*Offering:* As the heart which is animated by the spirit of gratitude seeks to do all in its power for its benefactor, so the offering by which we strive to fulfill this task follows in natural order the thanksgiving. Various kinds of offerings then may be joined to the thanksgiving. First, it is but fitting that we offer as a holocaust of praise, and with all the ardour of our hearts, our most loving Lord Jesus and the Blessed Virgin Mary with all their merits, and also ourselves with all our thoughts, words and actions, in gratitude and thanksgiving for benefits received, and in particular for those we have considered during the meditation, immolating likewise in this mystic sacrifice all hearts that are pleasing to God. We shall offer all these also as a sacrifice of propitiation or reparation for sin, and in intercession to obtain the graces necessary to bring us to the possession of God Himself. Finally, we shall make this entire oblation to God as a holocaust to contract with Him an intimate union of heart, and to thank and honour the Divine Majesty. When offered for these four ends, which specify the various affections and intentions of the heart, each of our thoughts, words, and actions will be pleasing to God in a fourfold way, and enriched with four different kinds of merit.

*Petition:* The Petition very appropriately comes after the Offering, for it is but just to demand that for which the price has been been offered. Now we see from the enumeration of the four kinds of oblations we have already mentioned, that he who prays offers himself to God with all his merits in union with Our Lord Jesus Christ and the most Blessed Virgin as a sacrifice in atonement for sin, and as a pacifying oblation to obtain new benefits. I will say nothing here of the two other kinds of oblations which do not concern us at present. Hence, after the offering, we should earnestly ask for the pardon of our sins, and then for all the graces we need to bring us to the ineffable vision and enjoyment of God Himself. We should ask in particular for true contrition for our past sins, humility, the Theological virtues, especially a true love of God, finally, the virtue we require most, and the victory over our predominant passion or temptation. All these and whatever else we may stand in need of we are to ask for ourselves. We should likewise make petitions for the whole Church, and as far as possible, for the entire human race, so that no one may be excluded from the law of charity.[237]

*Confidence:* But what we should principally aim at in our petitions is to have an unshaken confidence, by which we shall firmly believe without any misgivings that we will obtain what we ask through the merits of Jesus Christ.[238] This confidence can be easily acquired by the consideration of the three following reasons which we have developed more fully in the chapter on hope, and which no sane man can resist.

*First Reason:* God, since He is infinitely good, is from His very nature strongly inclined to do good and show mercy. He has given ample proof of this, when without being asked, solely of His own Divine goodness, He delivered His only Son to death for me. Consequently, if, even before I asked Him and when I was plunged in the mire of sin and incapable of meriting the least favour, God gave His Son for me, would it not be unreasonable and foolish for me to doubt that He will now grant my request, when instead of offending Him I ask pardon of my sins and other favours highly pleasing to Him which are much less than His Divine Son?

---

[237] "Do not think that offering this petition continually is useless. Some people think it a hardship not to be praying all the time for their own souls. Yet what better prayer could there be than this? You may be worried because you think it will do nothing to lessen your pains in Purgatory, but actually praying in this way will relieve you of some of them and anything else that is left—well, let it remain. After all, what does it matter if I am in Purgatory until the Day of Judgment provided a single soul should be saved through my prayer?" St. Teresa of Avila, *Way of Perfection*, Ch 3, Pub.

[238] "The principal instruction that St. James gives us, if we wish by prayer to obtain grace from God, is, that we pray with a confidence that feels sure of being heard, and without hesitating: 'Let him ask in faith, nothing wavering.' [James 1: 6] St. Thomas teaches that as prayer receives its power of meriting from charity, so, on the other hand, it receives from faith and confidence its power of being efficacious to obtain: 'Prayer has its power of meriting from charity, but its efficacy of obtaining from faith and confidence.' [2. 2. q. 83, a. 15] St. Bernard teaches the same, saying that it is our confidence alone which obtains for us the Divine mercies: 'Hope alone obtains a place of mercy with Thee, O Lord.'" St. Alphonsus Ligouri, *Prayer: The Great Means of Salvation and of Perfection*, Ch 3, Pub.

Indeed, this reason should so convince me, if I am not altogether devoid of reason, that I ought to ask with confidence all things conducive to my salvation.[239]

*Second Reason:* It is certain that Our Lord Jesus Christ has delivered Himself up to death for me, as if I was the only one to be saved. For the redemption of others in no way affects mine, and I have not been deprived of any of the merits of the Blood of Jesus Christ, any more than if it were all shed for me alone, without including anyone else. St. Paul appears to have felt this when he said: "I live in the faith of the Son of God, Who loved me, and delivered Himself for me."[240] Now, it is certain that I have not committed the iniquities of all men. Indeed, compared with them mine are very few. But I can offer to the Eternal Father all the Blood shed by His Divine Son to obtain pardon for them: or in other words, I can treat with Him about the remission of my sins, as if no one else required to be pardoned but me. How then, can I be so blind and senseless as not to see that I ought to reject all diffidence, and pray to God with the most perfect confidence? This second reason is no less solid than the first. It rests on the doctrine of truth itself. If anything should astonish us, it is the weakness of our hope.

*Third Reason:* But of all others, the most powerful incentive to our hope is the promise of Our Divine Lord, by which He pledged Himself to us when He said: "Whatsoever you ask when ye pray, believe that you shall receive, and they shall come unto you."[241] By those words, Our Lord wished to raise my hope so high that it is impossible to imagine any words more suitable and efficacious.

*Conclusion:* Now, what does He require of me? That I believe He is willing to grant my request. And what is easier than to believe it? For if by His very nature He is disposed to do good, as is clear from the first reason; if, besides, He delivered Himself up to death in order that His death should be the price of the goods which I ask, as appears from the second reason; if, in fine, He has engaged Himself by a solemn promise to grant me these goods as indicated in the third reason; what is easier to believe than that they will be given to me when I ask them? For if I fulfill the condition to which He has attached the accomplishment of His promise, can I have any

---

[239] "Ask, and it shall be given you: seek, and you shall find: knock, and it shall be opened to you." Matt. 7:7, Pub.

[240] Gal. 2:20

[241] Mark 11:24

doubt but that I shall obtain what He has promised? Certainly not. This indeed should be sufficient to convince me how foolish it would be to ask the means of salvation with little confidence.

Consequently, stimulated by these three reasons, we should make use of this last part of prayer, on which the success of the whole depends, in the manner recommended by St. James: "If any of you want wisdom, let him ask of God Who giveth to all abundantly. But let him ask in faith, nothing wavering."[242] In this way we shall end our summary of the practice of prayer.

---

[242] James 1:6

# III

## Devotion in General

It is certain that the heavenly exercise of prayer is the school of true devotion, and that devotion, which ought to be regarded as the principal act of the virtue of Religion, is the end or fruit of prayer.

Devotion is an act of the will by which one gives himself with promptitude to the service of God.[243] It is for many reasons a most excellent thing, but chiefly because it is the great support of the soul, according to the words of the Royal Prophet: "Let my soul be filled as with marrow and fatness," and he adds as a mark of this spiritual nourishment, "my mouth shall praise Thee with joyful lips."[244]

Indeed, devotion affects a man's whole being, and renders him apt and prompt in soul and body to exercise acts of piety. There is no fatigue, no interior pains, no exterior attacks, which the vivacity and promptitude of the will cannot overcome.

It is extremely useful on account of the hunger it awakens for good works, and the disgust it inspires for all that is not of God. For this reason we should be most careful like the Saints, to acquire it, and ought to remove all the obstacles that are in the way.

But it is important that Novices should know how to distinguish necessary and true devotion from that which is only apparent. Now

---

[243] "Devotion is simply a spiritual activity and liveliness by means of which Divine Love works in us, and causes us to work briskly and lovingly; and just as charity leads us to a general practice of all God's Commandments, so devotion leads us to practice them readily and diligently." St. Francis de Sales, *Introduction to the Devout Life*, Ch 1, Pub.

[244] Ps. 62:6

devotion as we have already stated is an act of the will; hence that devotion will be true and pure which consists in the good disposition of the will.[245] As regards *sensible* devotion, which is so called because it is felt in the sensitive appetite, and affects the senses in an agreeable manner, it is not always necessary or true.[246]

However, it can be true, and this happens when it arises from the good disposition of the will. But true devotion of the will exists very often without producing this effect, as the Apostle testifies when he says: "I see another law in my members fighting against the law of my mind."[247] This warfare he had previously described by saying: "I do not that good which I will; but the evil which I hate, that I do."[248] By these words, *I will the good, I hate the evil,* he indicates the force of his will, and the true devotion which animated him to do good and to avoid evil, yet he felt inwardly at the same time the most violent opposition of the appetite.

Now as true devotion was not wanting to Saint Paul when he experienced in his appetite only repugnance for Divine things, Novices are not to believe that they lack it, if they sometimes feel no taste for the things of God, or even when they feel an aversion for them.

On the contrary, true devotion seems to be then doubly solid, since aridity does not prevent them from performing the good works which are usually accompanied with feelings of sensible fervour, and the sensitive appetite is conquered by the energy of the will.

However, one should always endeavour to apply himself with promptitude and energy to exercises of piety; and for this end to remove as

---

[245] "Another man reckons himself as devout because he repeats many prayers daily, although at the same time he does not refrain from all manner of angry, irritating, conceited or insulting speeches among his family and neighbours. This man freely opens his purse in almsgiving, but closes his heart to all gentle and forgiving feelings towards those who are opposed to him;… devotion that is true and living presupposes the love of God, rather it is nothing else than a true love of God. It is not, however, love as such. In so far as divine love enriches us it is called grace, which makes us pleasing to God. In so far as it gives us the strength to do good, it is called charity. But when it grows to such a degree of perfection that it makes us not only to do good but rather moves us to do it carefully, frequently and promptly, it is called devotion." St. Francis De Sales, *Introduction to the Devout Life*, Ch 1, Pub.

[246] "Whenever we are assailed by these strong impulses stimulating the increase of our desire, let us take great care not to add to them ourselves but gently cut the thread by thinking of something else. For our own nature may be playing as great a part in producing these feelings as our love." St. Teresa of Avila, *Way of Perfection*, Ch. 19, Pub.

[247] Rom. 7:23

[248] Rom. 7:15

far as possible all the obstacles that are in the way.[249] If after this, devotion fails to secure the inferior part, it will not be a loss but a combat that will add to our crown.

Now that we have explained the nature of true and pure devotion, it is necessary for us to know the sources from which it is usually drawn. These are, the consideration of Divine things, meditation on the benefits of God, and in particular serious reflection on the various mysteries which relate to the Sacred Humanity of Our Lord Jesus Christ. For although devotion has the Divinity especially for its object, yet the Divinity accommodates Itself to our capacity through the medium of the Humanity.

But it often happens that the sentiment of devotion is more abundantly excited by other means, under the special influence of the Holy Spirit. Some, for instance, are more touched and moved by the thought of heaven, others by death, others again by judgment. But whatever the means may be, it ought to be referred to God as its end, Who is the source from which all true devotion emanates.

---

[249] "The answer of St. Thomas of Aquinas to one of his sisters is very well adapted to the present subject. She asked him, 'How she could save her soul' he answered 'by willing it;' if you desire it, you will be saved, if you desire it, you will make progress in virtue, you will render yourself perfect. All then depends on our willing it, i.e. on our willing it seriously and effectually, and on exerting ourselves with all possible diligence to secure our salvation. For Almighty God is always ready to assist us; but if our own will is wanting, all the exertions of our superiors are unavailing. It is you yourself, therefore, that must take your salvation to heart — it is your own affair." Fr. Alphonsus Rodriguez, *Practice of Christian and Religious Perfection*, Vol. 1, Ch 2, Pub.

# IV

# Devotion to the Most Blessed Eucharist, The Blessed Virgin and the Saints

## I. The Blessed Eucharist

It is usual to call these persons devout who apply themselves in a special manner to the worship of the Most Blessed Eucharist, or the honour of the Saints. They are strongly drawn to this form of worship by a particular affection, or at least they strive to embrace it with great promptitude.

Indeed, the most delicious Bread of the Eucharist is eminently calculated to excite our hunger, and consequently to move us to promptitude.[250] For if flesh attracts the lion, if the tender grass invites the sheep, why should not the man of faith be attracted and invited by Jesus Christ concealed in the Most Adorable Sacrament?

Now if what is sweet attracts us, St. Thomas tells us that: "In the Eucharist spiritual sweetness is tasted in its proper source."[251] Moreover the Blessed Eucharist is a strong incentive to love, and all the stimulants of love cause a rapid movement. Hence, we see all those who are very devout to the Blessed Eucharist drawn to this celestial food with great ardour.

---

[250] "Estote quod videtis, et accipite quod estis." [Be what you behold, and receive what you are.] St. Augustine, *Sermon 272*, Pub.

[251] *Opus 57*.

Moreover, since every good is contained in the Eucharist and we are all in dire want, it follows that our extreme poverty should urge us to honour in a special manner this most august Sacrament.

For these and many other reasons, the custom has been introduced amongst Religious of making their prayer always in presence of the Blessed Sacrament. Novices should apply themselves to this exercise with piety and devotion in the manner prescribed by their Master so as to become familiar with it.

Their lot indeed is a happy one in being chosen to assist as faithful servants before so great a King, and to implore His mercy for themselves, for others, for their Order, for the whole Church, and the conversation of infidels.

This laudable practice and other similar acts will awaken in the hearts of Novices an ardent desire to approach the Holy Table, and to prepare themselves well for so great a favour.

Hence arises also the profound reverence which they manifest towards this august Sacrament. For they are not satisfied with honouring the Holy Eucharist whenever they come near It exposed publicly, but they even adore the hidden presence of Our Lord Jesus Christ as often as they pass through places adjoining the Altar, or catch sight of the Tabernacle, by making a genuflection or profound inclination.

Many other practices also have been introduced by custom among Novices which we cannot relate here. We earnestly entreat all Novices to observe these practices faithfully, and transmit them unchanged to those who shall succeed them. We exhort Novices also to serve Mass in an angelic manner, and to consider it a great honour and advantage to assist often and minister at the Holy Sacrifice.

## II. The Blessed Virgin

After the worship of the Blessed Eucharist which is a worship of *Latria*, there is the worship of *Dulia*; and above all, that which is due to the Blessed Virgin. This worship is called *Hyperdulia* on account of the singular excellence of her who is its object.[252]

---

[252] "We honor persons for their worth and excellence, and since God is the most excellent, we give Him the highest honors, differing from others not merely in degrees but in kind—divine honors that belong to Him alone. And justly so, for the vilest animal upon the earth is a

To understand how conformable to our state is devotion to this august Virgin, we have only to consider her constant protection, and the benefits which she bestows on us daily. For, we firmly believe that we never have obtained anything from the Divine goodness, and never shall, save through the intercession of this most pure Virgin. God wills that all graces should come to us through Mary.

But even if we received no more from her than the rest of Christians do, her sublime glory and ineffable beauty would claim our loving homage and constant devotion.

If the Lord, as the Church sings, "has been charmed with the attractions of this Daughter of Jerusalem;"[253] is it not just that we the Servants of this great King, should ardently desire that grace and beauty which ravished the heart of God?

"Her stature is like to the palm-tree"[254] for she is most exalted and borders on the Divinity. "Her breasts are like to clusters of grapes"[255] teeming with an abundance of sweet juice, to signify that she suckles her own children, and unites in herself the lowest things with the most sublime.

Her exterior is full of grace, and she has charms that win all hearts. Men and angels have admired her beauty, and seeing her mount towards heaven have exclaimed: "Who is this that cometh up from the desert, flowing with delights, and leaning upon her beloved?"[256]

"Like cinnamon and aromatical balm,"[257] she has shed around an odour which has filled earth and heaven, and its sweetness even rejoiced the heart of God Himself.

---

thousand times more nearly our equal than the most perfect creature, man or angel, is the equal of God. In speaking of worship, theologians generally distinguish three kinds, namely: latria, or that supreme worship due to God alone, which cannot be transferred to any creature without committing the sin of idolatry; dulia, or that secondary veneration we give to saints and angels as the special friends of God; hyperdulia, or that higher veneration which we give to the Blessed Virgin as the most exalted of all God's creatures. It is higher than the veneration we give to the other saints, but infinitely inferior to the worship we give to God Himself. We show God our special honor by never doubting anything He reveals to us, therefore by 'faith'; by expecting with certainty whatever He promises, therefore by 'hope'; and finally by loving Him more than anyone else in the world, therefore by 'charity.'" *Baltimore Catechism*, Vol 4., Lesson 1, Q. 9, Pub.

[253] Little Office of the Blessed Virgin, Resp. 6 Less.
[254] Cf. Cant. 7:7
[255] Cf. Cant. 7:7
[256] Cant. 8:5
[257] Ecclus. 24:20

INSTRUCTION OF NOVICES

All that the Divine Wisdom has done in this vast universe is under the feet of Mary. She is exalted "like a cedar in Libanus"[258] above the Seraphim who look on her with admiring reverence.

How amiable and serene is that gracious Queen! Indeed, the beauty which emanates from her throne rivals in splendour the purity of heaven, and inundates with a flood of the sweetest delight all the inhabitants of the heavenly Jerusalem.

Her bounty also overflows on earth in abundant torrents "as a shower upon the herb, and as drops upon the grass."[259] It has never been heard of in any age that her mercy was wanting to the widow and the orphan.

She is by excellence the "Wise Virgin," and one, or rather the first of that select number of virgins whom Jesus called prudent. She fills the earth with her wisdom, and teaches in a most delightful manner the prudence of the just.

Happy those who attach themselves to her; happy those who contemplate in the silence of the heart a beauty so ravishing, a splendour so magnificent. "The noble sons of Sion and they that were clothed with the best gold,"[260] vie with each other in seeking her without ever growing weary.

Novices then, on their part, should direct to this end all the powers of their soul, and attach themselves to the service of this great Queen.[261] For she is beautiful as the dove that sits beside the plentiful streams;[262] "from her garments she exhales an odour which infinitely surpasses the most precious perfumes; roses and lilies form about her an eternal spring."[263] It is here, near Mary, that they should remain and drink in the fragrant air that will refresh them.[264]

They should not be content with an ordinary devotion to this Queen, whose beauty is incomparable, whose greatness surpasses the heavens, and

---

[258] Ecclus. 24:17
[259] Deut. 32:2
[260] Lament. 4:2
[261] "Love for Mary constitutes the Carmelite method of perfection. 'To Jesus through Mary' is the formula of this method." Very Rev. Lawrence Diether, *The Imitation of Mary*, Book 1, Ch. 3, Pub.
[262] Cf. Cant. 5:12
[263] Little Office of the Blessed Virgin.
[264] "He, the Holy Ghost, the more He finds Mary, His dear and indissoluble Spouse, in any soul, becomes the more active and mighty in producing Jesus Christ in that soul, and that soul in Jesus Christ." St. Louis Marie de Montfort, *True Devotion to Mary*, P. 1, Ch 1, Pub.

who is the glory of our state. Ordinary Christians even do not fail in this. But they should strive earnestly like true children to preserve in their hearts a constant remembrance of this Mistress of the world. They should offer to her each day as soon as they awake, as well as to her Divine Son, all their affections, thoughts, words, and works.

They should prepare with the greatest fervour for her feasts, and apply themselves to particular exercises suitable to honour those beautiful days. Whenever an opportunity occurs of doing something for her glory, they should instantly avail themselves of it.

Let them frequently ponder on her life and actions which are so worthy of imitation, in order to imbibe therefrom instructions useful for themselves and others. For it is quite certain that true devotion consists more in imitation than in prayers.[265]

However, they should be very exact in reciting their accustomed prayers in her honour, the Rosary, the daily oblation, and whenever an occasion arises they should strive with all their hearts to celebrate her praises.

Finally, they should never separate the thought of Mary from that of Jesus, as this is a most efficacious means of acquiring Christian perfection, and repelling or guarding against all kinds of evil.[266] If Novices cannot have the thought of Jesus and Mary habitually in their minds, let them at least recall their sweet names very frequently: "What God hath joined together, let no man separate."[267]

All that we have said of the most Blessed Virgin is indeed but little in comparison with her merits and our obligations. The end we had in view was to make Novices understand how shameful it would be for them to be negligent and lax in the service of this great Queen.

---

[265] "A life of intimate union with God, in imitation of Mary, characterizes the Carmelite" Very Rev. Lawrence Diether, *The Imitation of Mary*, Book 1, Ch. 3, Pub.

[266] "All our perfection consists of being conformed, united, and consecrated to Jesus Christ; and therefore the most perfect of all devotions is, without any doubt, that which the most perfectly conforms, unites, and consecrates us to Jesus Christ. Now, Mary being the most conformed of all creatures to Jesus Christ, it follows that, of all devotions, that which most consecrates and conforms the soul to our Lord is devotion to His holy Mother, and the more a soul is consecrated to Mary, the more is it consecrated to Jesus." St. Louis Marie de Montfort, *True Devotion to Mary*, P. 2, Ch 1, Pub.

[267] Matt. 19:6

## III. SAINTS

After the glorious Virgin Mary, Novices should hold her most worthy spouse Saint Joseph in the highest veneration. And indeed he well deserves it, on account of his exalted dignity, and the benefits he has bestowed on us.[268]

We recommend them also to honour in a special manner those Saints and other devout Servants of God whom their Order regards as its Founders and Patrons. For although we approve of the imitation of other saints, yet it is but just that we should give the preference to those whom God Himself by a special providence has proposed as our models, since their imitation will aid us very much in acquiring the perfection of our Institute.

---

[268] "To other Saints our Lord seems to have given grace to succour men in some special necessity; but to this glorious Saint, I know by experience, to help us in all: and our Lord would have us understand that, as He was Himself subject to him upon earth—for St. Joseph, having the title of father, and being His guardian, could command Him—so now in heaven He performs all his petitions... Would that I could persuade all men to be devout to this glorious Saint." St. Teresa of Avila, *Autobiography*, Ch 6, Pub.

# PART IV

# The Exercises of the Religious Life

# I

# Exercises in General

## 1. Observance of the Exercises

The mortification of the passions, the acquisition of the virtues, and the study of prayer lead us to aspire to Divine union, by means of the exercises of our Institute and the direction of Superiors. Now, Novices ought to be so convinced of this as to believe firmly that there are no other exercises that could be imagined more suitable for attaining the end they have in view, than those that are prescribed by their Order.

Indeed, they would seriously impede their own spiritual progress and injure the common good, if they imprudently imagined that they required other acts than those that are prescribed for each hour of the day, to acquire monastic perfection. For, how could they apply themselves with the necessary energy to what they believe to be but of little use to them?

Those are most liable to be deceived in this matter who have already applied themselves to spiritual exercises in the world, and imagine they have acquired some experience therein. For, since they are still ignorant of the monastic life, and consequently of forming a sound judgement on matters relating in it, satan transforms himself into an angel of light and highly extols to them those opinions they have already formed, to the great detriment of their perfection.

For this reason, Novices should lay aside all the knowledge they acquired in the world, and, now that they have changed their state, feeling convinced that they are not yet grounded in the first principle of the spiritual life, they should take to themselves the words of the Apostle: "If any man think that he knoweth anything, he hath not yet known as he ought to know."[269]

Starting then with this principle of self-knowledge, let them abandon themselves with entire submission to their Master. And no matter how talented or educated they may have been, they should be so well disposed to make no account of it, but rather as little children to suck in the new milk from the Religious life. For they may rest assured that if they cling to the knowledge they acquired in the world, without the sanction of obedience, they will render themselves incapable of acquiring Divine Wisdom.

Indeed the Apostle of the Gentiles had learned much in the world, at the feet of Gamaliel. Festus went so far as to reproach him for his vast science by saying: "Paul thou art beside thyself: much learning doth make thee mad."[270] Yet having learned at the feet of Jesus Christ the wisdom of heaven, he said: "I judged not myself to know anything among you, but Jesus Christ, and Him crucified."[271]

Let them remember that they have entered the school of Jesus Christ, and endeavour with all their might to perform in the most perfect manner the acts that are prescribed. The holy fathers advise us to perform each action as if we were to die immediately, and to render an account of it to God. Now, what perfection would we not impart to all our works if we were to act under the influence of this salutary advice?

But even if we ignore this counsel altogether, we shall soon discover by considering the matter a little in the light of prudence, what a signal folly it is not to perform each act prescribed for us by God with the greatest perfection. For, if it is certain that God so imposes on me this act, that He demands it of me at the present moment, or approves of it and no other, how can I apply myself with a heart to other acts different from it?

Certainly, when I perform an act prescribed, I embrace all the good that can befall me in the present life, and I exclude all the evil that can happen to me; so much so, that if any portion of eternal felicity is ever obtained in this life, it seems to be entirely contained in the present act. Now, if God in prescribing this act for me by the voice of my Superiors, thereby excludes all other acts, this one alone is good for me. Hence it is my whole good, because no other good can be my portion, since it is not the will of God. Moreover, what evil can hurt me, when by this act I make

---

[269] 1 Cor. 8:2
[270] Acts 26:24
[271] 1 Cor. 2:2

myself more pleasing to God than if I were working miracles; or rather, since this act is for me the only way to please Him, and all others, as He assures me, are disagreeable to Him? Let enemies rush upon me; let death even menace me. What happier fate could I have than to die at the very moment that I am giving pleasure to God? Will he be condemned who is judged at the very moment he is pleasing his judge?[272]

From these considerations we can well understand how far they depart from the will of God and the way of salvation, who, while reciting the Divine Office, or making mental prayer, or applying themselves to any other exercise prescribed by obedience, allow themselves to be distracted by solicitude for other acts different from those they are engaged in. Would that they reflected seriously on the reasons we have alleged: "O that they would be wise, and would understand, and would provide for their last end."[273]

If then, as we have shown, Novices can find the expression of the Divine Will in each of their least observances, and consequently the acquisition of all good and the rejection of all evil; they ought to have such a love for their Institute, and be so well disposed with regard to each and every act prescribed therein; that, holding what the Saints call singularity in abhorrence, they will be ever ready even to shed their blood for the maintenance of the least point of the observance.

This greatness of soul with regard to the observance of laws is proper to the children of God, and helps wonderfully in the acquisition of Christian perfection. On the other hand, we cannot expect much from those who perform the prescribed acts of the Order in a pusillanimous spirit.

For it is certain, that the exercises which of their own nature are salutary, become perverted, and changed into spiritual poison by the laxity with which they are fulfilled. To be convinced of this, it is only necessary to consider the daily injuries that result from routine and want of effort in the performance of common acts.

Let the children of the living God then never expose themselves to the danger of finding death in the bread which ought to give them life, and extinguish the spirit by the very acts which should reanimate it.

What have they come into Religion for, if not to act with valour, and to excite one another to the combat by a most exact observance of the regular

---

[272] "Always try to find out wherein lies the greatest perfection." St. Teresa of Avila, *Way of Perfection*, Ch 3.
[273] Deut. 32:29

acts? Thus of old: "the priests stood in their offices; and the Levites with the instruments of music of the Lord, which King David made to praise the Lord;" because He is good, "because His mercy endureth for ever, singing the hymns of David by their ministry."[274]

Indeed, the exact observance of laws whether Divine, monastic, or merely human is of such importance that it is the source of incalculable good, even in the present life. Witness the Spartans who won by it their glory and happiness; or the Romans who by it extended their empire.

But no glory is comparable to that of the Machabees, who in fighting for the laws of their country became a people and a powerful nation. The fury of tyrants exhausted, but in vain, every device and torment to extort from them the omission of a single observance.

Of this race was the illustrious Eleazar: "a man advanced in years and of a comely countenance."[275] His friends offered him meats which were allowed by the law to be eaten, in order that he might pretend to have eaten the forbidden meats which the King had commanded, and thus save himself from death. He at once replied that he preferred to descend into the grave, and suffer an honourable death.[276]

Such is the magnanimity with which Novices should arm themselves for the observance of even the minutest practices in the fulfillment of the exercises which we are about to indicate.

## II. Daily Exercises

Let Novices be very prompt in rising in the morning for the Office and mental prayer. Each one should strive with a holy emulation to be the first to seize the clapper or bell, call the others, and arrive at the Oratory.

Before going to sleep they will select the subject of meditation, and endeavour to think only of it.[277] On awakening let them at once recall the

---

[274] 2 Paral. 7:6

[275] 2 Mach. 6:18

[276] Cf. 2 Mach 6:21, 23, 28

[277] "Before getting into bed we take Holy Water, and sprinkle some upon our bed: we then kneel down and commend ourselves to God… When we awake during the night we should take care to lift up our hearts to God by making some short aspiration; but it must be remembered that we are not allowed to occupy ourselves with any thought, even of God, which would prevent our sleeping." *Carmelite Exactions*. "It happens to many who are given to prayer or contemplation that, by overwork of the understanding before going to bed, they cannot sleep,

presence of God and the virtue of the week, and carefully reject every other thought. During the preparation for prayer, or at the prayer itself, they will direct all their thoughts, words, and actions to the glory of God as prescribed in the *Instructions*.

Immediately after the morning exercises, they will retire to their cells to put them in order. They will be very careful to keep them clean and tidy, and when convenient, will arrange them in the morning before prayer.

While thus in retirement in their cells, they shall kneel down and recall to mind the good desires they conceived during prayer, confirm them by a resolution, and examine themselves on the faults they have committed.

Some time after at the signal of the bell, they will assemble in the place appointed by their Master for hearing Holy Mass. When Mass is over, they will go to fulfill the duties assigned them by obedience, or retire to their cells for spiritual reading, meditation, or other exercises that may be prescribed by their Master.

After having assisted with the other Religious of the Convent at the Canonical Hours, examination of conscience, dinner and grace, they will take recreation with their Master for an hour.

During recreation they will not speak of their own accord but will listen to Father Master or the President; if they are interrogated by him, they will answer. If they desire to ask a question themselves, they will first ask permission.

At the end of recreation, they shall retire to their cells unless obedience employs them elsewhere.

During the exhortation, whenever Father Master interrogates them on the presence of God, that is, on the manner in which they occupied themselves with our Lord during the day, and on the virtue which they resolved to practice more particularly for the week, each in his turn will kneel down to answer.

During the interval between the exhortation and evening meditation, they will apply themselves to spiritual reading and prayer. For the rest, they ought to know that it is a custom well established in Religious Communities, to make good use of the time that remains after the fulfillment of the obligations of our state, by consecrating it to prayer before the Blessed Sacrament or the image of the Blessed Virgin. We can call this by the grace

---

thinking still on what they have thought of or imagined, for the enemy will then try to suggest good things to them, that the body may suffer through loss of sleep, and this is a thing to be entirely avoided." St. Ignatius of Loyola, *Letters of St. Ignatius*, Vol. 1, Letter 8, Pub.

of God our *perpetual sacrifice*. We strongly recommend this practice to all Novices.

When the signal is given for evening meditation, they will go to it with the rest of the Community. After the other common acts are ended, they will retire in silence to their cells, where they will occupy themselves in spiritual reading and meditation until the signal for repose is given, when they will go to rest.

## III. Weekly Exercises

Every Saturday each Novice will select a virtue to practice during the week. In making this choice, the preference should be given to the one he knows he is most wanting in. Let him use much diligence to acquire it by the frequent practice of interior and exterior acts aided by prayer. He should be careful to read the chapter which treats of it.

Before choosing the virtue, Novices will do well to examine the vice, passion, or temptation which troubles them most. They shall then select the opposite virtue, and devoutly implore the intercession of the Saints in their efforts to obtain it.

A Novice can continue to exercise himself for several weeks successively in the same virtue, until with the help of God, he has made some progress in it.

As soon as Novices awake in the morning they should endeavour to arm themselves with some pious thought suitable to aid them in acquiring the virtue selected, and banish from their minds all thoughts about other things.

They shall approach Holy Communion as often as they are allowed.

They shall go to confession every week to the Ordinary Confessor of the Novitiate and present themselves four times every year to the Extraordinary Confessor.

## IV. Monthly Exercises

In the Novitiates of some Religious Orders a commendable custom exists of issuing a challenge to all, at the beginning of each month, for the acquisition of the virtue which Father Master will consider the most useful for the general good of the Novitiate. The form of the challenge will be as follows. He who during this month shall practice the virtue of ............... with the greatest fervour, will enjoy the fifth part of the merit of all the others.

When the challenge has been read, each one will take a copy and hang it in a conspicuous place on the wall of his cell. He will read it every day during the month that he may recall it to mind, and to excite his fervour in practicing it.

The Novices may also, from time to time with the permission of their Master, issue among themselves other more important challenges. This is generally done on extraordinary recreation days, and when they are leaving the Novitiate to go to another Convent.

It is also customary for Novitiates to send reciprocal challenges, in order to reanimate their fervour and "excite emulation for the better gifts."[278]

On the eve of his monthly Patron, each Novice will fast with the permission of Father Master, and on the feast itself, he will receive Holy Communion and read the life of the Saint.

The Novices shall be careful not to allow any month to pass without making their monthly Retreat, giving an account of their dispositions, and practicing one of the extraordinary mortifications. They will also perform very frequently, under the direction of their Master, the ordinary mortifications.

## V. Yearly Exercises

Before the greater feasts, such as Easter, Pentecost, Corpus Christi, the festivals of our Blessed Lady, as also before the holy seasons of Lent and Advent, the Novices shall prepare themselves with the permission of Father Master, by particular interior and exterior exercises. Let them be faithful to this custom.

On days of extraordinary recreation, and on solemn feasts, it is customary for Novices to challenge each other mutually to a more exact observance of the regular life. They make a covenant with their Master and his companion that for every fault of which they shall be admonished or

---

[278] Cf. 1 Cor. 12:31

corrected they will say certain prayers in token of gratitude. This practice is indeed very salutary.

Each Novice will make the spiritual exercises under the direction of his Master, once a year, if he is allowed.

During that month that precedes the Profession, the Novices will prepare themselves for this solemn act by longer prayers and divers other exercises. They will also ask on their knees the other Religious to aid them by their prayers in such an important affair.

# II

## Direction of the Acts

In order that the exercises of the monastic life, and in particular of the Novitiate, may produce more fruit, Novices ought to direct them to God with great fervour, not only in the morning in a general way, but also, as far as human frailty will permit, before each action of the day. The method to be observed in this offering, with which Novices ought to be very familiar, can be the same on all occasions. In the morning, however, the long form should be used, but at other times it may be shorter.

### Example

O God of infinite goodness to Whom I am indebted for all things, I unite myself most lovingly and intimately with Our Lord Jesus Christ, the Blessed Virgin, all the Angels and Saints in heaven and the just on earth, and offer myself entirely to Thee, with all the thoughts, words and actions of my whole life but especially of this day; and I desire by them solely and ardently to please Thee alone. Would that I had at my disposal to offer Thee the innumerable millions of most perfect hearts which Thou mightest have created, and who, with those I have already mentioned, would have pleased Thee in the past, and glorified Thee for all eternity. All these, O my God! I desire from the bottom of my heart to offer Thee anew at each breath I draw, as a sacrifice of expiation for my own sins and the sins of the world; in thanksgiving for all the benefits both general and particular I have received from Thee; in impetration for all the graces I need to bring me to eternal happiness; and finally as a holocaust to Thy glory, to unite me inseparably to Thee, and make Thy Divine Majesty better known and loved.

It is for these four intentions that each thought, word and action, united to all those millions of hearts, and enriched with a fourfold merit, ought to be offered to God. But after God they should be directed to the Blessed Virgin; and as this fourfold sacrifice is not suitable to her since it belongs to the worship of *Latria*, which is due to God alone, the offering to her will be made as follows:

O Most Blessed Virgin Mary! I offer myself entirely to Thee and Thy honour, with all the thoughts, words and actions of this day and my whole life, and all those other hearts I have already mentioned, as far as it is lawful or possible for me to do so, and I earnestly desire by all these to please Thee.

This double offering addressed to God and the most Blessed Virgin becomes quite easy after a few days' practice. But in the beginning, and especially in the morning when it is formed with more attention and energy for the whole day, it ought to be made with greater fervour, in order to impress it deeply on the heart.

In addition to this general intention, he should also elevate his heart to God at each action, by interior acts suitable to the work in which he is engaged, such as the following:

## Examples

*For the Canonical Hours.*—O my God! I desire to sing Thy praises, and I earnestly invite the most blessed Virgin, all angels and men, with every other creature, and the countless worlds Thou mightest have drawn out of nothing to join with me in praising Thee.

*For Mental Prayer.*—The same form may be used as for the Canonical Hours.

*For Chapter.*—O my God! I have sinned against heaven and before Thee. Have pity on me, a sinner. Grant, O Lord! That I may repent sincerely of my faults. Grant that they may be brought to light and expiated by efficacious remedies.

*For Confession.*—The same as for Chapter.

*For Meals.*—O my God! I am called to the Refectory; would that I were called to martyrdom instead! Grant, O Lord! that I may practice temperance.

*For Recreation.*—O my God! it is necessary that I should give some relaxation to the body in order that I may be better able to work for Thee. If Thou didst so desire it, I would as willingly go to the torture for Thee. Grant that I may comport myself with perfect modesty.

*For Sermon or Exhortation.*—It is to Thee, O my God! that I am about to listen; may Thy words impress themselves on my soul, in order that by them I may become better. Grant that I may retain them in my memory, and that Thy truth may shed itself sweetly on my soul.

*For Holy Mass.*—I desire, O my God, to assist at this Mass, the dignity of which is infinite; grant that I may hear it with attention and reverence, and participate in the fruits of the holy Sacrifice.

*For Holy Communion.*—O Jesus! I am preparing myself to receive Thee; grant that my heart may be pure in order to be united more closely to Thee.

*For Retiring at Night.*—O my God! I must now take some repose; grant that I may do so without pampering the flesh, and that I may rise promptly to sing Thy praises.

*For Serving at Table.*—O my God! I am about to serve Thy servants, make me attentive and diligent in order to supply them with everything they need; let me not fail in this duty.

We have given these examples to show Novices how they should unite interior with exterior acts, and connect them all together by the general intention of which we have already spoken. For that intention of itself, although very fruitful in merits, does not enter into the details of things, which indeed is necessary in order to perform our actions perfectly.

# III

# Exercise of the Presence of God in Our Daily Actions

The presence of God, as we have said in the treatise on Prayer, is an application of the mind to God, conceived in an intellectual or imaginary manner. For if it were sufficient that God is present with us without our giving any thought to Him, then, not only we, but all creatures without any exception, would live always in the presence of God. But such is not the meaning of the holy Fathers when they speak of the presence of God. They understand it in the sense of our definition.

The mind can be applied to God in two ways. It may consider Him simply as a friend regards his friend, without doing anything further; or in considering Him, it may excite towards Him many affections and acts of virtue, as a friend who not only regards his friend, but also offers him gifts or promises them to him.

The first way is sometimes useful, as when one rests for a while from continual aspirations, and fixes a look full of love on Our Lord, but generally speaking, it is sterile and does not inflame the heart. Novices ought to make use of the second method more frequently.

Hence, whether they remain in their cells, go out, or work, they ought to address themselves to Our Lord by frequent aspirations or ejaculatory prayers;—offering themselves to Him, renewing their good resolutions, producing acts of virtue, now of humility, again of gratitude, hope, charity or contrition, consulting Him in all they do and asking His assistance in everything.

Indeed, they should strive to begin and finish their various works with Our Lord Jesus Christ, fixing their eyes on Him as the Guide they should follow, and uniting themselves to Him in every action by repeated movements of the heart.

Nor ought their exercise of the Divine presence to stop here, but it should be extended to their neighbour, so that they shall endeavour to see in their fellow-creatures the Brothers of Jesus Christ, as that is the name that He gave them, or children redeemed by His Precious Blood, and destined to reign eternally with Him. This practice will beget love, peace, respect, and many other precious advantages. As to the Superior and Novice Master, it is evident that they hold the place of Jesus Christ.

Let us go yet further, and say that Novices should give themselves to this practice in such a manner that they cannot fix their eyes on any of God's creatures, no matter what it is, without raising their mind and heart to God. In this way all creatures without exception will help to remind them of Him. Finally, let them be fully convinced that nearly all the science of the spiritual life is contained in the few counsels given in this chapter, so that if they neglect these, they can never hope to become spiritual men.

# IV

## Use of the Sacraments and Examination of Conscience

The frequent use of the Sacraments requires of Novices great purity of heart, and full knowledge of all that pertains to them. They ought to be as sanctuaries, exhaling by the innocence of their lives those sweet perfumes in which the Divine Majesty takes delight.

With regard to the Sacrament of Penance, they should be very vigilant not to allow an indifference about small faults to steal in upon them, which destroys all sense of sorrow for them. We do not speak here of grave sins, for, thank God, there is no question of them among Novices. But if they have not a horror, even of the slightest transgressions, they will never make progress in perfection. They shall prepare for Confession in the following manner:

Let them represent to themselves Jesus Christ, Our Lord and High-Priest, as really present, and treat with Him as they will afterwards treat with their Confessor. Then they will go to the Confessor, prostrate themselves at his feet, and with the deepest contrition declare the sins committed since their last Confession, in thought, word and deed, renew the general accusation of all the sins of their past life and mention some one in particular in order to supply certain matter for absolution. All shall follow this method of Confession without any exception.

They shall observe the same method, with the exception of the accusation of certain matter for absolution, in the daily examination of conscience. Let them make it before Our Lord as if He were there really present to hear them, in the way we have already indicated when preparing for the Sacrament of Penance. And in order to expiate their faults, they will impose on themselves some light penance in keeping with their failings, such as the Confessor is wont to do in similar cases.

Finally, they will also adopt this method when giving to Father Master as to God Himself, an exact and sincere account of all their spiritual affairs.

Let them carefully avoid all negligence before receiving the Most Holy Eucharist, and endeavour to prepare the habitation of their hearts for so great a King by many acts of faith, hope, and especially charity, devoting to this practice a certain fixed time. After Communion they should occupy themselves solely with Our Lord Who is really present within them. Let them remember that this time, as long as the Sacred Species remains, is most favourable to obtain an abundance of every good, and deliverance from all evil.

# V

# Manner of Preparing for the Clothing and Profession

Whenever anyone is going to receive the holy Habit of Religion or to make his Profession, he will prepare himself in the following manner. Indeed, the method should be the same for both, since if anyone, while asking the Habit, wavers in his mind with regard to his future Profession, he shows himself unworthy of such a favour.

There ought to be then only this difference between him who receives the Habit and him who makes his Profession; both are disposed to make their Profession, but the former cannot as yet do so.

Hence as regards constancy and disposition, since the will of the one ought to be the same as that of the other, it is only proper to give them the same instruction. For what the Professed makes a vow to fulfill, the Postulant who is clothed forms a very strong resolution to observe.

During the time appointed for the consideration of the important step he is about to take, the Postulant or Novice will represent to himself that he is near death, and by this very act is about to die. He may regard himself as a victim destined soon for the slaughter, to be consumed as a living holocaust and immolated to God. Then he shall make with as much fervour as possible the following acts:

O my God! I desire to be conducted to this happy death, and to die to myself, in order that by the destruction of my own life, I may have the happiness of living for Thee, for it is thus I shall become a holocaust.

## Manner of Preparing for the Clothing and Profession

I desire to be governed by Thy will alone, and to follow even in the smallest detail all that obedience shall prescribe, in order to immolate to Thee my understanding and my will by the practice of the most excellent of all the vows.

I desire to renounce all the pleasure of the flesh and the senses, and to embrace irrevocably an austere life, in order to sacrifice to Thee my body by the practice of chastity.

I desire to cast off all the riches and advantages of this world and embrace Christian poverty, which is the queen of the universe, in order to offer Thee all imaginable wealth.

And since this mystic sacrifice demands the most ardent and generous sentiments, I desire, O my God, to possess the hearts of Thy Own Divine Son and the most Blessed Virgin, and all the hearts of angels and men that are pleasing to Thee, and united with my own heart to offer them all to Thee in this act of immolation which I am about to make of myself to Thy eternal glory. I desire to make this offering with all the fervour of which I am capable.

O my God! to Whom I am indebted for all things under so many titles, for love of Thee I detest all the sins of my life, and I firmly resolve to serve Thee always and in all things.

Accept, O Lord, this victim filled with good desires. Yes, I offer Thee my understanding and my will; may Thy good pleasure be henceforth my only rule! I offer Thee my body; may austerity keep it in subjection. I offer Thee all the riches of this world for which I will no longer feel anything but contempt. May this triple sacrifice obtain for me that true liberty of spirit which I seek.

I wish to know nothing or to wish for nothing save Thee alone, in order to become obedient. I wish to love nothing but Thee alone, in order to become chaste. I wish to possess or desire nothing except Thee alone, in order to become rich in my poverty.

I entreat Thee then, O God of my heart, to use me in future as Thy slave. I ask Thee through the Precious Blood of Thy Son, not to let me degenerate from the perfection of this holy Order.

And Thou, O Virgin most pure, invincible support of this Religious Institute which rejoices in Thy protection, receive me, I beseech Thee, among the number of Thy white-robed children, to whom I wish to be associated by the vows which I purpose to pronounce at Thy Feet and those of Thy Divine Son.

They will often renew these acts during the time which precedes the Clothing or the Profession.

# APPENDIX

## Instructions for Rendering an Account of the Interior Dispositions to One's Spiritual Director or Superior

Let each Religious who is about to give an account of his conscience to his Spiritual Director or Superior bear well in mind how much importance St. Teresa set on this exercise, for removing the dangers of temptations, procuring greater care, diligence, and solicitude on the part of the Superior, and making more rapid and happy progress in the ways of God and of virtue.[279]

Wherefore, after her holy death, she spoke thus in a vision to one of her children:—"It is of the utmost importance for the perfection of regular observance, to give the Spiritual Director or Superior an exact account of the interior, and to observe the Constitutions on this point. When the true spirit shall begin to decay in this matter, the fervour of the Order shall likewise diminish and disappear."

---

[279] All religious Superiors are strictly forbidden to induce their subjects, in any way whatever, to make a manifestation of conscience to them. Subjects, however, are not forbidden to open their minds freely and spontaneously to their Superiors; nay, more, it is desirable that they approach their Superiors with filial confidence, and, if the Superiors be priests, expose to them their doubts and troubles of conscience also.—1917 Code of Canon Law, Can. 530.

Nearly the whole range of matter for the manifestation of conscience is included under the subjoined headings. When Novices have revealed all they think proper in this manner, let them ask the Superior or Director to question them more closely, if he thinks that anything should be more fully manifested, for the greater glory of God, and the more complete knowledge of their hearts.

The following questions then shall be proposed for examination:

Are you content in your vocation?

How do you practice obedience, especially that which subjects the judgment and reason?

How do you practice chastity, self-denial and the other virtues? What are the things that you love most and pursue with the greatest ardour?

Do you feel any trouble of mind? Are you violently agitated by any temptation? In what manner, with what difficulty or with what facility, do you resist it? What are the passions or vices to which you are most inclined, and which are most easily excited within you?

Have you criticized the Rule or any of the Constitutions, and pronounced an unfavourable judgment on them?

What do think of our Institute, and the means it employs to attain more efficaciously the end of the congregation?

What are your dispositions with regard to spiritual things? How much time do you devote to prayer? Do you give more time to mental or to vocal prayer, and from which do you derive greater profit? What is your method of prayer?

Does your use of spiritual things increase in you devotion and interior consolation? Or do you, on the contrary, suffer from weariness, aridity, and distraction? How do you act in these different states?

What fruit do you derive from the frequentation of the Sacraments, the examen of conscience, and other spiritual exercises?

Have you gained or lost since the last manifestation? What ardour do you actually feel for acquiring perfection?

With what exactitude do you observe the Rule and Constitutions, not only those that are common to all, but those also that are proper to your office?

Do you frequently perform mortifications, penances, and other exercises useful to spiritual progress? In particular, to what extent are you prepared to carry the Cross of Christ, or suffer injuries for His love? Do you feel any desire for them?

What profit do you derive before God from your intercourse with the Religious? Are you bound to anyone by a particular friendship?

Have you even a slight aversion for any of your Brethren? What are your sentiments with regard to your Superiors?

What space of time do you allow to elapse during the day without recalling the presence of God? How often do you make aspirations and ejaculatory prayers?

Do you make the direction and offering of your actions, especially in the morning, at the beginning of each action and during the act itself (if it is a long one), as prescribed in the *Instruction of Novices*?

Do you practice each day a certain number of little mortifications, and when you have omitted them through forgetfulness, do you supply for it at night before going to bed?

Have you made the spiritual exercises of the Retreat during the year, conformable to the Constitutions?